THE POLITICAL INTERESTS OF GENDER

'FISKMADONNA' by Ann Wolff

THE POLITICAL INTERESTS OF GENDER

Developing Theory and Research with a Feminist Face

edited by

Kathleen B. Jones and Anna G. Jónasdóttir

SAGE Modern Politics Series Volume 20
Sponsored by the European Consortium for
Political Research/ECPR

 SAGE Publications

London · Newbury Park · New Delhi

First published 1988
Black and white photograph of the coloured glass statue 'Fiskmadonna'
reproduced by kind permission of Ann Wolff

SAGE Publications Ltd
28 Banner Street
London EC1Y 8QE

SAGE Publications India Pvt Ltd
32, M-Block Market
Greater Kailash – I
New Delhi 110 048

SAGE Publications Inc
2111 West Hillcrest Drive
Newbury Park, California 91230

British Library Cataloguing in Publication Data

The Political interest of gender : developing
    theory and research with a feminist face.
    1. Political science
    I. Jones, Kathleen B.   II. Jónasdóttir,
    Anna G.
    320

ISBN 0–8039–8085–X
ISBN 0–8039–8086–8 Pbk

Library of Congress catalog card number 88–062061

Typeset by Photoprint, Torquay, Devon
Printed in Great Britain by the Alden Press, Oxford

Contents

Notes on Contributors

Kathy E. Ferguson is Associate Professor of Political Science and Women's Studies at the University of Hawaii, Honolulu.

Gun Hedlund teaches women's studies courses and is co-ordinator of the Center for Women's Studies at Örebro University, Sweden.

Helga Maria Hernes is Under Secretary of State at the Royal Ministry of Foreign Affairs in Norway.

Anne Hildreth is a doctoral candidate in the Department of Political Science, University of Iowa, Iowa.

Jane S. Jaquette is Professor of Political Science at Occidental College, Los Angeles.

Anna G. Jónasdóttir is Lecturer in Politics at Örebro University, Sweden.

Kathleen B. Jones is Associate Professor in the Department of Women's Studies at San Diego State University, San Diego.

Arthur H. Miller is Professor of Political Science at the University of Iowa, Iowa.

Birte Siim is Associate Professor at the Institute of Social Development and Planning at Aalborg University, Denmark.

Grace L. Simmons is a doctoral candidate in the Department of Political Science, University of Iowa, Iowa.

Kathleen A. Staudt is Associate Professor of Political Science at the University of Texas, El Paso.

Ursula Vogel is Lecturer in Government at the University of Manchester, Manchester.

Editors' Preface

This book of essays grew out of the 1986 ECPR Workshop of the Standing Group on Women and Politics, 'Theories of Gender and Power', co-organized by Anna Jónasdóttir and Gun Hedlund, which met at the University of Gothenburg, Gothenburg, Sweden. For five intensive days, feminists from all over the world met to consider basic issues in contemporary feminist theory and research on politics. We all recognized the similarity of our pursuits and the necessity for greater communication among us. In particular, we felt the need to increase the exchange of ideas among theorists in Northern Europe, and those working in and on Western Europe, North America and the Third World. The book is inspired by the desire to promote dialogue about the parameters of a truly international feminist theory and practice that represents the interests of gender in cross-cultural and historical perspective. In so far as this dialogue is institutionalized – we now regularly read each other's work and attend each other's meetings – the book's purpose has been realized. The hope is that this text will be the harbinger of more works that stress the cross-cultural project of developing feminist theory and research.

The majority of the essays were written by participants in the 1986 meetings. Several others, those by Jaquette and Staudt, Ferguson and Miller et al., were included because their work contributed so well to the book's thesis.

We would like to express our thanks especially to David Hill, Managing Director at Sage Publications, and to Michael Laver, Modern Politics Series editor, for their encouragement and assistance with this project. We also would like to thank the ECPR conference organizers for the 1986 meetings in Sweden that brought us all together in the first place.

1

Introduction:
Gender as an Analytic Category
in Political Theory

Kathleen B. Jones and Anna G. Jónasdóttir

The premise of this book is that the conceptual terrain on which contemporary political theory rests is inadequate when political analysis is approached from the perspective of gender. Although there is disagreement among feminists about whether the basic concepts of political theory are value-free, there is widespread agreement that, in the modern period, theoretical works have been notoriously silent about women. (See the differences of opinion represented in the essays in Evans *et al.*, 1986.) Following the implications of this book's premise, the authors contribute to the ongoing task of breaking this silence.

Whereas early classical political writers, like Aristotle, may have regarded women as naturally unsuited to rule, they at least felt compelled to speak about the differences between the sexes. On both the metaphorical and the empirical level, Aristotle and others argued that women's activities and attributes made women incompetent to engage in political activities. This made politics a definitively male enterprise (Saxonhouse, 1985). Later classical writers directly addressed the gender question too. In the initial phase of classical liberal theory, women – now understood as more like than unlike men – were used to complete the analysis of social authority structures, marking the transition from medieval to modern thought. Nevertheless, the apparent levelling tendency in their thinking did not prevent such writers from precluding women's participation in governing, since they argued that women necessarily were subordinate to men (Jónasdóttir, 1983). Until women's studies scholars began to produce their own readings of classical theory, the secondary literature also remained almost totally silent about what the classical philosophers wrote about women, men and the family, as well as about the connection between these topics and their political theories. (See, for instance, Wolin, 1961; Sabine and

Thorson, 1973; and compare with Okin, 1979; Elshtain, 1981; Saxonhouse, 1985.)

In contrast, since the breakthrough of liberal democracy, modern authors have proceeded from the position of not so benign indifference to the meaning and interests of gender. However, their theories and research have not escaped gender-based limitations. On the contrary, indifference has meant that the nature of political action and the scope of political research have been defined in ways that, in particular, exclude women as women from politics. Men as men do not suffer the same fate, although the extent of their activities also is circumscribed by the shape of political concepts. This is because, to a great extent, modern theorists adopted the conceptual framework they inherited from earlier times. This framework had been built on the premise, never seriously challenged even by liberal thinkers, that political action and masculinity were congruent, whereas political action and femininity were antithetical (Okin, 1979; Eduards, 1983; Hartsock, 1983; Jaggar, 1983; Pateman, 1983; Lloyd, 1984; Saxonhouse, 1985; Hernes, chapter 9). Jones argues in chapter 2 that this heritage has continued to shape the research parameters and methodological principles of contemporary political science, even among some feminist writers. Vogel (chapter 7) focuses on how modern juridical notions of liberty conceal ubiquitous forms of power that men exercise over women, both in the family and in the economy.

How would one engage in the construction of political theory and the design of political communities as if women, and gender-based interests, mattered? This volume comprises a set of responses to this query. The authors share the recognition that the definition of central concepts in political analysis is the result of complex historical and political processes; these work to illuminate and privilege specific dimensions and meanings of human discourse and activity, while at the same time hiding others. Our intention is to challenge the hypothesis that the central concepts of political thought, and its basic techniques, are value-neutral. In contrast to those who argue that it is simply the assumptions of a particular investigator, structured by his or her socialization, that are biased and distort the uses of an otherwise objective technique of analysis, the argument of most of the contributors in this volume is with the very conceptualization of political theorizing itself.

If the way that politics is defined limits the vision of politics of specific theorists, as Wolin argued long ago, it follows that the tools and methods for representing and explicating this vision are not disinterested. One of the tenets of critical theory that this volume accepts and explores is the view expressed by Habermas that human knowledge, both in the ways that it is produced and the view of the social world that it constructs, is always connected to and driven by some set of human interests of either a technical, interpretive or emancipatory nature. Even formal logic and the principles of reason are not 'mere' tools used in knowledge production. For example, a particular conception of rationality abstracts from a set of social practices engaged in by 'situated' thinkers, whose activities reflect a specific way of apprehending reality. Rational comprehension is understood to be based, literally and figuratively, on a 'grasping' of reality through information collected through sense experience. Among the interests reflected in this grasping is the desire for greater control over the natural and the social world. What counts as rational thought is at least in part related to the extent to which it provides a relatively unambiguous picture of an otherwise chaotic universe. Thought that does not afford this kind of clarity, thought that remains uncertain about the boundaries between self and other, for example, does not appear to qualify as rational in this sense.

In recent years, feminist theorists have been claiming that there is something distinctive about women's interests and the activities that they represent. Among the interests that have been identified in contemporary and historical research are the concerns that emerge from women's disproportionate association with 'mothering and reproduction; . . . the political economy of the gendered division of labor; . . . the arrangements of the female body; . . . [and] spirituality and contact with the divine' (Ferguson, chapter 4).

In identifying these interests, feminists have also argued that what distinguishes 'women's interests' is not only the issues that are represented, but also the mode of representation. For instance, wedding concern with the activities of caretaking and nurturance to traditional notions of interest seems to diminish and distort the vocabulary of connectedness that gives expressive force to that concern in favour of the formalistic language of self-interested power-brokerage. Traditional concepts of interest do not seem adequate to define the political and moral values that women strive to achieve in having their interests represented.

Finally, feminists have been evaluating the relevance of the concept of interest itself. Some, like Diamond and Hartsock (1981), have argued that the language of interest, with its utilitarian connotations and connections to the 'rational calculus', can never be redeemed to serve feminist purposes. Others argue that abandoning the concept of interest cedes too much valuable political space and linguistic force to the dominant group. Theorists like Jónasdóttir (see chapter 3) claim that what is needed is a refocusing of the lens of interest to emphasize its formal dimensions – the notion that interest represents a group's 'being among' the members of a political community who are recognized as having a 'controlling presence'. This view leaves open to theoretical and empirical analysis the question of whether and how the specific, unique characteristics of different groups influence the political process, and shape the polity in different ways.

Regardless of the level to which the critique of the conceptualization of interest is taken in the above approaches, all of them concur in the indictment that contemporary political theory's silence about women, and its ignorance or distortion of gender, derive from the meta-theoretical postulates upon which the enterprise depends. This perspective takes the opposite view to that expressed by Judith Evans: 'It is not the techniques of political theory that constitute an obstacle to change, but the attitudes of political theorists, dictating which definitions will be adopted, and the manner in which techniques will be applied.' (Evans *et al.*, 1986: 3). Whereas Evans's analysis suggests that a re-socialization campaign is the properly therapeutic approach to removing the obstacles to the integration of a feminist perspective in political theory, our analysis confronts the problem of gender bias on a more fundamental level.

We take issue with her critique on two basic grounds. First, such a critique is based on a very narrow definition of 'techniques' of research that fails to consider the limitations of the meta-theoretical framework within which the application of research tools occurs. Recognition of fundamental biases in the methodological approach of bourgeois political science has a long history that is unacknowledged in Evans's view. For instance, Marxism – a paradigmatic shift in political analysis that Evans virtually ignores – attacked the methodology of political economy because of its acceptance of the atomistic world-view and ahistorical methodological individualism of liberal democratic analysis. This critique went well beyond the indictment of the particular class origins and socialization of specific theorists to locate class bias at the conceptual level of discourse. Marx's analysis of the commodity, defined merely as a unit of exchange in bourgeois theory, but which was in fact the expression of human labour power, is just one example of criticism of the distorting effects of the dominant epistemological assumptions of traditional theory. Feminists have advanced this critique by considering the ways in which orthodox materialist analysis still treats the operation of gender hierarchies as unproblematic, unless they can be re-defined in class terms.

Second, Evans's view trivializes the major intellectual challenges that feminist scholarship raises by claiming that *all* sexist bias reflects the early childhood experiences of particular researchers, or 'sociological factors such as the small proportion of political scientists who are women' (Evans *et al.*, 1986: 103). Increasing the number of women in the profession certainly can have a positive effect both on the legitimacy of women's studies as a research area for political science, and on the career development paths of women within the profession as a whole. It is even likely that increasing the number of women in the profession to the level of a 'critical mass' would make a substantial difference in both the contexts of discovery and the modes of justification in studies of politics in general. In the case of practical politics, the research of Gun Hedlund suggests that the existence of a relatively high proportion of women politicians seems to promote different strategies of activity and different views about women's interests that contribute to the development of a 'new relation to the political culture influenced by the fact that [women] no longer are tokens in the political system' (p. 100). But the view that the *mere* integration of more women in the field will be sufficient to realize the full transformative potential of the feminist challenge is naïve.

This criticism does not negate the fact that the personal attitudes of particular political theorists influence the construction of research designs. Certainly, identifiable misogynistic biases can distort the conduct of research. But attitudes reflect more than the personal psycho-histories of given theorists. They are themselves cultural products that express a given society's understanding of gender, on both the linguistic and material level. Feminist critics of mainstream political science are interested in the analysis of what others have called the 'prism of sex' (we choose 'sex/gender' for greater accuracy). This prism refracts the vision of politics that any given school of political thought endorses, often in ways that are not made explicit.

The contributors to this volume, then, address the problem of sexism in the discipline of political science by considering an alternative approach to the conceptualization of politics. They contribute to the growing body of work by feminists (Stiehm, 1984; Scott, 1986; Jones, 1987) that has attempted to reconstruct the methodology of political research by reformulating basic categories of political thinking in order to allow gender to infect the ways we conceptualize political reality with the insights of a feminist vision. This means much more than considering women individually as political actors, or merely adding 'women's issues' to the litany of demands citizens make of the state. It means, materially and metaphorically, conceptualizing the political arena in terms of gender. The research of Hedlund and Jaquette suggests the importance of using gender-focused models in empirical studies of political behaviour.

An important task that confronts feminist theory is the clear definition of what taking gender as an analytic category entails, and how it structures political thought. In a recent essay in *The American Historical Review*, Joan Scott charges feminist theorists with often having muddled through their work with imprecise or euphemistic definitions of gender. In some cases, gender merely stands for 'women'. The use of the term 'gender' instead of 'women' in the title of works lends greater scholarly legitimacy to the research enterprise by 'dissociat[ing] itself from the (supposedly strident) politics of feminism' (Scott, 1986; 1056). In other cases, Scott argues, gender is meant to imply the social relations between the sexes, or is defined as a 'social category imposed on a sexed body'. But in these latter cases, Scott insists, the interpretive utility of the idea of separate spheres, one male and the other female, is rejected, since this usage of gender suggests that the world of women is 'part of the world of men, created in and by it'.

But Scott is only partially accurate in her interpretations of these positions. Moreover, she has failed to explore other possible constructions and usages of gender that are particularly relevant to political theory, which is concerned not only with how gender symbolizes power, but also with how it, quite literally, embodies power. Thus, in contrast to Scott, many of the contributors in this volume consider the potential utility of the concept of 'women's culture', or some variation of the separate spheres formulation, for describing and explaining the operation of sex/gender interests in politics, while, at the same time, endorsing the general hypothesis that gender implies the social relations between and among the sexes. Thus, they attempt to use gender as a basic analytic category of political thinking without rejecting, a priori, the explanatory utility of the idea of separate spheres.

Paraphrasing Scott, the way that the premises and standards of scholarly work in political science will be changed by including and accounting for women's experiences depends upon the extent to which sex/gender can be developed into a category of political analysis. What, specifically, does the development of sex/gender as an analytic category in political theory entail? How does this volume contribute to that enterprise?

The aim of theorizing about sex/gender is to understand this system itself, in all its historical and cultural forms. This is in stark contrast with Scott's project, whose end-point is the definition of gender as a signifier of other relationships of power, or as primarily constitutive of power. Yet, as Scott herself argues, it is imperative to resist reducing sex/gender to some other social structure, and to preserve gender as an independent analytic category in its own right (1986: 1062).

Equally important is the necessity to distinguish between different expressions of power – economic, political, sexual and linguistic. Without these distinctions we are left with the Foucaultian dilemma: power is so dispersed, ubiquitous and fluid that one has no clear notion either of what its substance is, or of the norms for determining adequate paths of resistance to it (White, 1986).

Feminists have contributed in significant and different ways to the project of theorizing about sex/gender. Early theories of patriarchy focused on sexuality and reproductive roles as factors determining the exploitation of women (Firestone, 1970; Millett, 1970; O'Brien, 1983; Delphy, 1984). Later analyses of work and the economy contributed further to the investigation of the dynamics of the oppression of women (Eisenstein, 1978; Rowbotham, 1978; Young, 1980; Hartmann, 1981). More recently, feminists influenced by the psychoanalytic theories of object relations, and the linguistic/ symbolic accounts of the post-structuralist school, have turned to a consideration of the ways that gendered subjects are constructed. They have been concerned also with understanding the influence of gendered signifiers on the articulation of the rules and meaning of social relationships (Dinnerstein, 1976; Chodorow, 1978; Flax, 1983; Keller, 1984; Irigaray, 1985; Moi, 1985; Harding, 1986). Scott, for instance, proposes that we treat gender as a 'constitutive element of social relationships' as well as 'a primary way of signifying relationships of power' (1986: 1067).

Yet all these attempts to theorize about sex/gender, and to apply these theories to the reconstruction of the framework of social and political thought, have been limited by their lack of historical specificity, or, at the conceptual level, by the failure to distinguish among the various levels of lived experience, for instance, between work and sexuality. The tendency has been either to treat sex/ gender as an epiphenomenon, secondary to determining economic relations; to describe it ahistorically; or to empty it of meaning in its own terms.

One of the key questions posed by feminist research is how the same structures of oppression – work, despotic political authority, systems of social stratification – affect women and men both differently and in the same ways. What distinguishes the feminist project is that it asks 'why differently?' The answer must have to do with the fact that the structurally different conditions of women and men are due not only to capital taking advantage of women as child-bearers and cheap labour, etc.; the division of labour and the sexual segregation of work activities are due also to the fact that men and women as sex/gendered actors enter into exploitative relationships which possess a relative independence. It is important to emphasize that in every dimension of social experience, as well as in the sphere of the intimate, women and men are present as embodied, sex/gendered beings, that is, as women and men. Naturally, the shape of this presence varies historically and cross-culturally. Feminist theory that stresses the reclamation of the 'power of difference, of womanliness as women define it' (Offen, forthcoming) has the greatest potential for supporting research which considers the ways that the structure and representation of gender vary with different and temporal contexts.

It is a peculiar irony of modern political theory that precisely at the moment of its embracing the ideals of freedom and equality for all, the specific presence of women and men in the political field is denied. Rather, the notion of the political agent as an abstract individual, or as the sexless and genderless member of an organized interest group, is institutionalized as the norm of political behaviour. Marx, of course, offered one of the most extensive critiques of the construction of 'alien politics' in his 'On the Jewish Question' (Thomas, 1985). Recent feminist theory has contributed further to this critique of liberal politics by arguing that the concept of autonomy as personal independence and the abstract conceptualization of individual human rights suppress a 'gendered but egalitarian vision of social organization' that is more consistent with the dominant modes of feminism in modern European history, and increasingly in the ideologies of women's liberation in the non-Western world, as well as with the project of fully incorporating women *as* women within a more diverse and pluralistic world (Offen, forthcoming; Ferguson, chapter 4; Vogel, chapter 7).

Both Siim (chapter 8) and Hernes (chapter 9) use the idea of the mediation of relations between the citizen and the state through the reality of gender differences in order to examine the sometimes contradictory effects of changes in welfare state politics in different political systems. Miller *et al.* (chapter 6) explore how gender consciousness, not merely sex differences, is becoming increasingly significant to the explanation of electoral behaviour in the United States. More research like this is needed on what factors contribute to the development of gender consciousness in terms of a wide variety of forms of political action in different historical and cultural contexts. Hedlund, for instance, explores (in chapter 5) how significant different forms of gender consciousness are to understanding the self-perception of elected officials in Sweden. Jaquette and Staudt (chapter 10) argue that the subordination of women's own definition of their interests to the exigencies of population policies perpetuates programmes that often have negative results for feminist politics.

The central argument of this volume is that to consider gender as an analytic category in political theory – that is, to perceive gender as at least an analytically distinct set of social relationships – re-defines and enlarges the scope of politics, the practice of citizenship and authority, and the language of political action, as well as recognizes the political dimensions of sexuality. The following chapters are examples of research that contributes to this re-definition and enlargement.

References

Chodorow, Nancy (1978) *The Reproduction of Mothering: Psychoanalysis and the Sociology of Gender*. Berkeley: University of California Press.

Delphy, Christine (1984) *Close to Home: A Materialist Analysis of Women's Oppression*. London: Hutchinson.

Diamond, I. and N. Hartsock (1981) 'Beyond Interests in Politics: A Comment on Virginia Sapiro's "When are Interests Interesting? The Problem of the Political Representation of Women"', *American Political Science Review* 75: 717–23.

Dinnerstein, Dorothy (1976) *The Mermaid and the Minotaur*. New York: Harper & Row.

Eduards, Maud (1983) *Kon, makt, medborgarskap: Kvinnan i politiskt tankande fran Platon till Engels (Sex, Power and Citizenship: Woman in Political Thought from Plato to Engels)*. Stockholm: Liber.

Eisenstein, Zillah (1978) *Capitalist Patriarchy and the Case for Socialist Feminism*. New York: Monthly Review Press.

Elshtain, Jean Bethke (1981) *Public Man/Private Woman*. Princeton, NJ: Princeton University Press.

Evans, Judith *et al.* (1986) *Feminism and Political Theory*. London: Sage.

Firestone, Shulamith (1970) *The Dialectic of Sex*. New York: Bantam.

Flax, Jane (1983) 'Political Philosophy and the Patriarchal Unconscious: A Psychoanalytic Perspective on Epistemology and Metaphysics', in Harding and Hitinkka (eds), *Discovering Reality*. Dordrecht: D. Reidel.

Harding, Sandra (1986) *The Science Question in Feminism*. Ithaca, NY: Cornell University Press.

Hartmann, Heidi (1981) 'The Unhappy Marriage of Marxism and Feminism: Towards a More Progressive Union', in Sargent, Lydia (ed.), *Women and Revolution*. London: Pluto Press.

Hartsock, Nancy (1983) *Money, Sex and Power: Toward a Feminist Historical Materialism*. New York: Longman.

Irigaray, Luce (1985) *This Sex Which Is Not One*. Ithaca, NY: Cornell University Press.

Jaggar, Allison (1983) *Feminist Politics and Human Nature*. Totowa, NJ: Rowman and Allenheld.

Jónasdóttir, Anna G. (1983) 'Hon for honom – han for staten: Om Hobbes och Lockes kvinnosyn' ('She for Him – He for the State: On Hobbes' and Locke's view of women'), in Eduards (1983).

Jones, Kathleen B. (1987) 'On Authority, OR Why Women Are Not Entitled to Speak', *Nomos* xxix.

Keller, Evelyn Fox (1984) *Reflections on Gender and Science*. New Haven, Conn.: Yale University Press.

Lloyd, Genevieve (1984) *The Man of Reason: 'Male' and 'Female' in Western Philosophy*. London: Methuen.

Millett, Kate (1970) *Sexual Politics*. New York: Doubleday.

Moi, Toril (1985) *Sexual/Textual Politics: Feminist Literary Theory*. New York: Methuen.

O'Brien, Mary (1983) *The Politics of Reproduction*. Boston: Routledge and Kegan Paul.

Offen, Karen (forthcoming) 'Defining Feminism', *Signs*.

Okin, Susan (1979) *Women in Western Political Thought*. Princeton, NJ: Princeton University Press.

Pateman, Carole (1983) 'Feminist Critiques of the Public/Private Dichotomy', in Benn and Gaus (eds), *Public and Private in Social Life*. London: Croom Helm.

Rowbotham, Sheila (1978) *Woman's Consciousness/Man's World*. London: Penguin.

Sabine, George and Thomas Thorson (1973) *A History of Political Theory*. Hinsdale, Il.: Dryden.

Saxonhouse, Arlene (1985) *Women in the History of Political Thought*. New York: Praeger.

Scott, Joan (1986) 'Gender: A Useful Category of Historical Analysis', *American Historical Review* 91: 1053–75.

Stiehm, Judith (1984) *Women's Views of the Political World of Men*. New York: Transnational.

Thomas, Paul (1985) 'Alien Politics', in Ball and Farr (eds), *After Marx*. Oxford: Oxford University Press.

White, Stephen (1986) 'Foucault's Challenge to Critical Theory', *American Political Science Review* 80: 419–32.

Wolin, Sheldon (1961) *Politics and Vision*. London: Allen and Unwin.

Young, Iris (1980) 'Socialist Feminism and the Limits of Dual Systems Theory', *Socialist Review* 50–51: 169–88.

2

Towards the Revision of Politics

Kathleen B. Jones

The conceptual framework of contemporary Western political thought reflects a vision of politics that is gender-myopic. To classical thinkers like Plato, Aristotle, Hobbes, and Locke, it would have been inconceivable to ignore questions of gender in the formulation of basic theories of politics. Even when they distinguished sharply between male and female nature, they accepted the view that understanding the world of women was critical to understanding the nature and aims of the political. Most classical theorists claimed that biological and cultural imperatives not only precluded women's participation in authority structures, but also impaired women developing the qualities and attitudes associated with political efficacy and the activities of citizenship. Nevertheless, such claims reflected an acute sense of the centrality of gender to the rationalization of political life. Contemporary theorists like Dahl, Lipset, Eckstein, Deutsch, and even Lukes make gender questions peripheral to political analysis. Consequently, women and 'the female' have been hidden in contemporary political theory, and in the contemporary histories of political thought written from an androcentric viewpoint (Saxonhouse, 1985: vii). Despite the geometric progression of works by feminist scholars in political theory, the discourse of contemporary theory remains largely unchanged.[1] Theories continue to be constructed as if women, and their interests as a group, were conceptually irrelevant to political discourse. More accurately, mainstream theorists today define the political terrain in genderless terms.

This essay will examine epistemological and methodological biases in political science research. It will consider the ways in which the political behaviour of women and the political relevance of women's interests have been either ignored or distorted; it will evaluate the adequacy of contemporary studies of women and the political process. Finally, it will suggest ways to correct the conceptual and methodological limits of this research.

The major concepts of contemporary Western political thought are built on an acceptance of the idea that the public is fundamentally distinct from the private and the personal. This distinction informs the discipline and shapes the analytic tools of traditional political science. It contributes to making women and their political interests invisible. Its history and its influence on the definition of political norms and behaviour can be traced from the Greeks to twentieth-century political texts.

Beginning with the Greeks, the conceptual distinction between public and private reflected the classical understanding of the private realms of the household (*oikos*, or the sphere of reproduction) and the economy (the sphere of production) as realms of necessity. Relations of superordination–subordination prevailed 'naturally' in these arenas of human activity. Aristotle argues, for instance, that those who are superior are meant by nature to rule those who are inferior. By contrast, the realm of the *polis* was a sphere of freedom described by relations of equality. Aristotle notes that in political relationships 'ruler and ruled exchange positions, wishing to be equal in nature and differing in nothing' (*Politics*, I, 1259b 4–6).

The distinction between public and private is based also on the recognition that life in the *polis* is marked by considerations of moral choice, or what Aristotle called the concerns of the 'good life'. The activities of the private sphere provide the material and physical necessities of life. Although the work of private life, including women's work in the family, is an essential contribution to the life of the *polis*, it is categorically different from political action in the *polis*. Political action is characterized by reasoned discourse. Citizens participated in political acts that affirmed their rationality and autonomy. They were political actors who articulated publicly and authoritatively the values that the *polis* embodied. Since women were assumed to be associated by and through nature with the private sphere, they were excluded functionally from the practice of freedom that defined political life.[2]

In the Homeric tradition, the model of the citizen-soldier excluded women from public life. In the philosophical tradition, the model of rational discourse defined the practice of citizenship. The consequences of this conceptual bias acted, along with other material forces, to structure political life and citizenship in ways that categorically segregated women and the needs with which they were associated from public life (Slater, 1968; Saxonhouse, 1980; Hartsock, 1982, chap. 3). In the metaphor of Jean Bethke Elshtain, women were made publicly voiceless, having been excluded from the vocabulary of politics (Elshtain, 1982).

Thus, written into the classical definition of politics itself were premises that precluded women's participation in public life, even though female interests were recognized as essential to the stability necessary for the pursuit of virtue (Saxonhouse, 1985: 84–90). Moreover, hierarchical, patriarchal relations were held to be the natural characteristics of rule in the private sphere. Consequently, women's exclusion from public life was predicated on their 'natural' inability to transcend their biological and economic subordination in the household.[3] The distinction between rulers and ruled became a sex-specific one. Politics, by definition, became a world in which men acted and spoke.

The concepts that structured political discourse throughout the classical period were based on this assumed dichotomy between the public and private realms. Moreover, the public realm was characterized as an arena of freedom within which the tyranny of 'nature' could be circumscribed. Because women were associated with the private realm, public life became, in the classical tradition, not only without women, but against women and the devalued virtues of the 'oikos'. The anti-female ethos of public life was rooted in an epistemology that was effectively, though not intentionally, misogynistic.[4]

None the less, classical writers subscribed to the notion of politics as participation in an 'ethical' collectivity. Consequently, in so far as it could be demonstrated that the 'necessary' barriers to participation – of sex, class, and so on – were, in fact contingent ones, articulation of a more universalized definition of public activity and the norms of public life remained possible.[5] Even Aristotle allowed for the fact that, in certain circumstances, the natural rule of the male over the female may have to be subverted in order for the 'best' to rule, and for the virtuous act to be done. In the works of Augustine, for example, the idea of politics as ethical action was prominent. He distinguished between the City of God, in which hierarchy and inequality have been eradicated, and the City of Man, where lesser human characteristics became dominant. In the City of God, women are no less citizen-members than men, although in the City of Man they may be ruled by men. But since temporal politics has been eclipsed by the superiority of the spiritual polity, this apparent political equality has limited purchase in rethinking the meaning of the public life of citizens as gendered beings. Citizenship in the virtuous City of God lies beyond the body, beyond sexuality, and beyond the historical reality of people as men and women.

Machiavelli divorced the terms of political discourse and the norms of political life from virtue in the normative sense. Virtue became 'virtu', or excellence in the skills of leadership and state-building, where excellence was measured in terms of the effective and efficient use of power. To the extent that Machiavelli reduced politics to an instrumentalist enterprise, an exercise of will and power, women were excluded even more completely from public life.

Metaphorically, politics now existed as the arena of action in which the chicanery and cunning of the manipulative Prince (male) kept at bay, as much as was humanly possible, the vagaries of Fortuna's (female) rule over human affairs. Practically, since public life was not only founded through but dependent on brute force or military might, women's participation in 'militarized citizenship' (Pocock, 1975) was precluded. But it is especially important to consider the implications of the Machiavellian substitution of efficiency for all other ethical norms that could legitimate political action. Normatively, Machiavelli's politics excluded a mode of policy making that considered public choices in terms of justice, morality, and human relations instead of the rational calculus of means appropriate to political stability. Moral principles became 'feminine', politically irrelevant virtues. A politics based on this instrumental framework – on rules, skills, and techniques devoid of principles other than utility – was a sexually segregated field of action.

Machiavelli's calculus of power seems more descriptive of twentieth-century 'Realpolitik' than of the seventeenth- and eighteenth-century liberal theories of constitutionalism that followed. Although theorists like Locke and Hobbes considered authority and the boundaries of public life to be essentially 'contingent' institutions, the fact that authority was derived from consent and was bounded normatively by natural laws reunited ethics and politics. Moreover, in theory, these social contract theorists' principles forced them to reject any view that the structure of society was based on a 'natural' hierarchy of power and privilege. They attacked patriarchal authority as the exercise of arbitrary power over others, and, hence, violative of the law of nature that no one had the natural right to rule another. In this sense, their theories were remarkably gender-sensitive, since they addressed directly the question of women's relationship to the state (Vogel, in Evans, 1986).

Hobbes's radical individualism, and his insistence that all authority relations were based on convention, not nature, made his analysis of women's political status unique. Locke's theory distinguished more sharply between political rule and familial rule: he did not require a homogeneity of form and substance between authority in the political sphere, and all other forms of rule, as Hobbes did. Nevertheless, to the extent that the theories of Hobbes and Locke remained wedded to certain patriarchal assumptions about the structure of authority in the private sphere, women's citizenship, in the legalistic sense, was circumscribed arbitrarily. Hobbes, for example, erased married women from the political role that his postulates about the natural equality of humans suggested when he claimed the necessity for the family to be represented by one person, and allowed for the conventional preference for the husband to prevail. Locke's rejection of patriarchalism is less coherent. Although he argued in the *Second Treatise* that the rule of husbands over wives and children naturally belongs to males as the 'abler and stronger', he provided a liberal gloss to this patriarchal argument with the claim that a woman will enter voluntarily into a marriage contract that legitimately subjugates her to her husband's will (Locke, *Second Treatise*, 44; Brennan and Pateman, 1978: 183).

Liberal theory's postulate that authority depended on consent threatened the idea that authority in any institution could be derived from nature. Indeed, Locke and Hobbes used a gender-based critique – the critique of patriarchy as an inappropriate metaphor for authority – to complete the logic of their analysis of legitimate authority derived from consent. Hobbes, in particular, was emphatic in insisting that no one, not even women, could be excluded from the grants of natural rights. Yet, these theorists ultimately employed what Vogel calls a new patriarchalism to justify excluding women, especially married women, from the status of persons with civil and political rights. The contractual theory of marriage, and certain assumptions about women's special status that required their being protected 'for their own good', worked to inscribe classical liberal theories with biases that precluded extending the same individual rights to women that the logic of these theories seemed to require (Vogel, chapter 7).

At the same time, the emphasis upon individualism and instrumentalism in liberal theory ultimately limited the transformative and egalitarian possibilities even of extending the scope of citizenship to more and different people. As Marx observed about the French Revolution, the very blindness of liberalism to the material conditions structuring the life situations of different classes of individuals compromised the political equality in which liberalism presumably was grounded. Furthermore, even when it granted political rights to individual citizens who happened to be women, liberal theory ignored the different question related to the representation of women because they are women.[6] Its commitment was to a political equality derived from certain universal and uniform features of human existence that follow from the human capacity to reason. Since sex differences were regarded as irrelevant to determining the status of citizenship, the activities of citizenship must occasion the same forms of political representation for women and men. Citizenship was defined as a genderless activity.

Ultimately, the extension of political and civil rights to women as individuals incorporated women into public life in ways that did not alter either the structure or the ethos of the polity. Although writers like Mary Wollstonecraft and Condorcet advocated political and educational reforms that could improve the position of individual women, they remained silent about institutional arrangements in the market and in the private sphere that made the authority structure of the liberal state class, race and gender biased (Vogel, in Evans, 1986: 31; Korsmeyer, in Gould and Wartofsky, 1976). Exploitative relations of production and reproduction were left intact. Such writers acknowledged the deleterious effects of distinct patterns of socialization for males and females, and railed against any notions of reason being sex-linked. Rationality was a genderless capacity of all human beings, if only they were given the opportunity to develop it. But these liberals adhered to a model of rationality based on an instrumental calculus of logic and decision making. To them, sentiment, emotion, compassion, and love were vices that deflected the development of reason from its true path. The calculating self-interested ego of the burgeoning capitalist order became the norm for male and female moral development and citizenship. Women had to be educated to the same ends as men, or their lives would be hopelessly sunk below the level of rational creatures. Rather than criticize the standards of citizenship that prevailed, these writers urged that women be socialized and educated to them. 'Let women share the rights and they will emulate the virtues of men' (Wollstonecraft, 319).

For Wollstonecraft, citizenship meant participation in deliberations about the actions of the state. As much as she objected to Rousseau's marriage of military virtue and citizenship, she also rejected the scope of activities defined for women in his concept of republican motherhood. Wollstonecraft insisted that women become active citizens, not just the mothers of citizens. But she failed to consider systematically the ways in which social relations of personal life were affected by the exigencies of market society. The class structure of capitalism limited the impact of changes in juridical norms, or the expansion of educational opportunities for women (Eisenstein, 1980: 89–112). Moreover, she ignored the disciplinary logic of the modern state that subjugated citizens to the homogenizing force of nationalism.

Despite his disclaimer in *The Subjection of Women* that 'what is now called the nature of woman is an eminently artificial thing', even John Stuart Mill contended that women were naturally better suited for the responsibilities of housework and child care. Except if their class position permitted them to hire other women to perform these activities, women were to be confined to the home. Mill argued that working-class women's labour market participation would not be economically significant enough to offset the emotional costs of their abandonment of their 'natural' duties as homemakers and mothers. It never occurred to Mill to consider the political functions of the sexual division of labour within the family, or to alter such arrangements in the home (Mill; Pateman, in Duncan, 1983: 208–10)

Nor did such liberal writers challenge the limitations of instrumental modes of decision making. They accepted the notion that the order of society depended on the balanced resolution of conflicts of interest which gave preference to no one group over another, treating all alike. Yet there were characteristic interests constructed by women's disproportionate immersion in the 'female' world of the household. These interests related to the physical–social circumstances surrounding woman's different relationship to her body, to her intimate involvement with the nurturing of the young, and to an ongoing, historically structured connection to the concrete realities of everyday existence.[7] Representation of these interests seemed less amenable to translation into the demands of abstract, disembodied subjects.

Indeed, the liberal concept of justice implied an impartial application of rules for balancing competing interests in order to secure the common good. It depended, in part, on the subordination of particular or private interests to the public interest. But the claim was made by liberals that this sense of justice was developed through 'participation in as wide a range of public institutions as possible. . .'. Since women were confined to the family, and continued to be so located even in Mill's and Wollstonecraft's theories, they could 'never learn to weigh the public interest against selfish inclination' (Pateman, 1980: 31). In short, their interests in the private sphere conflicted necessarily with the pursuit of justice.

Challenging the limits of instrumentalism, or liberal ideas of justice, required seeking a solution to the problem of representing women in ways that neither attempted a banishment of women through bio-technical transformation, nor abandoned public life to men, since men had the appropriate 'natures' to behave competitively as required. A partial solution was suggested by feminist theory's growing emphasis on the claim that the peculiar quality of 'female experiences' seemed to necessitate fundamental changes in the scope and dynamics of public life itself if women were to participate fully in political discourse. These experiences demonstrated that citizens were not only voters – they were also sexual beings, caretakers, workers, in short, embodied gendered persons who participated in politics with heart, hand, and will.

The political language of liberalism proved incapable of expressing the broadened scope of citizenship that could include such fullbodied participation (Petchesky, 1983). Rousseau's solution had entailed a rigid segregation of roles that excluded women from citizenship, even though it acknowledged the critical functions that women performed as mothers of citizens. He embraced, as civic virtues, the values of sentiment and tradition that had been associated historically with a feminized sensibility, but he located women outside the public realm (Elshtain, 1986). The dilemma confronting modern political theory was how to recognize the political relevance of sexual differences, and how to include these differences within definitions of political action and civic virtue without constructing sexually segregated norms of citizenship. In short, how to construct a theory of political equality and citizenship that granted the individual personhood of women without denying that women had differing needs and interests from men (Rowbotham, 1986). This dilemma has been highlighted by contemporary feminist theorists' deconstruction of the codes of sexual difference and the resistance to any superimposed reading of an unambiguous 'female essence' emerging automatically from the structure of female experience (Elshtain, 1987; Grant).

The discourse of liberalism, with its emphasis on individual rights and abstract rules, fundamentally limited its vision of politics and political action. Its *laissez-faire* political economy segregated whole areas of social relations from public policy. Its acceptance of a sexual division of labour as natural exacerbated the consequences of this segregation for women especially. Those interests that could not be represented as claims of individuals for equal treatment before the law were ignored by the political system. Despite the fact that the social construction of gender made women's situations, like those of class and race, politically central to the dynamics and scope of their citizenship, liberal theory's postulate of ideal unsituated actors abstracted from these contexts by conceptualizing citizenship as the activity of isolated, self-interested, disembodied individuals (Nelson, 1984: 225).

The ideal of citizenship that liberal theory developed was derived from a set of interconnected assumptions about human nature. The state of nature was conceived, by early liberal writers like Hobbes and Locke, to be a state of perfect equality. In it, each individual enjoyed the same natural right to be free from arbitrarily coercive power. Although rights belonged equally to each individual, and natural law, disclosed by reason, prohibited each from harming another's right of life, liberty, or property, there was no naturally existing authority to settle destabilizing disputes that were understood to arise necessarily from conflicts of individual wills. Hence, Locke wrote, men put themselves into society in order to protect themselves from these insecurities and instabilities. Individuals quit their natural state of freedom, and agreed to be governed by the majority, in order to secure their individual rights. Consent was the necessary condition to ensure the legitimacy of the contract. But the apparently equal consent of each masked the fact that different material conditions constructed the terms of the contract variably, not only for certain individuals, but for similarly situated groups of individuals. To treat these different people as if they were the same before the law allowed existing material conditions of inequality of prevail.

The limited vision of politics in liberal theory was contradicted by the concrete ways that the development of the modern state and the market system connected more and different activities to the public realm. The effect of the development of the system of market production on the social relations and ideology of the family, the evolution of modern penology, the institutionalization of medicine, and the regimentation of sexuality are a few examples of the increasing politicization of everyday life that liberal individualism made opaque (Foucault, 1978; 1979). The political vocabulary and conceptual framework of liberalism further obscured the fact that traditional categories of public and private, as well as established views of political action, were limited. Its reduction of claims of conflicting 'interests' to conflicts of individual rights masked the social forces that structured these claims. The nature of these demands pointed to the limitations of the 'rights' conceptualization of moral reasoning.[8]

The permeability of the 'private' realms of household, market, sexual relationship, and so on, demonstrated that these different activities were connected to the public sphere. It also revealed that acknowledging the political dimension of these activities simultaneously required a basic re-definition of the concept of citizenship. More than anything else, making gender central to the development of political discourse required the articulation of norms and values that could move civic virtue beyond one-sidedly militaristic (warrior-citizen) or narrowly rationalistic codes. It meant searching for a language to express efforts to see citizenship as a 'create[d] space for meaningful action by persons in situations in which they find themselves' about the basic ends of their collective political identity (Elshtain, 1987: 248).

The politics of sexuality challenged implicitly the assumption that equality was equivalent to genderless laws. Rowbotham notes how early twentieth-century feminists' 'demands for protection at work or birth control could not be contained within an egalitarian framework in which individuals were seen as simply equivalent' (Rowbotham, 1986: 80). These dilemmas about the meaning of equality are evident again in the contemporary debates about abortion, affirmative action, military service for women, pornography, comparable worth, as well as in dialogue about the welfare state and defence spending. Potentially, they challenge the neutrality and universality of a concept of citizenship that proposes to include everyone without prejudice, but ignores the ways in which gender, as a socially constructed, historical reality, reflects different ways of being and knowing that fundamentally affect the practice and meaning of civic duties and responsibilities, and the enjoyment of civil and political rights (Jones, 1987).

Contemporary scholars have ignored the dilemmas entailed in employing the traditional concepts of political analysis. Instead, they have accepted the definitions of politics and political activity implicit in Western liberal theory. They have developed methodologies designed to describe and explain women's political behaviour within the framework of an epistemology that provides, at best, only a partial and distorted view of political life. The remainder of this chapter will survey recent research in political science.

One can describe the development of political science research on women in terms of three stages: invisibility, limited visibility, and visibility. The centuries-old exclusion of women from positions of power and from public life was mirrored in their exclusion from most political research. With the obvious exception of studies of notable historical women public figures – Queen Elizabeth, Joan of Arc, Catherine the Great, and others – political researchers generally accepted the notion that the 'scientific' study of politics could be conducted without bias by assuming that women's political behaviour was either non-existent or irrelevant. Despite the fact that women had participated in unique and important ways in the revolutionary transformation of the modern world, political scientists studied the dynamics of modernization in ignorance of this fact (Rowbotham, 1972).

In the first two decades following the founding of the American Political Science Association, the profession's main journals devoted approximately 1 per cent of their contents to the explicit examination of women's political activities (Shanley and Shuck, 1975: 633). Only after women were enfranchised did the subject of women's political participation become a concern of scholars. However, as

Baxter and Lansing have noted, many of these early studies were limited to the attempt to gauge the impact of women's voting on politics (Baxter and Lansing, 1983: 5). Because these studies demonstrated a markedly lower rate of registration and voter activity for women, many scholars took this as evidence supporting the image of the apolitical woman, rather than an indication of the persistence of extra-legal obstacles to women's citizenship (Shanley and Shuck, 1975: 640; Bourque and Grossholz, 1974: 255–66).

The behavioural revolution promised to transform the study of politics into a true science. In place of the narrow focus on the operations of political institutions, behavioural political science offered careful descriptions of the regularities of political behaviour. But this apparent shift in focus did not constitute any considerable alteration in the definition of what was considered political. Throughout most of the 1950s and 1960s, political research on women either was non-existent, or was limited to the treatment of gender as a background variable in behavioural studies (Lovenduski, 1981: 83–97). The notable exception was Maurice Duverger's 1955 classic, *The Political Role of Women*. Nevertheless, conventional studies of political participation were unaffected by Duverger's analysis. Instead, they continued to assume that the field of politics was stereotypically male. 'Although he abjured the simple description of the structure and operation of public institutions, in his study of political behavior the behavioral political scientist concentrated on the behavior of those people within or aspiring to posts in those very same public institutions which had fascinated his predecessors' (Shanley and Shuck, 1975: 639). If women failed to participate at the same rate and in the same ways as men, this was considered proof of their inadequacies rather than of sexist bias in the definition of what was political, or evidence that there remained material obstacles to the full participation of women as a group.[9]

The major project of the second stage of limited visibility has been to expose the sexist exclusion of women from traditional political science research. The result has been the proliferation of a significant body of scholarship, largely by women in the profession, challenging the assumption that women participate in politics significantly less than men, and attempting to explain persistent differences in patterns of participation in non-sexist ways.[10] Included in this stage also was the publication of works that explored the behaviour of women as political élites and that began to consider the public policy process surrounding 'women's issues'.[11]

Despite this important work by and about women, the epistemological and methodological framework of most of this research remained wedded to traditional definitions of politics and political behaviour. The work of this phase represented the amassing of considerable evidence concerning women's contributions to politics. However, paraphrasing Gerda Lerner's analysis of this stage of women's history, these researchers applied questions from traditional political science to women, and tried to fit women's behaviour into the empty spaces of political science scholarship (Lerner, 1979: 149). The obvious limitation of this work is that it left unchallenged the adequacy of the traditional categories of political analysis either to describe or to explain women's political attitudes, behaviour, and 'interests'. Instead, the pervasive assumption of this research was that 'those stereotyped characteristics held up as the masculine ideal (for example, aggressiveness, competitiveness, and pragmatism) are the norms of political behaviour as well' (Bourque and Grossholz, 1974: 229).

A case in point is Susan Welch's essay, 'Women as Political Animals'. Welch proposes to challenge the dominant research finding 'that women participate less in political activities than do men' (1977: 711). Analysing the differences in degree of participation for thirteen types of political activities, Welch finds that when situational and structural factors are controlled, 'women as a whole participate as much as men' (p. 726). The impetus behind this endeavour is clear: to refute the theory that women differ from men on scales of political activity. Indeed, Welch demonstrates clearly that factors like employment outside the home and education are more explanatory of male and female participation patterns than is the variable sex. Nevertheless, the hidden bias of such research limits the feminist implications of its findings. The implicit assumption of this study, and similar research of the limited visibility type, is that male standards of participation are universal norms of political activity. By implication, the more women act like men – that is, register, vote, contribute to campaigns, attend political meetings, and work for parties – the more they demonstrate their involvement in politics and their sense of political efficacy.

The assumption that quantity (more voting) is what counts and the acceptance of male norms have serious consequences. Measurement of voting and participation is a much simpler task to perform than is examination of the goals and results of such activity. It is certainly possible that the consequences of increasing women's voting might be the pursuit of policies which are decidedly anti-feminist. Welch established a linear relationship between class, education, and traditional political participation. Recent voting behaviour studies have suggested that traditional political activities may be correlated with political conservatism (Nie, Verba, and

Petrocik, 1976; Jaquette, 1974). Therefore, what studies like Welch's may be describing is the development of an alliance between élite women and élite men who together need to protect their stake in society against the redistributive needs of economically and socially underprivileged women and men.[12]

To describe more accurately the significance of women's participation in traditional ways, studies must be conducted that explore the direction and outcome as well as the rate of participation. This of course requires utilizing qualitative methodologies, like detailed case studies, as well as quantitative research (Jayaratne, 1983). It also requires the careful examination of other topics directly connected to policy – such as welfare politics, the operation of the criminal justice system, state regulation of sexuality and reproduction, employment and economic development, immigration laws, and so on. The experience of citizenship is strongly determined by the rhetoric and development of public policy in these arenas, as well as by the activities of lobbying and voting. The argument put forth here is that we should not limit our investigation of citizenship only to forms of participation that have been defined traditionally as political, or to those that are able to be measured easily through standard quantitative analyses.

Research like Welch's accepts uncritically the adequacy of the concept of participation and the parameters of the field of politics described by such activities as voting, campaigning, or party work. But as the earlier sections of this chapter demonstrated, the theory of citizenship reflected in these modes of participation is a male-defined/male-oriented one. It is derived in abstraction from, if not in opposition to, women's experiences of the public world, as well as their connection to a whole range of activities in the private sphere. Any theory of participatory citizenship must address the issue of the political integration of women from within a conceptual framework that does more than fit women 'into the categories and value systems which consider man the measure of significance'.[13] For women to become fully visible in politics, an epistemology is needed which shifts from male-oriented to female-oriented modes of political behaviour, communication, and decision-making styles derived from the actual experiences and interests of women, while at the same time remaining suspicious of the universality and self-definition of any experience (Grant, 1987: 110, 112).

Failure to develop a critical feminist epistemology results in research that supports implicitly a patriarchal hierarchy of values. For example, Virginia Sapiro argues that if women have been less politically involved, it must be because they lack the skills, experience, and language which generate political knowledge and a sense of political efficacy. Women, she writes, 'are diverted away from knowledge and expertise in many important areas, including politics. . . . Women's language is the language of the noninfluential, of those who are deferential and dependent.' It is women's ghettoization in the private sphere that Sapiro contends teaches them 'to be something other than full citizens' (Sapiro, 1983: 172). The questions Sapiro raises have to do with changing women and adapting them to public life, rather than changing politics to accommodate the multiplicity and vitality of women's voices.

Sapiro's programme for integrating women would necessitate changes in the private sphere in order to free women for political activity. These certainly are important and necessary changes. But apart from expanding the scope of the public policy agenda in this manner, incorporation of women would leave the political terrain unchanged essentially. Other researchers, however, have argued that representation of women's unique 'interests' would necessarily entail recognition of the inadequacy and partiality of traditional conceptions of the political community as an instrumental alliance. They argue from a perspective that regards female experience as the foundation of an alternative, not underdeveloped, vision of politics. For instance, Diamond and Hartsock contend that 'women's relationally defined existence . . . results in a social understanding in which dichotomies are less foreign, everyday life is more valued, and a sense of connectedness and continuity with other persons and the natural world is central'. The representation and integration of this vision entails the 'development of more encompassing categories of analysis for political life' (Diamond and Hartsock, 1981). It also requires a radical reconstruction of public life in ways that would preclude the need to devalue women's social understanding of politically meaningful activities, as well as promote the transformation of sexist divisions of labour in the private sphere.

Andre Gundar Frank has written extensively about the hidden bias in Anglo-American theories of development. Theorists of modernization, Frank contends, have failed to recognize that the history of capitalist development has contributed to the systematic underdevelopment of much of the world. Instead, they have argued that the path to modernization is a singular one that moves nations inexorably toward greater equality and freedom. If nations fail to reach this goal, the failure is explained generally by problems of maladaption endemic to these countries themselves. Not only is the historical creation of international inequality ignored, but the identification of pre-modern societies with oppressive, backward social structures is presumed (Frank, 1979: 103–13). Moreover, the fact that the greater equity of modernized states is predicated on the exploitation of the majority of the world's population is overlooked.

Similarly, those researchers who argue that women's experience is exclusively a distorted, powerless, ineffectual, voiceless reality are guilty of a parallel amnesia. They forget that men have defined the territory of politics, established the rules of political discourse, and limited the scope of political interests so that women's powers and strengths could be seen only as their opposites (Dinnerstein, 1976; Chodorow, 1978).

What a feminist political science must do is develop a new vocabulary of politics so that it can express the specific and different ways in which women have wielded power, been in authority, practised citizenship, and understood freedom. This means that we accept Gerda Lerner's advice to discard the 'oppressed group model' for defining women's roles. This model emphasizes too exclusively the idea that, since women have been segregated from male political territory, women's consciousness and experiences have been ones of pervasive alienation. Women's occupations, status, experiences, rituals, and consciousness clearly reflect patriarchal definitions and norms. But that is not all. Although in a distorted way, the situations of women reflect a different perspective on society: an attempt to attain autonomy and emancipation in the face of systematic oppression, and to speak in what Carol Gilligan has called a different voice.

Re-defining our concepts of politics, activity, and community necessarily challenges the assumed bifurcation of the public and the private into two radically isolated realms. It also provides a foundation for a theory of political activity that could include women, 'female' virtues, and 'female' interests, without having to adhere to an ahistorical or essentialist reading of women's lives.

Several researchers have provided models of doing research with the interests of gender at the centre of the epistemological frame.[14] For instance, a number of studies have suggested how contradictory and complicated the picture of citizenship becomes when we explore the impact of the welfare state on women's lives. Barbara Nelson has shown how structural factors effected the construction of a two-tiered system of citizenship in the United States: relatively powerless, predominantly female client-citizens, and more powerful, disproportionately male electoral-citizens. Gender relations mediate citizen's experience of state activities (Nelson, 1984).

Helga Hernes argued that, despite highly developed social service programmes, women's status as citizens in Scandinavian countries was still marked by inequality, under-representation, discrimination, and subordination. Women had been incorporated into the state as client-citizens, or as low-level service worker-citizens – as recipients and deliverers of benefits under programmes designed for them largely by a male-dominated establishment. But they, and their interests, generally were absent from the corporatist system that established the priorities of the public sector. Consequently, the nature of women's citizenship was marked primarily by their transition from private to public dependency. Since women were more likely to be the immediate beneficiaries of a stable public sector, Hernes hypothesized that women were more likely to be the supporters of public growth and regulation. The irony was that women were supporting the growth and development of an institution that incorporated women without necessarily incorporating greater representation for them in the arenas and institutions shaping their lives (Hernes, 1984).

Birthe Siim has explored this further in her comparative study of the impact of welfare state systems on the nature of women's citizenship. The growth of the public sector and the state's increasing role in providing services has not transformed women into dependent citizen-clients universally. Rather, Siim argued, in the Scandinavian countries women's roles as consumers of state-provided services made them less dependent on the state as clients than in systems like those of the United States and Britain where weaker welfare systems increased women's dependent reliance on the state as clients. She has also contributed to the re-definition of political activity by criticizing Hernes's bias toward conceptualizing political influence as participation in formal 'power from above' types of politics, as opposed to women's activities in social movements, or power from below (Siim, chapter 8). Men and their interests may continue to dominate in the formal arenas of power, but women's ability to construct alternative arenas of influence is not lacking altogether, and may augur for the future forms of participation that are less bureaucratic, more democratic, and personalized (Ferguson, chapter 4).

Contemporary feminists are reluctant to stress the differences, in activities and norms, that appear to distinguish women's interests from men's. The fear is that this stress might undercut the demand to eradicate inequities in the methods of recruitment that discriminate against women having access to the dominant institutions of politics. However, neither the blind demand for access, nor the uncritical embrace of 'maternal thinking' will enable us to usher in the feminist future. What is needed is the development of categories of analysis protean and inclusive enough to describe adequately the position of different women in different political systems.[15] It is in this light that we need to consider the implications of women's 'disinterestedness' and exclusion from the 'power of "what has always been"' for the development of alternative social frameworks (Reeves, 1982: 156, 151; Balbus, 1982; Hartsock, 1982; Jaquette, 1983). This book contributes to the broadening of our theoretical conceptualization of the relationship between women and politics, and to the development of a body of empirical research that applies a new perspective to the investigation and analysis of this relationship.

This chapter has argued that the conceptual framework of traditional political science is a distorted one. It has demonstrated that both traditional political science research and some feminist research have utilized limiting categories of analysis. Because they have accepted uncritically the conceptual terrain developed in Western political theory as a universalistic one, these scholars have tended to reproduce a sexist epistemological framework.

Women's voices about the meaning of politics must be sounded if political science as a discipline is to be anything more than a dismal science. The demand for different measures of value and public virtue becomes an imperative in the post-nuclear world. Instrumental reason and the calculating ego of bourgeois politics seem antiquarian and destructive in comparison to the centrality of the specific qualities of individuals and objects that women's lives have emphasized. That empathy should substitute for efficiency as a modal political virtue no longer seems naïve. We must meet the challenge to discard the old categories of politics and to engage in the 'painstaking search of known sources for unknown meanings' (Lerner, 1979: 14). The concept of difference must not be annihilated but critically reappropriated as a rhetorical strategy of resistance to the hegemony of homogenizing norms.

Notes

1. At the 1984 APSA Roundtable on the Future of Political Theory none of the editors of the major theory journals represented mentioned the issue of gender and politics as the sort of topic that would push the discipline in new directions. When the audience questioned this omission the response of one of the participants was that this was hardly surprising, given the sex of all of the editors.

2. For a discussion of these ideas see Arendt, 1961. See also Okin, 1979.

3. For a discussion of the impact of participatory modes in 'non-political' life see Pateman, 1970. For a consideration of women's situation and the development of an alternative moral sensibility see Gilligan, 1982.

4. Despite the fact that Plato is often regarded as a radical exception to this exclusion of women from politics, since he permits women to become philosophers in *The Republic*, his incorporation of females into the upper strata depends upon his eradication of everything that is distinctive and troubling about the female body

and soul. It is certainly not women as women who become rulers of the 'best polis' (Book V).

5. However, to the extent that notions of 'public' authority define ideas about the development of 'moral' agency and a more complete human identity, the concept of politics may still depend upon a degree of antipathy toward the 'private' realm and the norms of rationality found within it, even if these norms are no longer associated exclusively with the female. See Hartsock's discussion of Greek citizenship as domination 'of those outside the community' (Hartsock, 1982: 202–3). See also Jones (1987) on reconceptualizing authority, and Elshtain's interesting discussion (1981) of Christian political discourse as an alternative mode to the classical celebration of public life as the arena of ultimate value.

6. Vogel explores the competing paradigm of romanticism reflected in the works of von Hippel, Schlegel, and Schleiermacher. These writers repudiated the 'dictates of universal, uniform and immutable standards', defending instead the ideals of diversity and difference derived from their acceptance of a gender-related conceptualization of individuality and community. They argued for the idea of gender-related differences in emotional and cognitive faculties without connotations of superiority or inferiority. But since they located the site of liberation outside the public sphere – in the radical implications of changed personal relations of private life – Vogel contends that their vision of liberation became one-sided. Their derogation of the political tended to reinforce existing material and legal inequalities (Vogel, 1986: 34–42; see also Sapiro, 1981: 702).

7. This is not to suggest that 'women's needs' were limited to the concerns with nurturance, affective ties, and the other dimensions of physical and emotional 'survival' associated with home and personal life. There were other issues of discrimination and exploitation at work and in politics which affected women. But these latter issues could at least partially be corrected through traditional 'interest group' politics: improved wages and working conditions, the franchise, and so on. The former group of 'needs', and aspects of the latter which are related to the political–cultural dimensions of the organization of labour 'transcend instrumental cooperation for the attainment of joint ends' (Diamond and Hartsock, 1981: 718; see also Balbus, 1982).

8. See Petchesky, 1983. Joan Tronto has explored the implications of criticism of liberal moral theory (Tronto, 1987).

9. The works of Lane (1959), Lipset (1960), and McCloskey (1968) are representative of such studies.

10. Representative works of this stage are Jaquette (1974), Anderson (1975), Goot and Reid (1975), Githens and Prestage (1977), and Lovenduski and Hills (1981). The predominant assumption of such research is that political participation is a function of one's 'stake' in the political system. In this view, women's 'stake' increases either as women's activity outside the home increases (for example, labour market activity), or as a result of the politicization of issues in which women traditionally have had stake. Hence, as Lovenduski and Hills argue, '[w]omen's participation at the level of voting, standing for office, and entering the political elite are all sensitive indicators of their position and stake in a particular society' (1981: 3). They acknowledge, however, that mainstream political science 'is handicapped when attempting a systematic consideration of the political participation of women' because it lacks a 'dynamic theory of participation' (p. 4). One of the elements which such a theory would have to incorporate – assessment of the adequacy of traditional indices of political activity – is not analysed by these authors, however.

11. For élite studies, see relevant essays in Jaquette (1974), and Githens and Prestage (1977), as well as sections of Lovenduski and Hills (1981). See also Kirkpatrick (1974), Tolchin and Tolchin (1974), Boneparth (1977), Diamond (1977), Mayo (1977), Kelly and Boutelier (1978), Mezey (1978), and the research cited in Randall (1982). The studies of 'women's issues' include Brownmiller (1975), Boles (1979), Adams and Winston (1980), Boneparth (1981), Diamond (1983), and Mansbridge (1986).

12. Some scholars suggest that traditional political participation be read as a measure of political co-optation. Voting is seen as an act which attests to one's confidence that the system's traditional access points will be sufficient to ensure that an individual's or group's interests will be met. See Murray Edelman, *The Symbolic Uses of Politics* (1964).

13. Gerda Lerner, 1979: 151. Joan Hoff Wilson makes similar criticism of the 'equalizer' school of women's history which accepts modernization theory and its male standards of achievement and change (Wilson, 1982: 881; see also Joan Kelly, 1976; 1977).

14. See Jónasdóttir's analysis of the validity of applying the concept of interest to women's political activity (Jónasdóttir, chapter 3).

15. For a criticism of liberal-individualist demands for access see Eisenstein (1980); Jones (1984). Jenny Bourne's discussion of the limits of Western feminist political priorities for exploring the salient issues in the lives of Third World women is also relevant (Bourne, 1983: 20–1).

References

Adams, E.T. and Winston, C.T. (1980) *Mothers at Work*. London: Longman.

Anderson, Kristi (1975) 'Working Women and Political Participation, 1952–1972', *American Journal of Political Science* 19: 439–54.

Arendt, Hannah (1961) 'What is Authority?', in Hannah Arendt, *Between Past and Future*. New York: Viking Press.

Aristotle *The Politics*. Oxford: Oxford University Press.

Balbus, Isaac (1982) *Marxism and Domination*. Princeton, NJ: Princeton University Press.

Baxter, Sandra and Marjorie Lansing (1983) *Women and Politics: The Visible Majority*. University of Michigan Press.

Boles, Janet (1979) *The Politics of the ERA: Conflict and Decision Process*. New York: Longman.

Boneparth, Ellen (1977) 'From Lickin' and Stickin' to Strategy', *American Political Quarterly* 5: 287–300.

Boneparth, Ellen (1981) *Women, Power and Policy*. Oxford: Pergamon.

Bourne, Jenny (1983) 'Towards an Anti-Racist Feminism', *Race and Class* 25: 1–22.

Bourque, Susan and Jean Grossholz (1974) 'Politics as Unnatural Practice', *Politics and Society* 4: 255–66.

Brennan, Teresa and Carole Pateman (1978) '"Mere Auxiliaries to the Commonwealth"', *Political Studies* 27: 183–200.

Brownmiller, Susan (1975) *Against Our Will: Men, Women and Rape*. New York: Simon and Schuster.

Chodorow, Nancy (1978) *The Reproduction of Mothering*. Berkeley: University of California Press.

Diamond, Irene (1983) *Families, Politics and Public Policy*. New York: Longman.

Diamond, Irene (1977) *Sex Roles in the State House*. New Haven, Conn.: Yale University Press.

Diamond, Irene and Nancy Hartsock (1981) 'Beyond Interests in Politics: A Comment on Virginia Sapiro's "When Are Interests Interesting?"', *American Political Science Review* 75: 717–23.

Dinnerstein, Dorothy (1976) *The Mermaid and the Minotaur*. New York: Harper.

Duncan, Graeme (1983) *Democratic Theory and Practice*. Cambridge: Cambridge University Press.

Duverger, Maurice (1955) *The Political Role of Women*. UNESCO.

Edelman, Murray (1964) *The Symbolic Uses of Politics*. University of Illinois Press.

Eisenstein, Zillah (1980). *The Radical Future of Liberal Feminism*. New York: Longman.

Elshtain, Jean Bethke (1981) *Public Man/Private Woman*. Princeton, NJ: Princeton University Press.

Elshtain, Jean Bethke (1982) 'Feminist Discourse and Its Discontents', *Signs* 7: 603–21.

Elshtain, Jean Bethke (1986) *Meditations on Modern Political Thought*. New York: Praeger.

Elshtain, Jean Bethke (1987) *Women and War*. New York: Basic Books.

Evans, Judith *et al.* (1986) *Feminism and Political Theory*. London: Sage.

Ferguson, Kathy (1984) *The Feminist Case Against Bureaucracy*. Pennsylvania, PA: Temple University Press.

Foucault, Michel (1978) *The History of Sexuality,* vol. I. Pantheon Books.

Foucault, Michel (1979) *Discipline and Punish: The Birth of the Prison*. New York: Vintage Books.

Frank, Andre Gundar (1979) 'The Development of Underdevelopment', in Charles Wilber (ed.), *The Political Economy of Development and Underdevelopment*. New York: Random House.

Gilligan, Carol (1982) *In a Different Voice*. Cambridge, MA: Harvard University Press.

Githens, Marianne and Jewel Prestage (1977) *A Portrait of Marginality: The Political Behavior of the American Woman*. New York: David McKay.

Goot, M. and E. Reid (1975) *Women and Voting Studies: Mindless Matrons or Sexist Scholarship?* Beverly Hills: Sage.

Grant, Judith (1987) 'I Feel Therefore I Am: A Critique of Female Experience as the Basis for a Feminist Epistemology', *Women and Politics* 7: 99–114.

Hartsock, Nancy (1982) *Money, Sex and Power*. New York: Longman.

Hernes, Helga (1984) 'Women and the Welfare State: The Transition from Private to Public Dependence', in Harriet Holter (ed.), *Patriarchy in a Welfare Society*. Oslo: Universitetsforlaget.

Jaquette, Jane (1974) *Women and Politics*. New York: John Wiley.

Jaquette, Jane (1983) 'Weber, the Pluralists and the Rational Calculus: Women and Power in Western Political Analysis'. Paper presented at the Annual Meeting of the Western Political Science Association.

Jayaratne, Toby (1983) 'The Value of Quantitative Methodology for Feminist Research', in Gloria Bowles and Renata Dueli Klein (eds), *Theories of Women's Studies*. London: Routledge and Kegan Paul.

Jones, Kathleen (1984) 'Dividing the Ranks: Women and the Draft', *Women and Politics* 4: 75–87.

Jones, Kathleen (1987) 'Aspects of Citizenship in a Woman-Friendly Polity'. Paper presented at the Annual Meeting of the International Society for Political Psychology, July 1987.

Kelly, Joan (1976) 'The Social Relations of the Sexes: Methodological Implications of Women's History', *Signs* 1: 809–24.

Kelly, Joan (1977) 'Did Women Have a Renaissance?', in Renata Bridenthal and Claudia Koonz (eds), *Becoming Visible: Women in European History*. Boston, MA: Houghton-Mifflin.

Kelly, Rita Mae and Mary A. Boutelier (1978) *The Making of Political Women: A Study of Socialization and Role Conflict*. New York: Nelson-Hall.

Kirkpatrick, Jeanne (1974) *Political Woman*. New York: Basic Books.

Korsmeyer, Carole W. (1976) 'Reason and Morals in the Early Feminist Movement', in Carol Gould and Marx Wartofsky (eds), *Women and Philosophy*. New York: G.P. Putnam's Sons.

Lane, Robert (1959) *Political Life*. New York: Free Press.

Lerner, Gerda (1979) *The Majority Finds Its Past*. Oxford: Oxford University Press.

Lipset, Seymour Martin (1960) *Political Man: The Social Bases of Politics*. New York: Anchor Books.

Lovenduski, Joni (1981) 'Toward the Emasculation of Political Science: The Impact of Feminism', pp. 83–97 in Dale Spendor (ed.), *Men's Studies Modified: The Impact of Feminism on the Academic Disciplines*. Oxford: Pergamon Press.

Lovenduski, Joni and Jill Hills (1981) *The Politics of the Second Electorate*. London: Routledge and Kegan Paul.

McCloskey, Herbert (1968) 'Political Participation', in D.L. Sills (ed.), *The International Encyclopedia of the Social Sciences*. London: Macmillan and Free Press.

Mansbridge, Jane (1986) *Why We Lost the ERA*. University of Chicago Press.

Mayo, M. (1977) *Women in the Community*. London: Routledge and Kegan Paul.

Mezey, Susan Gluck (1978) 'Does Sex Make a Difference? A Case Study of Women in Politics', *Western Political Quarterly* 40: 492–502.

Nelson, Barbara (1984) 'Women's Poverty and Women's Citizenship: Some Political Consequences of Economic Marginality', *Signs* 10: 209–31.

Nie, Norman H., Sidney Verba, and John R. Petrocik (1976) *The Changing American Voter*. Cambridge, MA: Harvard University Press.

Okin, Susan Moller (1979) *Women in Western Political Thought*. Princeton, NJ: Princeton University Press.

Pateman, Carole (1970) *Participation and Democratic Theory*. Cambridge, MA: Harvard University Press.

Pateman, Carole (1980) '"The Disorder of Women": Women, Love and the Sense of Justice', *Ethics* 91: 20–34.

Petchesky, Rosalind (1983) *Abortion and Woman's Choice*. New York: Longman.

Pocock, J.G.A. (1975) *The Machiavellian Moment*. Princeton University Press.

Randall, Vicky (1982) *Women and Politics*. London: Macmillan.

Reeves, Nancy (1982) *Womankind: Beyond the Stereotypes*. Aldine Press.

Rowbotham, Sheila (1972) *Women, Resistance and Revolution*. Vintage Books.

Rowbotham, Sheila (1986) 'What Do Women Want? Woman Centered Values and the World as It Is', *Dalhousie Review*, 649–65.

Sapiro, Virginia (1981) 'When are Interests Interesting? The Problems of the Political Representation of Women', *American Political Science Review* 75(3): 701–16.

Sapiro, Virginia (1983) *The Political Integration of Women*. University of Illinois Press.

Saxonhouse, Arlene (1980) 'Man, Woman, War and Politics: Family and Polis in Aristophanes and Euripides', *Political Theory* 8: 65–82.

Saxonhouse, Arlene (1985) *Women in the History of Political Thought*. New York: Praeger.

Shanley, Mary and Victoria Shuck (1975) 'In Search of Political Woman', *Social Science Quarterly* 55: 632–44.

Slater, Philip (1968) *The Glory of Hera*. Boston: Beacon Press.

Tolchin, S. and M. Tolchin (1974) *Clout: Women, Power and Politics*. New York: Coward, McCann and Geoghegan.

Tronto, Joan (1987) 'Political Science and Caring: Or, the Perils of Balkanized Social Science', *Women and Politics* 7: 85–97.

Vogel, Ursula (1986) 'Rationalism and Romanticism: Two Strategies for Women's Liberation', in Judith Evans *et al.*, *Feminism and Political Theory*. London: Sage.

Welch, Susan (1977) 'Women as Political Animals', *American Journal of Political Science* 21: 711–30.

Wilson, Joan Hoff (1982) 'Review of *Liberty's Daughters*, by Mary Beth Norton and *Women of the Republic*, by Linda Kerber', *Signs* 7: 881.

Wollstonecraft, Mary (1792) *A Vindication of the Rights of Woman*. Harmondsworth: Penguin, 1975.

3

On the Concept of Interest, Women's Interests, and the Limitations of Interest Theory

Anna G. Jónasdóttir

Within feminist theory and research 'interests' is a much used but little-examined concept. This remains true despite – or perhaps because of – the fact that concepts like 'interest/s', 'interest group', and so on, are among the most controversial within the whole field of scientific studies of politics.[1] Yet in everyday speech and strategic political discussions, the different connotations of 'interest' – she is 'interested in' women's issues; she 'has an interest in' political work; or, it is 'in the interest of' women that effective measures are taken against rape and battering' – seem to be understood immediately. Their meaning is understood by reference to the various contexts in which the terms are used.

It is true that disagreement about terms reflects the academic propensity for wordplay, but mainly it reflects differing, often unarticulated, theoretical and meta-theoretical approaches, that is, different conceptions of how social relationships and their histories are constituted, and how and to what extent we can obtain reliable information about these things. Yet, if we avoided using 'contested concepts' altogether, we would neither be able to study nor relate to the realities of political life. Thus, when feminist researchers use expressions like 'women's interests' we land in the middle of a scientific quagmire, suffused with contradictory meanings. Our analyses are affected by all the classical controversies, although, at the same time, our specific questions carry new conceptual challenges. These challenges have now propelled us into conflict.

Some feminist researchers argue, against traditional political thinking, that women *as women* should be considered a group with 'representable interests'. Other feminist researchers, who otherwise have differing views, question this argument in a somewhat uniform manner; still others reject the concept of interests entirely. In this latter view, the idea of interests, which since the Renaissance has constituted in one form or another a sort of backbone to almost all

political theory, is thus declared to be something that feminist
theory must transcend.

Women's Studies and Views on Interests

The aim of this chapter[2] is to discuss the applicability of the concept
of interests to women's concerns today. Two American articles from
1981 have focused particularly on this question: Virginia Sapiro's
'When are Interests Interesting? The Problem of Political Representation of Women', and Irene Diamond and Nancy Hartsock's
discussion of Sapiro's article, 'Beyond Interests in Politics'. Sapiro's
question is whether women today have representable political
interests *because* they are women and not primarily independent of
that fact. She finds the former to be plausible, while Diamond and
Hartsock criticize her very premises and reject interest theory
altogether in favour of a theory of needs. In addition, traces of how
and if interest terminology suits studies on women occur both
explicitly and implicitly in several works. For example, in her book
Women and the Public Interest. An Essay on Policy and Protest
(1971), American sociology's grand old lady, Jessie Bernard,
anticipated the view of Diamond and Hartsock when she argued
against using interest group theory as being inappropriate in studies
of women and children. Instead, she recommends a view that
proceeds from the traditional concept of common public interest, a
perspective that Diamond and Hartsock do not discuss in these
terms. They project a collective order where views of interests, in
total, do not apply.

In two essays (1974, 1984) Jane Jaquette also questions the
pertinence of the interest perspective to women's reality, the basis
of which, according to her, is the home and the family. Politics does
not take women's concerns into account nor do women feel at home
in politics. Rosalind Pollack Petchesky (1980, 1983) makes a
parallel argument when she questions the relevance of the concept
of rights to the demands of women. Since 'rights' are part of the
framework of the theory of interests, her argument applies broadly.
In a manner comparable to Sapiro, Helga Hernes (1982) considers
various aspects of the problem of interests. She is concerned with
making the theory of interests relevant to women. If democracy is to
be really inclusive we need a shift from viewing women and
women's organizations in traditional politics as a source of power
for men to a view that acknowledges women's resources and
women's organizations as a power basis of their own.

In addition to these primarily theoretical works, the conceptual
problems around women's interests have been explored in empirical

studies of political behaviour and of the concrete campaign issues of the women's movement. Abby Peterson (1981) for instance, provided a theoretical foundation for analysing 'women's issues' within voting studies, and Drude Dahlerup (1984) stipulates the right to vote as an objective interest of women, quite conscious of how inflammable that concept is. Arthur Miller, Anne Hildreth, and Grace Simmons (chapter 6) distinguish between 'gender identification' and 'gender consciousness' and find that women (in the USA) are increasingly viewing their social situation in political terms as they have successively developed an awareness of shared interests.

In this chapter, I consider the questions (and answers) that have been raised concerning the concept of interest, women's interests, and the limitations of interest theory. My main objective is to argue that the concept of interest is useful if re-defined. Moreover, conceived of in a certain way, the concept is particularly significant in analyses of the society we actually live in. But it has its limitations. All the values that women strive for cannot be contained in the historically conditioned, utilitarian conception of interests. Thus my ambition is to attempt to transcend the either/or situation that the Diamond and Hartsock versus Sapiro debate suggests. At the same time I will indicate solutions to several of the problems concerning 'interests' with which women's research grapples. I find that the concept of 'needs', which Diamond and Hartsock suggest should take the place of 'interests' as a conceptual core in feminist political theory, does not alone cover the dynamic essence of feminist political claims. On the other hand, taken together as two elements in a related whole, needs and interests lend a special historical significance to political theorizing about sex/gender in contemporary society.

For almost two decades women have been mobilizing in order to assert their interests as sexed and gendered persons which, in turn, has enabled them to begin to politicize their women-defined needs and the needs that arise out of their relatedness to other people and to nature. But to speak *politically* – that is, with reference to authoritative decisions – only in terms of needs leaves open the question of who is to define what those needs are and who is to act on behalf of them. A crucial point, however, is that interests as an active counterpart to needs, is not altogether salient when applied to the vast array of needs that exist in human beings and their relationships. Referring as it does to controlling situations, to instrumental agency, interest seems to claim its own opposite if some of our deepest needs – those for love and commitment – are to be fulfilled and developed.

Sapiro addresses a number of important issues in her essay, but her reasoning is weak for she is unaware of the above-mentioned limitations of interest theory. Moreover, her notion of what kind of social contrapositions validate women as an interest category is far too narrow. The main question is not whether or not to politicize 'the production of children'; the essential interested parties to be problematized here are not women versus the state, but women versus men, that is, sex/gender versus sex/gender with all the complexity entailed by that particular social structure.[3] The field of competing interests which is at the bottom of the problem in question is sexuality as a composite social process of generating, nurturing, and empowering people. How the sexuality process is related to the state, historically and theoretically, is a closely related question, but a distinct one.

In the following, I will begin with a short survey of the most significant controversies surrounding the concept of interest, both as they are reflected in political studies in general, and also in relation to the new themes conveyed by feminist theory and research. Next, I will look at the historical determination of the concept of interest in order to scrutinize the issues exposed by feminist research. Finally, I intend to give a short presentation of a new way of conceiving the interest 'problématique' and ways of applying it. Using examples from women's research and reality, I will show how the idea of using 'interests' as having a special historical significance can loosen certain Gordian knots in our formation of political theories, and contribute to a clearer understanding of several problems.

Points of Conflict

The most heavily charged conflict within discourse about the concept of interests in modern times concerns the question of *objective and subjective interests*. How are objective interests determined? Is the concept scientifically meaningful at all, or are subjective interests, that is, an individual's conscious wishes and preferences, the only ones with which we can actually work?

The two main positions, which are also divided internally, have been designated as pluralistic and Marxist (Balbus, 1971). Against the Marxists, who assert objective class interests, the pluralists counter that what are considered to be a group's or individual's objective interests always rest upon the researcher's subjective values and thus are unscientific.[4] Within feminist research, the dilemma has much the same contours. Can we claim that women have certain objective interests regardless of what women themselves think?

Another controversy that has provoked extensive discussion concerns the presumed opposition between the *public interest and special or private interests*. Public interest, in the sense of the state's external interests vis-à-vis other states, and, internally, the state's interest vis-à-vis various groups in the population, constitutes the historical basis of the political concept of interests (Gunn, 1969). Quite early, during the eighteenth century and the French Revolution, it was claimed that public interest was a fiction. What did exist were the interests of separate social classes (defined in *Phil. Wörterbuch*, 1975). During the twentieth century it has been claimed that the notion of public interest is both realistic and necessary. Writers like Pendleton Herring (1968: 171) stress that public interest should not be seen as the result of negotiations between two or more parties – more or less like a labour market situation – but rather as 'more than the sum of competing interests'. Modern criticism of 'public interest' has developed from two opposing perspectives, one Marxist and one libertarian/atomistic. The former sees public interest in a class society as reflecting the special interests of the ruling class. According to the latter, the concept of public interest is both scientifically meaningless and politically dangerous; only the interests of rational individuals are able to be defined, represented and, thus, are real.

Another view of interest groups and their bases which is empirically and historically oriented takes a middle position between Marxists and pure atomists. This view takes into account certain, primarily economic, group interests; medieval rankings, merchant and craft guilds are supposed to have modern successors. Within this line of thinking the criterion for belonging to 'the interest group universe' is to be 'concerned with public policy' or, in other words, to 'have a stake in the political process' (Ehrmann, 1968: 486).[5] Independently of how relevant this view could be, if re-formed, from the point of view of feminist theory, one of Ehrmann's arguments should be underlined and expanded. He asserts on the question of the legitimacy of interest groups that 'whether groups contribute to the operation of the political system or undermine it cannot be determined in the abstract' (1968: 490). Much in the same way we can claim that whether or not certain social groups (or groupings), as for instance women and children, do have group-specific interests, or are concerned with public policy cannot be determined in the abstract or as a matter of principle. Theorizing in terms of interests (as all theory that aims at description and explanation of reality) must be historically and empirically informed.[6] Of course the question of what constitutes evidence is always a methodological problem. How, for instance, should we define a 'stake' in politics or 'concerns with public policy', or how do we measure impact on politics? In our case, for the time being, the pervasive mobilization of women in all areas of society would be a valid indicator for beginning such theorizing.

There has been less comprehensive discussion about a suitable classification system or *typology of interests*. One common way of doing this has been to differentiate between *material* interests, in the sense of economic, and *ideal* interests, in the sense of abstract support for a set of principles. It has been emphasized that this division is unclear since the economic and ideal aspects overlap each other, at least in part. Traditionally, the women's movement and its organizations have been included among the idealist types; they have been defined as 'promoting a cause'. According to this view, women *as women* (or men as men) are assumed not to have any common material interests. No social, historically relevant, material interests based on sex/gender are supposed to exist. But the habit of reducing 'material interests' to 'economic interests' must be transcended.[7] Sexuality (or the sex/gender relationship) can be seen as generating specific bio/social, material interests. The meaning, and social and historical dynamics of sexuality as a basic category, have yet to be fully explored and explained by feminist theorists (compare note 2).

As soon as sexuality is posed as a basic category in the political theory of interests a new controversy enters the field of conceptual conflicts. In addition to the question of ascribing to women objective interests regardless of their subjective consciousness, the problem has arisen whether *all women*, across all class and race lines, can be said to have *certain common interests*. In spite of numerous deep divisions within feminist thinking, a majority of feminist students as well as activists are in agreement about maintaining some sort of minimal common denominators: the interest in not allowing oneself to be oppressed as a woman, or, in fighting patriarchy. Consequently, although there is dispute about the specific contours and contents of sex/gender interests, most feminist theorists support the premise that gender is a fundamental organizing principle of social life and of human consciousness.

The final conundrum in this debate about interest as a concept can be called the question of *female/male interests versus various role-based interests*. In these or similar terms we are confronted with questions about whether, for instance, promoting public care for children and the elderly are to be considered women's issues, while others, such as those of economic policy or military concerns, are seen as men's issues.

The History of the Concept of 'Interests'

The origin of the concept of political interests[8] must be seen against the background of the rise and development in Europe of the national state, the capitalist system of production, and the emergence of the bourgeoisie. The term 'interest' comes from the Latin 'inter esse', meaning 'to be' (esse) 'among' or 'between' (inter). The notion of 'public interest' replaced some older ones with a similar function. In particular, ideas like 'common good' and the 'salus populi' were supplanted by this new notion.

The new revolutionary middle class demanded a place in the public sphere. They wanted 'to be among' those who defined the public interest. The social and political theory – classical liberalism – which directly or indirectly grew out of this social transformation heavily stressed both the primacy of the individual's interests and the need for combining, consolidating, and literally fortifying these interests by means of the authority of the state. Defining the person as an individual who existed independently of society as a whole was a fundamental premise of this philosophy, and revolutionized thinking about state, society, and the nature of human existence. 'Interests' were taken as an expression of the 'natural' human being's unique qualities and capacities. An individual could determine his own life with the help of reason's and nature's measuring-stick, independent of all spiritual and earthly despotic powers. By the seventeenth century the foundation had already been laid for a structural analysis of society and history that used interest as a key concept. Philosophers contended that social interests, class interests, group interests, and personal interests constituted those dynamic forces in the structure of society which created historical changes.

In addition to the broad political and social analytical significance that 'interests' has had from the Renaissance onwards, it has also had for a long time a much more narrow economic or financial meaning (compare note 8). The idea of profit as the result of exchange has increasingly permeated notions of what 'inter esse' means. With the integration of utilitarianism in liberal theory, especially under the pervasive influence of economic exchange theory, the broader political and philosophical concept of interest has focused largely on the dividend aspect. The demand to 'be among' the state's actors was also motivated from the start by the idea of the individual's right to monitor the results of the political process since private individuals were affected by these results. This shift in focus has tended to obscure the controlling agency aspect in interests, that is, the aspect of who it is that determines what the dividends should be and by what powers the political process is conditioned. This has fostered a type of theorizing that looks on interest 'divorced from its sources'.[9] The question is now whether we are moving into a new historical period where the emergence of conscious gendered interests and outlooks are undermining the validity of not only the liberal view of both public and private interests but also of the Marxist critique of that theory from a class point of view. Perhaps, as women enter the arenas of social and political struggles the very nature of their entrance will require a re-thinking of the relevance of the categories of interest much in the same way as the 'common good' was challenged earlier.

In sum, it can be said that the concept of interest has had, from the beginning, a double significance consisting of two connected, though often hidden, aspects: the *form aspect* – the demand to 'be among', or the demand for participation in and control over society's public affairs; and the *content or result aspect* – concerning the question of those substantive values that politics puts into effect and distributes, including what this process results in related to various groups, needs, wishes, and demands.[10] Historically, this dynamic concept emerged as a politically relevant term in a period of rapid transformation: when new, innovative social groups (classes) and national states no longer accepted the existing political order or the characterization of general values as determined by an élite-defined 'common good' or a scholastic 'salus populi'. A basic hypothesis in this chapter is that women as a group are now, in a historically new way, calling into question the ruling 'salus populi masculini'.

The Present is also History

The parties involved in the modern controversy over objective and subjective interests generally use the term 'interests' as a synonym for words such as 'needs', 'wishes', 'preferences', and 'demands'. Thus the stress is on *content* – what (values) people need, wish, or demand in order to be satisfied. The formal aspect, the claim to active participation, tends to disappear. The dynamic doubleness of the interest concept – the simultaneous stress on both form and content, both agency and substantial wants – then also disappears.

In political science, in system theory for instance, concepts such as 'needs' and 'wants' are supposed to form a continuum extending from inchoate *needs*, through socially and politically articulated *wishes/preferences*, to politically linked (aggregated) *demands* on the political system. This is the ideal image of the representative democratic system. But an explosive issue lies embedded here. It is far from self-evident that the picture of citizens innovating and designing political issues is a valid one. Ever more important sources of 'politics-production' are the top levels of the system where, to modify Schumpeter's words, those 'men sit who are to do the deciding'. As Pitkin points out (1972: 291–2), such a political system, though defined as a (methodical) democracy, is not necessarily a representative one. Thus, the fact that women vote in elections as much as men do does not guarantee representation for women as women – that is, as gendered persons. The active presence and positions within the 'factory' of politics should be what counts as representation.[11]

There are strong arguments in favour of maintaining a certain distinction between interest in the sense of actively 'be/ing among' on the one hand, and interest as the satisfaction of needs and desires on the other; for example, *agency* and the *result of agency*. The main advantage of such a distinction is that it permits the resolution of the conflict surrounding objective and subjective interests. The concept's *formal aspect* becomes primary so that the content of needs and desires is, from the point of view of interest, an *open question*. In a certain way this means that only 'subjective' interests exist; in other words, only human agents (or persons, see Connolly, 1983: 69) have interests. This does not mean, however, that interests are determined by chance only. Understood historically, and seen as emerging from people's lived experiences,[12] interests about basic processes of social life are divided systematically between groups of people in so far as their living conditions are systematically different. Thus, historically and socially defined, interests can be characterized as 'objective'. Unless we keep the form aspect of interest (and of politics in general) visible, we might come to believe that the history of political forms had come to an end. We might continue to think, as Lipset once claimed, that formal-equal liberal democracy is the culmination and completion of political history.

Ideas concerning Interests in Feminist Theory and Research

One of the points of conflict, mentioned above, had to do with the unclear reasons for speaking about women's and men's interests, and women's and men's issues in politics. The question is whether and how we can differentiate between general (human) interests, derived from individual historically determined positions and roles (people as parents, workers, and so on), and interests derived from the historically defined gendered reality of human existence. When we differentiate between women's interests and men's interests, and between women's and men's issues, we derive these distinctions partly from theoretical assumptions – often based upon some variant of the theory of the division of labour based on gender – and partly on the basis of extensive empirical data. One basic hypothesis in this chapter, developed at some length elsewhere (see note 2), is that a theory of the division of *labour* based on gender is necessary but not sufficient for describing and explaining different – and partially opposed – sex/gender interests. What is needed, as a further foundation, is an historical theory of the gender division of *love*.

A number of recent studies of politics have shown unequivocally that the background variable of gender is one of the most, sometimes *the* most differentiating factor in studies of political behaviour (Putnam, 1976; Halsaa-Albrektsen, 1977; Milbrath and Goel, 1977; Lafferty, 1980; Fuchs-Epstein and Laub-Coser, 1981; Hernes, 1982). And there is a clear pattern in this which is in total accord with both common and scientific hypotheses. Women, to a greater *degree* than men, and in different *ways*, initiate, pursue, and support issues concerning bio-social production and reproduction, that is, those questions having to do with control over, responsibility for, and care of people and other natural resources (Edsall, 1984; Holmberg and Asp, 1984; Togeby, 1984; Jonasson, 1985; Walker, 1986).

In many cases, authors of empirical studies are satisfied with statistically and typologically identifying certain feminist issues without making any attempts at theoretical deductions. Others explain results theoretically. According to Abby Peterson a women's issue is defined through the value system of women's culture. It 'originates . . . from those interests or demands which the reproductive sphere poses against the productive sphere . . . , from the fundamental levels in the family which all women in this society share – i.e. the *content* of their work in the family. In this sense a women's question is objective' (Peterson, 1981: 6). Peterson further assumes that class membership, the different socio-economic conditions of classes, explains attitudinal differences between different groups of women. She summarizes four features that tend to characterize a feminist issue in politics: (1) women support the issue to a greater degree than do men; (2) the issue stands outside of the traditional right/left scale; (3) the issue tends to be met with emotional reactions in the political arena; and (4) the issue lacks certified cultural authority or at least has an ambiguous political status (Peterson, 1981: 9).

Looked at objectively, sex/gender-differentiated interests can thus be stated as those which pertain to women and men 'being among' (compare 'inter esse') different activities, working with different things, having different responsibilities, being involved with other people in different ways. What they are subjectively interested in, what their views are, and how they participate in other social matters 'originates in' (non-mechanically) their respective sensuous practices. Understood in this way, the objective is neither mysterious, nor difficult to work with. Nor is it separate from the subjective experience of it.[13] Aside from the bearing of children (and in a narrow meaning the copulative sexual act itself), division of labour according to gender is not and has never been absolute, nor is the connection between experience and attitudes mechanically necessary. It is in this connection that the concept of 'gender' is most important. Men who live and work in the 'female' social sphere have all the opportunities for adopting a 'female' consciousness. Likewise, women's political involvement is not an a priori given, nor is it limited to so-called 'reproduction' issues. For instance, in a Danish study of young people's political behaviour, Lise Togeby (1984) shows that today's young women are very involved in employment issues. Thus the *historical character of gender interests* is actualized. Their changeability can be seen as a further dimension of the problem of the concept of interest.

Women and Men as Interest Groups[14]

In 'When are Interests Interesting?' Sapiro sets out to demonstrate that women can demand gender interest-based representation in politics without going against generally agreed ideas about the bases of demands for group representation. Sapiro claims that we are 'accustomed to the idea that divisions of labor and stratification in public life define group interests in politics' (1981: 704). Thus, she asserts, we can draw a parallel with the gender division of labour and stratification (power and status hierarchies) in private life, since the private sphere is affected by and affects issues in public/political and policy debates. According to Sapiro, the ordinary indicators, that is the socio-economic differences in *public* life, also show that the politically relevant situations of men and women are very different. But despite these easily proven parallels it is politically and intellectually challenging to consider reproductive practices in private life as the foundation for conflicts of interest. For example, Sapiro refers to studies that show that women have lost in election campaigns when they define themselves as representatives of women or when they bring up women's or feminist issues (1981: 711).

Sapiro discusses women as a group and representation in general.

She does not distinguish between franchised (numerical) represent-ation and resource-based (corporate) representation. This may be because she mainly argues from the political realities of the United States, where an established lobbying system and a weak party system render this distinction less clear than in Scandinavia. Hernes (1982), on the other hand, deals in particular with the problem of corporate representation, and I would argue that it is here that analyses of sex/gender problems in terms of interests become really controversial within traditional political science. Dahlerup (1980: 19) has offered the hypothesis that political parties have always tried to avoid a clear politicizing of the question of the position of women, and have instead connected sex/gender conflicts with family politics or some other sub-issue. There is a parallel problem within scientific studies of politics, namely one of resistance to conceiving sex/gender – women and men – as socially and politically relevant corporations or fundamental parties in society. In Western capitalist societies with their liberal democratic states, neither sex/gender groups nor sexuality, as a field of activities, is openly acknowledged as a politically relevant social basis for competing interests. Even many women's organizations are hesitant or unwilling to see society in these terms, and mainstream political science reflects this situation by being silent.

Besides the gender-based differences in traditional (electoral and public) politics and those in work-based politics (see Siltanen and Stanworth, 1984), evidence shows that men and women are forming groups based on the politics of housework, parenting, and sexuality. In many cases, these are taking the form of fully fledged interest organizations. Since the early 1970s women have, in a second historical wave, organized both more and less formally; they have come together in small groups as well as in large-scale organizations in order to be conscious of and protect themselves from patriarchal power in all its various forms, in addition to developing women-centred strength and strategies. Now even men seem to be moving towards a new phase of organizing vis-à-vis women. As in the history of classes, where the capitalists usually organized formally only after the labourers had unionized, men as men (that is, as fathers and lovers) are now beginning to associate formally against what they see as the unfair advantages of women. Recently a voluntary association for so-called 'weekend fathers' has started in Sweden. The aim of this organization is to influence the judicial procedures surrounding divorces, in particular, the arrangements for judging parental fitness when determining child custody cases. It is also meant to be a forum where men can meet other men as fathers. In addition, a few male crisis-centres have existed for some years in Sweden.

Feminist Critique Rejecting Interest Theory

In their criticism of Sapiro, Diamond and Hartsock question whether views of, or ideas about interest should be 'interesting' for women and feminist research. They claim that feminist theory must make a 'clean break with the assumptions of the interest group framework' (1981: 720). Sapiro is criticized for being at once too comprehensive and too narrow in her definition, as well as vague in her theoretical premises. According to Diamond and Hartsock, there is a contradiction in Sapiro's claim that the inclusion of women's demands in the political system constitutes a fundamental challenge to society while still considering women as an interest group: 'if the inclusion of women in politics threatens the most basic structures of society, one cannot fit their concerns into the framework of interests'. They see Sapiro's inconsistency as an 'inevitable consequence of trying to work within the conventional categories of political analysis' (1981: 717). Her point of departure is in the 'hidden and untested assumption that women's demands can be integrated into political systems'. However, this, like the opposite assumption of 'the inherent impenetrability of political life', must be made much more specific and studied empirically (1981: 720). Diamond and Hartsock agree with Sapiro that women share common interests across class boundaries, and that the analyses of the power of the state and official policy must be expanded to include more than 'social divisions deriving from productive activity'. But they must also account for the 'profound implications of the social divisions deriving from *reproductive* activity'. Thus, what remains is a matter of studying the entire policy process and all the complexities of state power (1981: 720).

According to Diamond and Hartsock, what argues against accepting interest theory and considering women as one interest group among many is that analyses according to these criteria become entangled in the dominant class and sexist patterns of society. Such analyses leave no room for regenerating demands, no openings for fundamental changes, and Diamond and Hartsock point out that, historically, ideas about interests reflect a view that society consists of rational, economic men seeking to maximize their satisfactions. 'But', they continue, 'human beings are moved by more than interests. The reduction of all human emotions to interests and interests to the rational search for gain reduces the human community to an instrumental, arbitrary, and deeply unstable alliance, one which rests on the private desires of isolated individuals' (1981: 719). Such a view of social life is extremely partial. It is particularly difficult, for example, to imagine a mother's characteristically nurturing relationship to her children in terms of instrumental interests and individual gain (1981: 719). For the more comprehensive categories of analysis which they seek, Diamond and Hartsock refer to the Canadian political scientist and philosopher Christian Bay, who has in various works advocated 'needs' as an alternative to 'interest' and 'rights' (Bay, 1965; 1968; 1980).

This criticism is shared by Jane S. Jaquette (1974) who suggests that the explanation for women's lower rate of participation in politics is that they do not have a 'stake' in politics. This is either because politics does not concern itself with what women find important, or because it judges the engagement of women as naïve, trivial, or even dangerous. Women are alienated in politics: they do not feel at home in the party apparatus, with its interest groups and its corruptions. What is often asserted to be 'the true function of politics: that of brokerage among competing interests' does not appeal to women. Jaquette continues this theme of alienation in a later essay (1984), where she states that women's power, which is anchored in the home sphere, 'is like a "soft" currency in the international economy' (p. 23), that is, not 'convertible' in the public sphere. She questions whether women's daily needs and goals are compatible with the usual view of politics as utility maximization and economically rational interest calculations.

Similarly, Rosalind Pollack Petchesky (1980) discusses the concept of rights and 'women's right to choose' in connection with the goal of the women's movement – reproductive freedom. 'Rights' are closely associated with interests; they are, in fact, part of the theory of interests. Petchesky rejects the concept of rights in favour of 'social and individual need' as the key concept in the fundamental feminist-political analysis. She makes connections with certain branches of Marxism, for example, with Herbert Marcuse's ideas about the revolutionary potential in people living out their needs and assenting to their sensualism, as well as to Agnes Heller's theory of needs. In contrast to 'rights', which are abstract and bound to a given social order, 'needs' always refer to concrete, individual concerns, that can be seen as 'part of a total revolutionary program', according to Petchesky (1980: 670).

I agree that there *are* '. . . difficulties of approaching the study of women and politics within the conventional categories of political analysis' (Diamond and Hartsock, 1981: 717). I also agree that in order to develop new directions for theory and research where we spell out the radical implications of a sex/gender-based political representation, we need to transcend not only the result-oriented utilitarian notion of interest in its narrow sense, but also Sapiro's theoretical frameworks. However, the important question is *how* we cope with the conventional categories: from within themselves, or if 'going beyond' only means ignoring or passing by. I claim that we must do it from within so that these categories, after being tried, can be put aside as unfitting. They will nevertheless have provided a necessary point of departure and, to some extent, a substance with which we must go further. Doing it the other way takes an outside view, one that refers to a reified version of reality rather than constructing valid indicators of reality, whereas it is only through valid indicators of existing reality that we are able to form alternatives and new visions.

Implications of this Rejection
In the following comments I focus mainly on Diamond and Hartsock's arguments as being representative of the categorical rejection of interest theory.

Diamond and Hartsock fail to understand the point in Sapiro's assertion that including women *as women* into politics 'tears at the most basic structures and conceptions of society'. But it is misleading to describe women as 'simply another interest group' (Diamond and Hartsock, 1981: 717). It is more constructive to see women as one part in an historically determined, antagonistic relationship to *men*. The point of seeing women as a group whose position has given rise to special interests is not the same as equating them with, for example, the National Association of Motorists or even pensioners' associations. It means to question from the aspect of sex/gender, the 'individual' as *one*, and as an isolated unit, without throwing out the individual level as unimportant in social analyses. Besides implying a qualified criticism of the Marxist concept of class (as the one and only historically and theoretically relevant basic social category) the view of women as a group with certain shared basic interests means that the individual – the one – of liberal theory does not in fact exist.[15] And that alone is a challenge to a society that both practically and ideologically atomizes and individualizes people more and more. The definition of the determining set of social relationships – the 'ensemble of social relations' – that an individual is in Marxist theory, none the less remains an incomplete task. This task can be completed only by introducing a new basic analytical level: that of the sexually and generically related individual.

Diamond and Hartsock also give too one-sided a picture of the theory of interest. Ever since this idea appeared it has been linked with values other than merely economic and economically coloured profit motives. It could apply to the right to practise religion according to one's own beliefs, and the demand to be acknowledged as a full subject – politically, judicially, and in every other way. To argue that all such other practices only reflect the class-divided economy would be to lock oneself into a sterile deterministic way of thinking. In addition, we cannot dismiss in advance the relationship between mother and child as having nothing to do with interest, even in the sense of interest as a narrow utility-maximizing category. The mother–child relationship includes many different dimensions all of which are socially and historically moulded (and are thus, for instance, class-divided and culturally different), but one essential in this multiple relationship is nurturing and care in one form or another. Yet even a superficial look – not to speak of one's own experiences – at everyday practices makes it plausible that the parties in these relations are to some extent rational beings 'seeking to maximize their satisfactions' (Diamond and Hartsock, 1981: 719). The character of the mother–child relationship must, like all other social relations, be investigated empirically and not be determined on principle. If we do not base our conceptual definitions on how this relationship manifests itself and develops in various real social contexts, and during various phases of life, we run the risk of returning to the 'myth of the good mother'[16] – albeit in new guises. This is not to say that we should return to the myth of the omnipotent/evil mother either.

There is a final point about the difference between applying an interest perspective and a needs perspective in political studies. Diamond and Hartsock, as well as Petchesky, make the general claim that the theory of interests cannot reveal human desires, needs, and aims. To support this claim they cite, for example, Bay, who says that precisely this character of interest theory implies a vindication of the 'right of the strong to prevail in every contest' (Diamond and Hartsock, 1981: 719). This must be modified. The idea that human needs should constitute the point of departure for political analyses and considerations means that those affected do not necessarily need to be where the lines are drawn and decisions taken in society (compare 'inter esse'). Various weak groups should, for example, be able to have their needs met without first having to overcome their weakness and fight for their own positions of influence. Those groups poor in resources should not be penalized for their weakness. A society where this view is implemented as a general political principle is of course more humane than one where it is not implemented, or one where it is practised within the framework of private charity.

One fundamental difference between the interest point of view and that of needs, in regard to *politics* and to *political* theory, is that the former is necessarily a view taken *from below* as far as individuals and groups are concerned. The core of this perspective is the demand of persons to 'be among' – the demand to be present, literally (physically), or with their own wants represented. This is central to participatory democracy. *Political* thinking in terms of needs opens a different angle, a perspective *from above*, the perspective of socially engaged experts, of the political élite and administrators, the perspective of anticipation and of service democracy. Strictly speaking, the needs perspective, if applied *separately* from an interest perspective, does not require the existence of any channels of influence from below other than for positive or negative responses to decisions which have been taken and policies which are already worked out.[17]

Another Theory of Interest

In the following I try to sketch a particular use of the concept of interest and show both its fruitfulness and its limitations for feminist theory. I think it is important not to 'make a clean break with' the theory of interest, but rather to understand the limitations of its relevance. I would claim that all studies containing a feminist-political premise of 'offensive solidarity' (Haavind, 1982: 413), namely women's conscious acting as a group, require analyses in terms of interest. My remarks in this section are based upon a modified reading of Robert Q. Parks's essay, 'Interests and the Politics of Choice' (1982).

Parks's primary aim is to loosen the opposition between subjective and objective interests. He asserts that all the different types of 'interest speech' have a common denominator, one and the same 'speech-act meaning' or 'point'. 'Interest' always refers to control *over conditions* of choice, rather than to the consequences of choice.[18] The function of arguing in terms of interest in the real world of politics 'is to allow us to persuade, to assert, and to deny claims that an action or policy increases one's control over the conditions of choice. . . . instead of functioning as a standard of what is beneficial to or good for someone (which is assumed by definitions of interests in terms of outcomes)' (Parks, 1982: 549, 552).

Parks understands interests as 'that which increases my *control* over the range of options or conditions of choice, or [that which increases] my capacity to choose'. But interests do not 'involve merely *any* increase in the range of options or choices available'. An increase, for instance, in the number of toothpastes or soaps on the market from 20 to 100 could hardly be taken as in my interest under ordinary circumstances, according to Parks (1982: 557). The promotion of our interests, that is, increased control over conditions of choice, relates, on the one hand, to increasing our real possibilities to determine what values become the objects of choice, and, on the other, to increasing our abilities to see alternative choices clearly, free from distorted feelings, and aided by adequate concepts and sufficient information (Parks, 1982: 550).

Furthermore, he treats interests, explicitly, as an historically specific concept. It is in our society, 'with its politics of choice', that interest talk has its appropriate place: 'Our society has seen an unprecedented proliferation of choices thrust on the individual without any corresponding increase in our individual or collective ability to control the range or type of choices with which we must deal' (1982: 549, 563). We are living in a society where, in more and more spheres of existence, everyone is forced to make choices constantly – whether about work, education, living-quarters, sexuality, living partner, having or not having children, or merely between different types of soap. Under such circumstances it is the 'being among', the attention to, and the undistorted insight into those societal conditions that form our lives, that comprise the relevant point of interest. Thus Parks focuses on what I have chosen to call the formal aspect of the interest concept. To evaluate the consequences of, or satisfaction of choice – the content of the values we desire – does not require the concept of interest. For this the concept of needs, the satisfaction of needs, desires, and preferences is more apt.

At this juncture I would like to summarize the view of interest that I will explore in more detail in the two following sections by stating the following points:

1   The concept of interest is historically conditioned, and it both comprises the key to a particular theory of society as well as implies a particular view of humankind. These dimensions are connected with the normative character of the concept of interest, or, in Parks's words, its 'value slope'. 'Interest' ascribes to people in a certain form of society the norm of participating, the motivating power to try to expand their control over the conditions of choice.

2   Of the interest concept's two main aspects, form and content (or conditions for and consequences of choice), it is form that is the more relevant one. The advantage of this conceptualization is that the content aspect of human values and preferences is *kept open*: these are and will remain the object of conflicts, discussions, and compromises. But discussions of content are expressed best in terms of needs and desires, and not in terms of interests.

3   By focusing on the formal aspect, the subjective and objective dimensions of interest can be linked. 'Interest' always relates to some sort of *controlling attendance confronting conditions of*

choice (more than what gains one receives from a choice, or an increased number of alternatives to choose between). This means either 'be/ing among' those creating the alternatives, or knowing, by means of information, concrete thinking, and clear vision, what one chooses and has to choose between. This approach also implies an integration of the prevailing fragmented view of humanity. By focusing on conditions of choice and not only on the contents of those choices that are offered, people as producers/creators of their life conditions are united with people as consumers/choosers of ready-made packages.

4   But the concept of interest has a limited area of application. Certain of the most intensive human needs, especially those of love and caring for others, render the concept of interest as outlined above, strictly speaking, irrelevant. However, 'interest' should still not be rejected: its limitations should be recognized, as should the sort of landscape that lies, and should lie, beyond these limits. Many of the most important choices in life, like choosing one's work, one's partner, or whether to have a child, are hardly involved with increasing control over future choices. Instead, these choices are primarily about assuming responsibilities and committing oneself, giving up one's options. Of course, a utilitarian dimension is not altogether absent. On the other hand, involvement in relationships of mutuality and trust, and the commitment they foster, may create possibilities of choice which could not have been otherwise obtained (Parks, 1982: 562).

In agreement with Parks, we can differentiate between interest and choice on the one hand, and commitment on the other. Assuming that there are values that authorize a limitation in the control over possibilities of choice, we must weigh and compare the arguments which we deduce from such values and those related to interest. Parks thinks that the contrast between controlled choice and committed engagement is unavoidable in any type of society, but he assumes that larger conflicts between choice and commitment in important areas of life ordinarily need not arise. Applied to gender, this last point in Parks's argument is a weak one. There is reason to believe that such conflict situations are both more difficult and arise in significantly more areas for women than they do for men. Women are, for instance, caught in the oppressive contradiction between the home and the sphere outside the home in a way that men usually are not. In most industrialized countries women, even if they have to work outside the home for economic reasons, are still forced ideologically to 'choose' whether or not to do so. Therefore it is also 'their choice' who is to take care of the children,

how to make the household work, and so on. Moreover, women
seem to found their choices on motivational bases that tend to differ
from those of men (compare Gilligan, 1982).

The Historical Character of the Concept of Interests

In her essay on the difficulties experienced by the earlier women's
movement in placing the demand for women's franchise on the
'public agenda', Dahlerup cautiously takes up the problem of
objective interests. She writes:

> If we want to understand the suppression of issues, we must start from
> the assumption of *objective interests*. If we do not, we cannot grasp the
> most important form of issue-suppression, that of preventing issues from
> being raised at all. As Crenson starts with the assumption that people
> want to avoid being intoxicated by pollution, so the following case starts
> with the assumption that women as well as other disenfranchised groups
> have an objective interest in achieving the right to vote. But there is no
> reason to try to hide the fact that the question of objective interests is
> very delicate. (Dahlerup, 1984)

The problem which Dahlerup faces when relating her study to
Crenson's,[19] is that the assumption that women (or other groups)
have an objective interest in political participation is far from being
as obviously valid as the assumption underlying Crenson's study. In
the latter case interest is connected to objectively measurable living
conditions of (more or less intoxicated) people as bio-physical
bodies. The former case is about the societal conditions of people as
free-willed human beings.

If we conceive of the concept of interest as an historical category,
we should be able to support the proposition that the right to vote is
an objective interest in another way than just by making an analogy
with Crenson. We can see 'interests' as a categorical element in
political theory about the historical development of Western
society. Our argument would be more or less the following: the
objective in women's relation to the right to vote (and eligibility)
derived from the fact that the form of society which actualized the
issue was based increasingly on the will of 'the many', that is,
internally competing groups' choices of action alternatives. People's
actions were no longer justified or vindicated by appeals to rigid
traditions, or by offers from an absolute ruler. A real political
society had grown in Europe, replacing the 'old regime'.[20]

In a political structure where an increasing number of groups are
affected by situations of choice, where more and more areas
become a matter of choice, people's historical determination
becomes to 'be there' where choices are made. This is especially the
case in a society divided and dominated by class and gender; there it

is part of the conditions of social life that people are driven to try to expand control over those spheres that encompass choice. Further, this historical process is a process of concrete social struggle that cannot be seen as steps in a mechanic order, or as derivatives of rational logic. (See Ursula Vogel, chapter 7. The classical philosophers who wrote of individual rights and individual autonomy did not, in fact, extend their reasoning 'automatically' to women.) In our society now, however, women's objective political interests do not concern being individuals in the formal system. They attained that position successively. Swiss women finally got the right to vote in 1972. Women's objective political interests today concern building up and controlling *as sex/gender* a concrete presence or attendance in this system. This historical political situation – the development of sex/gender into a specific, historically relevant 'cleavage basis' in society – has come about through those practical life struggles with which women are involved.[21] It is reflected in the gap between their formal/equal rights and the oppressive and exploitative social realities in which they live and work. For instance, in the process of a public policy which increasingly intervenes into family and other so-called personal matters, with more and more family care and housework being taken over and organized by agencies outside home, the potential of conflicting interests between women and men has increasingly been unfolded and shaped.

Women should be able to act on the strength of being women and not mainly despite being women. They must be visible politically as women, and be empowered to act in that capacity, because there is the continual possibility (not necessity) that they may have needs and attitudes on vital issues which differ from those of men. This does *not* imply that women have no needs and preferences in common with men. Nor does it imply that these differences only reflect biological distinctions, but it *does* imply, as extensive facts in contemporary Western societies also indicate, that women and men are beginning to constitute themselves as two basic societal corporations. These developments, which have their origins in the second wave of the women's movement and its ensuing mobilization of women, can be found more or less within every area of social life. This means, further, that the sex/gender structure must be analytically conceptualized independently of class structure, race relations, and such.

Interests as Controlling Presence

As Dahlerup shows, the right to vote was preceded by lengthy attempts to get the issue present and noticed on the public agenda, to give it 'public attention'. Parks uses precisely the word 'attend' as an underlying and distinguishing feature of the concept of interests. 'Attend' and 'attention' have the double meaning of actual/physical presence and subjective notice or consciousness.

One type of structural barrier which hinders women's issues from reaching the public agenda is the fact that women have been excluded, and to a large extent still are absent, from those institutions that create these agendas, for example, the mass media, political organizations (in a broad sense), literature, public meetings (Dahlerup, 1984, p. 44ff). But the reverse situation applies also now: from well within such institutions women now seek space and an attention in the public debate in order not to be pushed aside *within* the institutional contexts. Today women have the simple legal right to be present in, for example, political and union organizations, and they have increased their numbers, sometimes significantly. But if they conceive of themselves and/or act as a gender interest group, that is, when they try to control their attendance in order to be able to shape those conditions which they live under in their capacity of human beings who are women, they run into obstacles. Women active in unions have written about how they are forced to start public discussions in order to bring attention to and prevent their issues and demands from being pushed aside or choked within the unions.[22]

In the early 1960s the Swedish essayist and journalist Eva Moberg used the expression 'conditional liberation' to describe the circumstances of women. They were allowed to be wage earners, and otherwise active outside the home – as long as they took care of 'their' domestic chores too. One could similarly speak of women's 'conditional membership' in regard to political parties and unions. Research from several different countries shows how women's presence and participation in these organizations are accepted as long as they do not express themselves or act from sex/gender-based interests.[23] This way of applying the concept of interest as form and in this notion of form differentiating between the *simple* and the *controlling* presence (or between the legal right and the active practising of shaping social reality) takes us right into the complicated question of objective circumstances and the subjective consciousness of these circumstances. It takes us into the 'first and most serious problem' for the women's movement to overcome (Dahlerup, 1984: 43): women's own lack of consciousness of oppression – a lack that is easy to understand.

Women take continual risks – not only the risk of losing control over their circumstances, but also the right of attendance itself if they consciously act in terms of sex/gender (compare note 23).

Women take similar risks in love relationships if they start conflicts, if they argue that male dominance in the relationship must be a question to be discussed and answered, or if they merely take control themselves of their shared life conditions. Examples of this could be women's claims to financial autonomy, or to full insight into the couple's common finances; demands that men take their emotional responsibilities as fathers; and not considering it self-evident that men's chances of getting work or pursuing a career should one-sidedly determine the family's place of residence or its life-style. Even *being interested in* and seeking knowledge about women's lives and the different conditions of the sexes can be considered threatening. Women are often left in the end without either partners or success.

The essence of the problem of the sexes is even more about the body-and-the-soul of concrete, socially related *individual people* than is the problem of class and race. In the struggle of the sexes even more areas of life and values are affected, and in different ways. The striving to 'be among' and, in the capacity of sex/gender group, to control this presence also demands that each individual person as far as possible gains perspective of his/her own actions and powers to exist and function as precisely sexed/gendered persons. This in turn presumes unity among women and mutually supportive alliances with sympathetic men as well.

One important strategic question is how far it is reasonable to consider agreement when it comes to common needs, values, and demands. With reference to the question of organization, perhaps large (offensive) women-only organizations can have no other function than to organize women's 'collective discontent' (Hernes, 1980: 265), and protect and promote general positions of equality. The longer-range women's struggle, goals, and strategy development must necessarily be fragmented and cultivated both formally and informally within all the various areas and contexts of social life, and even within the family. Because of the deep social cleavages of class, race, or ethnicity among women, I suppose it is realistic not to rely on genuine *sisterhood* between all women; nor even on *solidarity*. *Alliance* on certain issues is perhaps the only realistic kind of large-scale unitedness. Sisterhood, conceived as a bond of relatively deep affection, of friendship and sometimes love, is presumably only possible between *few*. Solidarity, understood as a relatedness which does not necessarily presume personal friend-ship but, when practised, involves sacrifices and sharing of burdens, should be possible among *many*. Limited alliances, both offensive and defensive, could be seen as the minimum of necessary united-ness among *all* women.

Limitations of the View of Interests

All the authors mentioned above who reject the theory of interests share the view that the issues of reproduction by their very nature do not lend themselves to utilitarian interest arguments. All of them take up the birth of children, love, and caring in mother–child relationships as particularly incomprehensible in terms of interests. However, considering all the conflicts and power struggles – not only for 'standing' (control) but even about the distribution of many limited resources such as time and money – which are constantly waged openly and covertly between parents and children, it seems to be more realistic to assert the composite notion of both utility and care, both control and commitment. And I refer not only to oppressive or to purely exploitative relationships, but also to those containing 'good conflicts', to use Jean Baker Miller's expression.

What on the other hand clearly overrides the traditional view of interest is that the parents' vocation, according to this planet's life programme, is to promote their offspring's interests *beside their own* (compare Ruddick, 1980/1984). According to the idea of interest which I argue for here, this would mean that parents should help their children to overcome successfully their dependency on the parents themselves and on parental authority. Children must learn to take control over *their* own conditions of choice, without the self-denial of parents as being relatively autonomous persons. This is difficult, especially perhaps for women who from infancy are taught altruism: women learn 'to be something for others', to identify themselves with other people's problems, particularly those of husband and children, and to make the well-being of the latter their own, often at the expense of their own presence. One result of this is that conflicts of interest in relation to others become problematic to articulate and work on (Gilligan, 1982; Ve, 1982: 418–19; 1984: 133; and Ferguson, chapter 4).

It is obvious that the satisfaction of many values in life presumes that one loses, or restricts considerably, control over future conditions of choice – being pregnant and giving birth to children, for example. Does the bodily part of motherhood, then, stand in opposition to a woman's interests? Strictly speaking, yes, according to the idea of interest outlined above. We also can formulate it so that by bearing children women involve themselves in promoting 'mankind's (and in extension also the state's and capital's) interest'. Pregnancy carries us into a union with nature (needless to say, this varies with different social forms); we enter into a process the course of which we can ourselves influence only to a minimal degree (and of course this degree differs socially/historically); we run risks to life and health both during and after pregnancy and birth; and to all this are added the ties and responsibilities during the child's upbringing and for the rest of his/her life. But the value of bearing life and helping it to be is so enormous that many happily restrict their own autonomy for its sake. What on the other hand promotes women's interests in this context is to safeguard the very real possibilities of being able to decide whether or not we want children, under what conditions we want to give birth to them, and within what parenting pattern and with what expectations we will raise them.

Conclusion

The theory of interests is partisan by nature (or particularistic). The focus of this theory is that each party in a community or an association strives to ensure his/her autonomy in the community and his/her voice in those policy processes that shape the development of the community as a whole. Thus the idea of interests issues from the view that social contrapositions and conflicts are both unavoidable and potentially fruitful. The notion of interest developed here which emphasizes its formal (as relatively distinct from the content) aspect is essentially more appropriate as a core concept in a theory of broadly based participatory democracy than is the concept of needs (the content) taken separately. These two related concepts should not be viewed as exchangeable but rather as referring to two different layers of social existence: agency and the needs/desires that give strength and meaning to agency. As a core concept in (a participatory democratic) political theory, needs must be mediated by interests. In no developed country have women reached the stage where they can give up the struggle for a real and controllable attendance as an identifiable group within the various groupings of society. Even within relationships of love and care this struggle is necessary in order to have a worthwhile life, a life with woman-human dignity.

In her article, Sapiro asks the question: 'why is an individual's relationship to the production of children not commonly accepted as a matter of political interest while one's relationship to other forms of production is?' (1981: 713). Put this way the question becomes rather misleading. In all welfare states, including the socialist ones, this relation is indeed accepted as being of political interest. Childbirth has always been of concern to the state, as an issue of population growth or decline, and has thus made motherhood a concern of the state (this is actually suggested by Sapiro herself; compare also Jaquette and Staudt, chapter 10). The problem is not whether to politicize the production of children (of course, from women's point of view, what is of decisive importance is *how* it is politicized); the crucial issue is the politicization of the gender/ sexual relations themselves. Women and men are obviously the producers of children and responsible for them, but women and men, or rather, people as sexual beings, are also the primary parties in the reproduction of themselves and each other as persons who have special human, natural/social, capacities for sexual love. Regardless of how the forms of society may change – for example in the direction of less 'compulsory heterosexuality' (Adrienne Rich, 1980) – perhaps we will never avoid a certain struggle of interests in this matter. We will perhaps never cease to exist in a delicate balance between, on the one hand, surrender, leaping into situations where control and reflective choice stand in direct opposition to what is valued most highly – profound love – and, on the other hand, a compelling need to monitor interest, control, and responsibility.[24] What can and must be changed is that women are affected and damaged much more and so differently from men in this basic process in social life.

Notes

I want to thank Jan Teeland for translating the original Swedish version of this chapter into English, and Kathleen Jones for other generous help with the language as well as the content of this revised version. I am grateful to Ingrid Pincus for lending a helping hand with the final English version. Finally I want to mention that without the grant from the Commission for Research on Equality between Men and Women/The Swedish Ministry of Labour, it would have been difficult for me to take the time to write my contribution, the original version of which was published in *Kvinnovetenskaplig tidskrift* 6 (1985): 2.

   1. I use 'scientific studies of politics' and 'studies of politics' to include the main ways of approaching politics: political science (which tends to look at politics from a state perspective), political sociology (which more often starts in society), Marxist studies of politics (which takes class structure as an important point of departure), and feminist studies of politics (whose common denominator is the perspective of sex/gender as a social relationship which organizes society).

   2. The subject of this chapter and the standpoints I take have a background in a larger study I am doing, on the theoretical conceptualization and explanation of what I call the formal/equal patriarchy of today. I am trying to move the feminist historical materialist (the 'synthesis' of radical feminist questions and Marxist method) analysis of patriarchy some very important steps further. I claim that if we really take the feminist questions seriously and in fact apply Marxist method as 'guiding threads' on *these* questions we come up with – not some Marxist answers (as Juliet Mitchell said in the very beginning of the theoretical project of socialist feminism) – but with a firm conviction that we must transcend the 'field of knowledge' of *political economy, class,* and *work.* Much more definitely than existing socialist feminist theory does, we must (on a basic or grand theory level) establish a specific theoretical 'problématique' (field of knowledge), that of '*political sexuality*': the *relationship between people as*

sexual and gendered beings, and *love*. How the realities of economy and class, and race/ethnicity (as well as those of other oppressive oppositions) reveal themselves in women's and men's lives must be stated then as empirical questions. (Among my working papers available in English are Anna G. Jónasdóttir, 1985; 1988.)

3. When I speak about women versus men as being the essential parties in the sexual process, I am not cancelling out lesbian or homosexual relationships. My point is that if we take sexuality (as opposed to economy) to be the complex fundament on which patriarchy, in its various historical forms, is based, the main parties in this *oppressive* sex/gender structure are women versus men (rather than women versus women or men versus men). This oppressive relationship, in turn, forms the conditions in which people practise other social relationships.

Furthermore, my standpoint implies a view opposed to that of, for instance, Hartmann (1981); she asserts that the basic relation of patriarchy is a relation between men. Defining it that way she misses the whole point of the new feminist use of the term.

4. As is well known, this theme has been one of the 'burning issues' within the multi-branched (methodological) debate on power studies. 'Interest' and 'power', in this debate, used to be defined in terms of each other, and are characterized by Lukes as 'essentially contested concepts'. For references and an introduction to this debate see, for example, Steven Lukes (1974). For an overview of the main contributions to the more limited (analytical) debate on the concept of interests in politics, see the references in note 1 of Parks (1982), and Reeve and Ware (1983). Benton (1982) argues that while 'power' can be conceived and applied without 'moral or political bias', the concept of interests is 'indispensably both cognitive and evaluative' (p. 8).

5. Sapiro's view is similar to this. She argues that it can be expanded from its present customary use to include sex/gender concerns, such as the production and reproduction of children.

6. One of the greatest weaknesses in modern, mainstream political science is the lack of such historically grounded theorizing about politics. The way in which *interests* is usually handled today is a good example of the 'poverty of theory'. On one hand there is a lot of philosophical (logically and/or morally oriented) conceptual analysis which is almost entirely unrelated to historical or empirical conditions; on the other hand the term 'interests' is much used in empirical studies, but usually without any clearly stated theoretical frame of references.

7. Ethel Klein (1984) provides certain evidence which is relevant here. According to her, women's support for feminism is part of their personal identity or consciousness (and, thus, as I see it, part of their bodies-and-minds as human-material entities); and 'consciousness . . . is derived from personal experiences that prompt people actually to change the political agenda' (Klein, 1984: 104). The significance of men's support for feminism differs from women's. 'For men, feminism is an abstract issue of rights and obligations', a cause that they can sympathize with (if they want to) on ideological grounds. 'Men's concern for feminism is similar to the concern that whites express about race discrimination' (p. 104). It should be added here that the survey questions that these results are based on are mainly about feminism in the meaning of efforts to end sex discrimination and sexism in general. To what extent nurturing (or 'mothering') fathers, for instance, come to such issues as child-care facilities 'from the path of personal experience', instead of that of ideology, is thus another question.

8. 'Interest' in the sense of financial interest rates or gains has its roots in the Middle Ages. Money lending was carried on for centuries before openly taking out

interest on borrowed money was allowed. The prohibition on interest was circumvented by allowing compensation for those damages a borrower might cause to a creditor's property. This compensation subsequently was called interest (see Patinkin, 1968). My references regarding the history of the concept of 'interest/s' include also works such as Gunn (1969); 'Interessen' in *Philosophisches Wörterbuch*; Hirschman (1977).

9. Allusion to P. Birnbaum (1976) 'Power Divorced from its Sources: a Critique of the Exchange Theory of Power', in B. Barry (ed.) *Power and Political Theory*. London: John Wiley.

10. My arguments in this essay imply a use of 'form' and 'formal' that transcends their common meaning of juridico-legal formalism, that is, legal rules for what individual citizens have to do, or are allowed to do, as members of the state/political community. In short I use 'form' and 'formal' as meaning: the power of forming or shaping societal processes. Thus, the fact that women are fighting for an openly acknowledged presence as *women* in those processes, and the idea, derived from this fact, that women and men as gendered persons are interested parties in the political processes, challenges the reified genderlessness of the existing forms. Women are demanding gender-based social 'intervention' into the seemingly gender-neutral institutionalized arrangements (forms) that shape, or direct, the substantial/material processes (the work process, the process of producing and reproducing people, etc.) of society.

11. This line of reasoning, as well as the whole discussion here of women and interest theory, leads into the question of the status of women as women (and of men as men) in relation to the state; or the question of sex/gender as a component capacity in citizenship. In the last few years a feminist theory of the state has begun to emerge. For further references and problems stated, see Siim (chapter 8) and Hernes (chapter 9).

12. A review of the literature shows that there are at least three different ways of linking interests to some source or base: (1) interests *are* the preferences of context-free subjects; (2) interests are related to some externally determined principles or standards, which in turn can be of two kinds: (a) some ethical principles or ideals, or (b) some objectively stated standards for human need fulfilment; and (3) interests emerge from people's social experiences, from the social arrangements in which people practise their lives. My own standpoint is of the third kind.

13. Even if there are other 'memberships', such as class and race, they do not *cancel out* gender ones. In fact, they are always mediated by it. Of course, the particular intersections of race, class, and sex/gender, and the ways these vary in different historical and cultural contexts, need to be articulated carefully in theory, and studied empirically.

14. The behavioural revolution in Anglo-American political science brought with it, among other things, much ado about how to define the concept of 'group' in general and 'interest group' in particular. This depended on methodological individualism being one of the main points of the behaviouralist credo. A central issue in the definition discussions was whether to define 'interest group' by considering some objectively confirmable characteristics of individuals (such as class position, sex, age) or if shared attitudes, or consciousness of some common concerns, between individuals was needed for 'interest group' to be a meaningful concept. Against this background Klein (1984), for example, distinguishes between women as an 'interest category' or a 'status' in the objective sense, and women as an 'interest group' in the sense of a class of people who, through a social and political movement, have become aware of some common concerns. In traditional political theory similar

distinctions have been made in terms of 'grouping' versus 'group' (Easton) and 'potential interest group' versus 'interest group' (Truman).

15. Siedentop (1983), for instance, criticizes existing political theory for taking the concept of 'individual' as a neutral or descriptive term synonymous to 'the social agent' in general, while it is, in fact, historically specific and related to another problematic concept – "the state". . . . *de facto*, development of the "state" [as one species of government] is a necessary condition for the emergence of the individual as a social role', according to Siedentop (1983: 61).

16. Allusion to the book with that title (1973/1974) by Hanne Haavind *et al.* in which the authors criticize several dubious scientific results and interpretations of the mother/child relationship.

17. There are at least two different discourses on need-based political theory. On one hand what might be called a reformist theory of social justice and on the other a radical, or Marxist, theory of social community. Representative authors of the first discourse are Bay (1965, 1968, 1980), Etzioni (1968), and Miller (1976).

A radical theory of needs and community, built on the work of Marx, has been developed by authors like Herbert Marcuse and Agnes Heller. For further studies on this subject see, for example, Kathleen B. Jones, 'The Marxian Concept of Community' (unpublished PhD dissertation, 1978).

My critical comments in the text refer mainly to the first-mentioned discourse (the justice theory of needs) as being the more relevant one for looking at existing welfare societies (and in fact Diamond and Hartsock link together the two by quoting Bay). On the other hand, it seems to me that the Marxists hitherto, when they claim that people's concrete needs should be the *raison de société*, also take for granted things that must be discussed. The whole dimension of agency and organization: the formulating of wants, potential conflicts, decision making, implementation, and so on, are hardly problematized at all. Of course we are here touching upon the question of the underdevelopment of *political* theory in Marxist thought, and there is no space here to go further into that question.

18. This way of defining 'interests' as control over the conditions of choice is both like and unlike the way Brian Barry (in his *Political Argument*, 1965) conceives interests: as generalized means (or actions) to ends (or results), and not the ends or results themselves (pp. 176, 183). The similarity is in drawing such a boundary and in putting the focus on action rather than the content; the dissimilarity is that Barry treats the two aspects as two *separate* or isolated things while my understanding here (and my reading of Parks) aims at treating the two aspects of interests (the form and the content) as dialectically related. Another dissimilarity is that Barry's concept 'generalized means' refers exclusively to money, while my action component in the concept of interest refers to a power of agency as a specific political 'means'.

19. Dahlerup refers to Matthew A. Crenson: *The Un-Politics of Air Pollution. A Study of Non-Decisionmaking in the Cities* (1971). This is one of the few empirical studies carried out with the help of the controversial non-decision theory. The conundrum concerns how one can, and from a scientific point of view should, investigate power in society. 'Objective' or 'real interest' is included as one of the controversial concepts. Compare note 4.

20. The expression is Tocqueville's, 'l'ancien régime'. He wrote about the 'great transformation', the transition from the Middle Ages to the new age in Western Europe. 'L'ancien régime' refers more specifically to the royal autocracy: the middle phase between the medieval decentralized social organization and the political/civil, gradually democratic modern societies.

21. The historical line of reasoning I am aiming at should not be confused with the

type of argument that says, for example, that women have the right of participation because they comprise half the population. To speak about objective interests in terms such as these would be to derive women's interests from some principle of quantitative justice. That is not analytically fruitful, even if it is sometimes ideologically forceful. In short, we can say that the notion of 'objective' or 'real' interests, actualized in Crenson's study, refers to biological criteria; the justice argument, as usually formulated, refers to an ahistorical general principle; while my notion of 'objective' interest refers to subjects or agents motivated by experienced historically specific forces.

22. See Balas *et al.* (eds), *Faglig kvinnepolitikk – hvor går LO? (Union Policies concerning Women – Where is the (TUC) going?)* Pax Publishers, Oslo, 1982, pp. 103ff. Several sections of this book support my arguments here.

23. In his book, *Democracy. The Threshold of Freedom* (1948: 61ff), Harold F. Gosnell relates how the principle of equal distribution of sexes amongst the delegates to a party convention was practised during the second and third decades of this century in a state in the USA, and how it was a disappointment for the women because the men, who were already in power, could see to it that 'difficult' women disappeared and that accommodating women were chosen for the places designated for women.

Lenin's berating of Clara Zetkin for allowing working-class women to discuss marriage problems at their meetings is well known. Less known is how she was actually treated in the party at home in Germany, how for example in 1908 (when German women obtained the right to organize politically), at the designation of a women's place in the party executive, she had to step back in favour of Luise Zietz, a woman who increasingly identified herself with the party executive and not with women. (Compare Karen Honeycutt (1976) 'Clara Zetkin: A Socialist Approach to the Problem of Woman's Oppression', *Feminist Studies*, 3–4, pp. 131–44, especially p. 139.)

Anita Dahlberg in *Jämt eller ibland – om jämställdhet (Always or sometimes – on Equal Rights)* (1984: 138) takes up for instance how the unions (read: unions dominating men) see a threat in women's 'internal solidarity'. Similarly, recent reports from the Swedish JÄMO (the ombudsman for the equality between the sexes) show that some of the women who have contacted that office because of discrimination on the job have afterwards been harassed by their bosses and also by their union officials.

24. Not even these dialectics exhaust the multiplicity of reality. Presumably, surrender sometimes *is* 'control' – as, for example, in sado-masochistic relationships.

References

Balbus, Isaac D. (1971) 'The Concept of Interest in Pluralist and Marxian Analysis', *Politics and Society* 1: 151–77.
Barry, Brian (1965) *Political Argument*. London: Routledge and Kegan Paul.
Bay, Christian (1965) 'Politics and Pseudo-politics: A Critical Evaluation of some Behavioral Literature', *American Political Science Review* 59: 39–51.
Bay, C. (1968) 'Needs, Wants, and Political Legitimacy', *Canadian Journal of Political Science* 1(33): 241–60.
Bay, C. (1980) 'Peace and Critical Political Knowledge as Human Rights', *Political Theory* 8(3): 293–318, 331–4.

Benton, Ted (1982) 'Realism, Power and Objective Interests', pp. 7–33 in K. Graham (ed.), *Contemporary Political Philosophy*. Cambridge: Cambridge University Press.

Bernard, Jessie (1971) *Women and the Public Interest. An Essay on Policy and Protest*. Chicago: Aldine/Atherton.

Connolly, William E. (1983) *The Terms of Political Discourse*, 2nd edn. Oxford: Martin Robertson.

Dahlerup, Drude (1980) 'Approaches to the Study of Public Policy Towards Women' (stencil). Aarhus, Denmark: Institute of Political Science.

Dahlerup, Drude (1984) 'Overcoming the Barriers: An Approach to the Study of How Women's Issues are Kept from the Political Agenda', pp. 31–66 in J.H. Stiehm (ed.), *Women's Views of the Political World of Men*. Dobbs Ferry, NY: Transnational Publishers.

Diamond, Irene and Nancy Hartsock (1981), 'Beyond Interests in Politics: A Comment on Virginia Sapiro's "When are Interests Interesting? The Problem of Political Representation of Women"', *American Political Science Review* 75(3): 717–23.

Edsall, Thomas B. (1984) *The New Politics of Inequality*. New York; London: W.W. Norton.

Ehrmann, Henry W. (1968) 'Interest Groups', pp. 486–92 in *International Encyclopedia of the Social Sciences*, vol. 7–8.

Etzioni, Amitai (1968) 'Basic Human Needs, Alienation, and Inauthenticity', *American Sociological Review* 33(6): 870–84.

Fuchs-Epstein, Cynthia and Rose Laub-Coser (eds) (1981) *Access to Power. Cross-National Studies of Women and Elites*. London: George Allen and Unwin.

Gilligan, Carol (1982) *In a Different Voice. Psychological Theory and Women's Development*. Cambridge, Mass.: Harvard University Press.

Gunn, J.A.W. (1969) *Politics and the Public Interest in the Seventeenth Century*. London: Routledge and Kegan Paul.

Haavind, Hanne (1982) 'Premisser for personlige forhold mellom kvinner ('Premises for personal relations between women') in H. Holter (ed.) *Kvinner i felleskap* (*Women Together*) Oslo: Universitetsforlaget, 1982.

Halsaa-Albrektsen, Beatrice (1977) *Kvinner og Politisk Deltakelse* (*Women and Political Participation*). Oslo: Pax Forlag.

Hartmann, Heidi (1981) 'The Unhappy Marriage of Marxism and Feminism: Towards a More Progressive Union', pp. 1–41 in Lydia Sargent (ed.), *Women and Revolution*. London: Pluto Press.

Heller, Agnes (1976) *The Theory of Need in Marx*. New York: St Martin's Press.

Hernes, Helga Maria (1980) 'Predicting Support for the Women's Movement: A Diffusion Model', *Scandinavian Political Studies* 3(3): 265–73.

Hernes, Helga Maria (1982) *Staten – kvinner ingen adgang?* (*The State – Women No Access?*) Oslo: Universitetsforlaget.

Hernes, Helga Maria (1984) 'Women and the Welfare State: The Transition from Private to Public Dependence', pp. 26–45 in H. Holter (ed.), *Patriarchy in a Welfare Society*. Oslo: Universitetsforlaget.

Herring, Pendleton (1968) 'Public Interest', pp. 170–5 in *International Encyclopedia of the Social Sciences*, vol. 13–14.

Hirschman, Albert Q. (1977) *The Passions and the Interests. Political Arguments for Capitalism before Its Triumph*. Princeton, NJ: Princeton University Press.

Holmberg, Sören and Kent Asp (1984) *Kampen om kärnkraften. En bok om väljare, massmedier och folkomröstningen 1980* (*The Struggle about Nuclear Energy. A*

Book about Voters, Mass Communication, and the Referendum 1980). Stockholm: Liber.

Jaquette, Jane S. (1974) 'Introduction', in J.S. Jaquette (ed.) *Women in Politics.* New York: John Wiley and Sons.

Jaquette, Jane S. (1976) 'Review Essay: Political Science', *Signs* 2(1): 147–64.

Jaquette, Jane S. (1984) 'Power as Ideology: A Feminist Analysis', pp. 7–29 in J.S. Stiehm (ed.) *Women's Views of the Political World of Men.* Dobbs Ferry, NY: Transnational Publishers.

Jónasdóttir, Anna G. (1985) 'Beyond "Oppression": On Exploitation in the Sex/Gender System'. Paper presented in the workshop 'Exploitation' at the ECPR conference (European Consortium for Political Research), Barcelona, 25–30 March.

Jónasdóttir, Anna G. (1988) 'Sex/Gender, Power and Politics: Towards a Theory of Patriarchy in the Formally Equal Society', *Acta Sociologica* 31(2): 157–74. (The Swedish version was published in the anthology *Feminism och marxism. En förälskelse med förhinder [Feminism and Marxism. A Love Affair with Impediments.]* Stockholm: Arbetarkultur, 1986.)

Jonasson, Birgit (1985) 'Åsikter i tre jämställdhetsfrågor' ('Opinions in Three Equality Issues'), *Kvinnovetenskaplig Tidskrift*, 6(2): 54–62 (Summary in English, p. 62).

Jones, Kathleen B. (1978) 'The Marxian Concept of Community', Unpublished Ph.D. dissertation, City University of New York, The Graduate School.

Klein, Ethel (1984) *Gender Politics. From Consciousness to Mass Politics.* Cambridge, Mass.; London: Harvard University Press.

Lafferty, William M. (1980) 'Sex and Political Participation: An Exploratory Analysis of the "Female Culture"', *European Journal of Political Research* 8: 323–47.

Lukes, Steven (1974) *Power. A Radical View.* London: Macmillan.

Milbrath, L.W. and M.L. Goel (1977) *Political Participation* (2nd rev. edn). Chicago: Rand McNally.

Miller, David (1976) *Social Justice.* Oxford: Clarendon Press.

Parks, Robert Q. (1982) 'Interests and the Politics of Choice', *Political Theory* 10(4): 547–65.

Patinkin, Don (1968) 'Interest', pp. 471–85 in *International Encyclopedia of the Social Sciences*, vol. 7–8.

Petchesky, Rosalind Pollack (1980) 'Reproductive Freedom: Beyond A Woman's Right to Choose', *Signs* 5(4): 661–85.

Petchesky, Rosalind Pollack (1983) *Abortion and Women's Choice.* New York: Longman.

Peterson, Abby (1981) 'Kvinnofrågor, kvinnomedvetande och klass' (Women's Issues, Women's Consciousness, and Class'), *Zenit* 70: 5–21.

Philosophisches Wörterbuch (1975) 'Form', pp. 409–12 in Band 1. Leipzig: VEB Bibliographisches Institut.

Philosophisches Wörterbuch (1975) 'Interessen', pp. 581–4 in Band 1. Leipzig: VEB Bibliographisches Institut.

Pitkin, Hanna (1972) *The Concept of Representation.* Berkeley, CA: University of California Press.

Putnam, Robert D. (1976) *The Comparative Study of Political Elites.* Englewood Cliffs, NJ: Prentice-Hall.

Reeve, Andrew and Alan Ware (1983) 'Interests in Political Theory', *British Journal of Political Science* 13(4): 379–400.

Rich, Adrienne (1980) 'Compulsory Heterosexuality and Lesbian Existence', *Signs* 5(4): 631–60.

Ruddick, Sara (1984) 'Maternal Thinking', pp. 213–30 in J. Trebilcot (ed.) *Mothering. Essays in Feminist Theory*. Totowa, NJ: Rowman and Allanheld. (Appeared first in *Feminist Studies* (1980), 6(2).)

Sapiro, Virginia (1981) 'Research Frontier Essay: When are Interests Interesting? The Problem of Political Representation of Women', *American Political Science Review* 75(3): 701–16.

Siedentop, Larry (1983) 'Political Theory and Ideology: The Case of the State', pp. 53–73 in D. Miller and L. Siedentop (eds), *The Nature of Political Theory*. Oxford: Clarendon Press.

Siltanen, Janet and Michelle Stanworth (eds) (1984) *Women and the Public Sphere. A Critique of Sociology and Politics*. London: Hutchinson.

Togeby, Lise (1984) *Politik – også en kvindesag (Politics – a Women's Concern Also)*. Aarhus: Politica.

Ve, Hildur (1982) 'Kvinnefellesskap og relasjonslogikk. Om altruisme som samhandlingspremiss' ('Women Together and Relational Logic. Altruism as a Premise for Interaction'), pp. 416–24 in H. Holter (ed.), *Kvinner i fellesskap/Women Together*. Oslo: Universitetsforlaget.

Ve, Hildur (1984) 'Women's Mutual Alliances. Altruism as a Premise for Interaction', pp. 119–35 in H. Holter (ed.), *Patriarchy in a Welfare Society*. Oslo: Universitetsforlaget.

Walker, Nancy J. (1986) 'Are Women More Peaceminded than Men?'. Paper presented in the workshop 'Political Theories on Gender and Power' at the ECPR conference, Gothenburg, 2–7 April.

4

Subject-centredness in Feminist Discourse

Kathy E. Ferguson

French feminist Luce Irigaray entitles one of her essays 'Any
Theory of the "Subject" has always been Appropriated by the
"Masculine"' (Irigaray, 1985a). In this she echoes the suspicions of
many other feminists that the notions of subjectivity dominant in
Western life are relentlessly male. The subjectivity claimed by men
and denied to women constitutes the self as bounded agent in the
world, the centre of all things, active, reflective, coinciding neatly
with itself. This subject often designates itself under the name
'humanist' to establish that which is essentially the same for all
humans, and which distinguishes the human from the other-than-
human world. Women in male humanist discourse have generally
been among those others, consigned to the world of the acted-upon,
of otherness colonized in the service of maintaining the sameness of
the subject.

The most readily available move for nascent feminist discourse to
make was (and is) to demand equal entry for women into the world
of the human. Humanist feminism, as Iris Young expresses it,
'defines gender as accidental to humanity' and urges both women
and men to 'pursue self-development in those creative and
intellectual activities that distinguish human beings from the rest of
nature' (Young, 1985: 174). Humanist feminists have often turned
to the law to claim the status of subjects, seeking the rights and
opportunities that such status carries. The law is an appropriate
vehicle for this project for two reasons: it can be a powerful club in
changing behaviour; and, more importantly, the law itself rests
heavily on the notion of the self as subject. Subjects are beings in
possession of themselves and their property, and legal rights serve
as property to be possessed. Rights are things that the subject can
have, independently of where or who the subject is.

A second move for feminist discourse to make, often voiced by
those sharing Irigaray's suspicion of the subject, is to turn women's
marginality in subject-centred discourse to advantage. 'Gynocentric
feminism', as Young presents it, 'defines women's oppression as the
devaluation and repression of women's experience by a masculinist

culture that exalts violence and individualism. It argues for the superiority of values embodied in traditionally female experience, and rejects the values embodied in traditionally male dominated institutions' (Young, 1985: 173). Traditionally female experience can be defined in many ways: by mothering and reproduction; by the political economy of the gendered division of labour; by the arrangements of the female body; by spirituality and contact with the divine. While it is of enormous importance to feminist epistemology to distinguish between arguments about what women are said to *be*, versus what women are said to *do*, both types of argument share the suspicion of subject-centred discourse, whether or not it includes women.

Between these two strategies of feminist discourse, the humanist and the gynocentric, the dilemma of feminism's relation to the subject resides. Humanist feminists point convincingly to the dangers of living in a society based on juridico-legal discourse and selves-as-subjects without possessing the same armour of rights: the laws and the courts do not oblige us by leaving us alone. Furthermore, those who lack a sense of themselves as agents, as capable of acting and taking responsibility for their actions in the public world, are put at enormous disadvantage: in a world made by and for solid subjects, not being one, or being less of one, can be devastating. For example, many of the women in Carol Gilligan's abortion study (Gilligan, 1982) or in Kim Chernin's interviews on body size (Chernin, 1981) suffer from a sense of paralysis, an inability to act, that leads easily to their victimization. The women interviewed by the authors of *Women's Ways of Knowing* spoke consistently of a 'quest for self and voice' (Belenky *et al.*, 1986: 133), testifying with their lives to the psychic and material pain accompanying an ill-defined sense of self.

Finally, it is very difficult to speak of liberation without some notion of a subject whose life will be improved in some way, or to envisage political change at all without some idea of who will bring it about and why. As a philosophy of liberation, feminism has often appealed to the powers of agency and subjectivity as necessary components of struggle. The project of 'expanding the concept of woman to the point where a woman can assert herself and make demands upon respect' (Frye, 1983: 93) has often been couched in terms of strengthening and validating the subjectivity of women.

But to turn from this traditionally female dilemma to a whole-hearted embrace of the modern subject is to follow too closely the path of the dominant male discourse. The subject, as Foucault and others remind us, is one who is *subjected*, brought to order by the disciplinary strategies of modernity. Modern subjects are constituted by a complex process of differentiation, fixation, interrogation; they are separated from the rest of nature, from the play of possibilities and pleasures in bodies and relations. The modern subject is a unity fabricated out of the diffuse flow of experiences and relationships, 'an empty synthesis . . . a profusion of lost events' (Foucault, 1977: 145). Women's consignment to the outworld of otherness by the work and words of men has reserved the full force of modern subjectivity for the dominant male groups. The subjugated and submerged discourses of those sharing the margins are ill-served by incorporation into the discourse of the same. Subjects keep their rights by force of the tyranny of sameness: one has rights by virtue of claiming to be the same as the rightful others, and one makes claims to difference at the expense of being assigned to the outskirts of the realm. To be equal is to be the same; to be different is to be inferior. Either way there is colonization, homogenization, and the erasure of diversity.

This dilemma suggests that feminists can neither turn their backs completely on the discourse of rights and subjects, nor happily embrace it. Thus comes the search for other strategies, other discourses, other possibilities. I can see three alternative discursive strategies that have emerged in opposition to juridico-legal discourse and the self-as-subject: a discourse of needs and of persons-in-relations; a discourse of nature/spirit and of the self-in-place; a discourse of semiotics/play and of bodies-and-pleasures. These are not unique to feminism; rather, they indicate feminism's obligations to and influence on other strategies of inquiry that position themselves as counterpoints to the dominant humanist tradition. Nor are they clear and distinct fractions within feminism. They are more like contrasting codes (Barthes, 1981: 133–61) or means of interpretation, directions of exploration that share a great deal but none the less differ as to the kinds of meanings they make possible. Each is an effort to establish an identity for women not as lesser subjects than men, but as subjects differently.

Codes of Need and Relation

This opposition strategy focuses on human need rather than rights, and on intersubjective connections between persons rather than on autonomous selves. From this perspective women's experiences, their daily activities which are likely to entail attending to the needs of others, are read as generating a psychology of connection with others and a relational morality. Carol Gilligan argues that women are more likely than men to attend to the concrete needs of particular others, more likely to judge themselves and others by the moral injunction to take care, to respond. Careful to differentiate moral themes rather than the sexes *per se*, she locates the differences she finds in 'the interaction of experience and thought, in different voices and the dialogues to which they give rise, in the way we listen to ourselves and to others, in the stories we tell about our lives' (Gilligan, 1982: 2). Concentrating on what (a selected group of) men and women make of their own experiences, she sees personal crisis as the trigger which either promotes or thwarts moral development. Nancy Hartsock calls upon women's life activity to construct a political economy of gender, one which builds from women's experiences of *eros*, community, and power. She explores writings by women on power where the emphasis is placed on energy, capacity, and potential rather than domination and exclusion. The material circumstances of women's lives produce in women an experience of self in relation to others, an opposition to dualisms, a valuation of the concrete, and 'a sense of variety of connectedness and continuities both with other persons and with the natural world' (Hartsock, 1983: 242). A feminist standpoint is to women's life activities as the proletarian standpoint is to workers' life activities, only 'deeper going' (p. 234). Feminist theory should both be grounded in women's material activities and be directed toward the political struggle necessary to create 'areas of social life modeled on this activity' (p. 261).

This shift from rights to needs and from separation to connection offers many possibilities for developing feminist discourse. The emphasis on human need and on political economy connects feminism to socialism and class analysis, a welcome affirmation in light of other contemporary feminists' turning away from the material. Drawing upon the lived structure of women's experiences rather than some essential trait of the female, this view is more historical and more open to recognizing diversity among women and men. Interpreting women's experience as revealing positive virtues rather than unrelenting victimization, arguments such as Gilligan's and Hartsock's articulate women's ways as models for a reconstituted public and private life. The focus on needs and persons-in-relations is also compatible with some version of rights, since people can be seen as having a right to their needs as well as a need for their rights, and could thus connect to and expand the dominant discourse.

But its weaknesses are the underside of its strengths. The ability to connect with the dominant discourse also entails the danger of succumbing to it: a weak version of the rights/needs connection could result in a politically limp sort of welfare state liberalism. Further, an exclusive focus on the intersubjective, on the ways that women experience their relations to others and the world, can be a way of side-stepping a coming to terms with the prediscursive. The world of intersubjectively constituted realities tends to give too much to the completeness and wholeness of our accounts of things, evading any discrepancies between the prediscursive and the discursive. That which does not fit into the web of communication '"no longer seems to be" but it still works its effects' (Connolly, 1987: 154). Also, a discourse of need and connection may rest too readily on the authority of the (female) subject, whose accounts of her own experiences (and of those of men) are taken as unique and privileged. But it is precisely the dominance of the subject that we were questioning in the first place. If to be a subject is to be subjected, if the self-as-subject is the constituted outcome of the disciplinary strategies of modernity, then women's subjectivity and intersubjectivity are not exempt from this problematic.

Like most feminist theorists challenging the discourse of rights and autonomous subjects, Hartsock and Gilligan embrace an anti-linear approach to knowledge. Yet both of them speak in a language of layers, levels, and stages that reintroduces conventional linear assumptions about knowing. Gilligan's stages of moral development holds on to Kohlberg's developmental scheme, while Hartsock's analysis of standpoints bows too heavily to Marx. Too willing to employ unproblematically words such as 'real', 'scientific', 'error', and 'counterfactual', Hartsock's arguments rest on assumptions that knowledge can be readily labelled as higher or lower, as appearance or reality. Such assumptions side-step the epistemological challenge that accompanies the suspicions of the autonomous subject: what if the 'real', like the subject, is a selective naming of events that is organized and produced in language? Such suspicions throw doubt on efforts 'to see beneath the surface of social relations' (Hartsock, 1983: 232) by locating in the underneath another face of power.

Codes of Attunement and Nature

The second alternative discourse focuses on human beings placed in relation to nature or spirit. There are many versions of this perspective, as there are also of the other alternatives. Some authors appeal to the (selected) heritage of the American Indians, stressing women's 'ancient wisdom' that men have suppressed but not completely obliterated (Wheeler and Chinn, 1984; Andrews, 1981). Others invoke the tradition of ancient goddess religions and the heritage of witchcraft as sources of personal strength and creative power for women, and as validation of nurturance for women and men (Ochs, 1983; Starhawk, 1979). Still others speak of a poetic bonding between women, other animals, and the earth, a bonding constituted partly by what men have made of us but not reducible to a residue of male power (Griffin, 1978).

These visions of a self-in-place with respect to a larger scheme of things issue a radical challenge to the hubris of humanism, which puts the human above all else. Invoking rather than side-stepping the realm of the prediscursive, these views seek to loosen the hold of language in order to bring into it the animal, the natural, and the spiritual. Joining politically with a radical version of ecology, such views generate compelling critiques of technology and of the reduction of the natural world to standing reserve. But once again their weaknesses are the underside of their strengths: the prediscursive is brought in by invoking the heavy hand of *telos*, by assuming a fit (at least potentially) between the prediscursive and the discursive which acts to blind us to our own participation in constituting that fit. Attributing disjunctions and ruptures to the (unnecessary) effects of male power, these sorts of cosmic feminisms are not readily open to an appreciation of necessary ambiguities and dissonances between our articulations of life and the life being articulated. Animated by a quest for attunement with higher unities, such perspectives tend to turn away from examination of their own role in constituting such unities by the act of reaching for them.

Cosmic feminisms tend to invoke premodern forms of faith in an inherent order already in nature. They hark back to what in another context has been called 'an ancient philosophy of accommodation' (Lopez, 1986: 40), one which evokes disorder in the name of a higher order. Susan Griffin, for example, associates women with motion, fluidity, and the capacity to make change: 'We are disorderly. We have often disturbed the peace. Indeed, we study chaos, it points to the future. The oldest and wisest among us can read disorder' (Griffin, 1978: 175). But the disorder is that which disrupts modern, humanist, rationalist understandings, while finding fit within a higher order of things. Giving an account of forests that is simultaneously an account of women, Griffin says 'Yet what you fail to know we know, and the knowing is in us, how we have grown this way, why these years were not one of them heedless, why we are shaped the way we are, not all straight to your purpose, but to ours' (Griffin, 1978: 220). Cosmic feminists are quick to see patriarchal strategies for smuggling male authority into language, but less able to see any similar process in their own 'picture thoughts' (Bennett, 1987: 21), their poetic, imprecise nature/woman imagery. Women, Griffin says, in their greater closeness to nature are less dependent on the immediate crutch and veil of language.

They are thus more in touch with the *telos* standing behind it: 'Behind naming, beneath words, is something else. An existence named, unnamed and unnameable' (Griffin, 1978: 190). The appreciation of the prediscursive is strong, but the realm of the prediscursive is read as having a consistent and available meaning, one that can absorb all apparent disruptions and mysteries into an inherent order of things. Differences – the concrete differences among women and among men, and the elusive differences residing in the margins of any unified field of meaning – are easily lost in affirmations that subdue discrepancies by enveloping them (Connolly, 1987: 155).

Politically, the evocation of unity and affirmation often translates into decision making based on consensus. In *Peace and Power: A Handbook of Feminist Process* (Wheeler and Chinn, 1984) the requirements for consensus are specified: respect for others, an ability to listen, the capacity for self-criticism, an ability to face and tolerate conflict. Small, decentralized women's groups have often found that consensus works well for them, allowing them to employ strategies that respect individuation while achieving unity. My point is not that consensus is unworkable, nor that it necessarily oppresses the individual in the name of the group. Rather it is that consensus, like any unified affirmation, names only one of many possible intersections of values and actions; it is 'a partial representation of the multiple and contingent relations between politics and ethics that arbitrate the arrangements of power' (Dumm, 1986: 18; also Foucault 1984). Given its inevitable partiality, consensus is not exempt from the double edge of any organizational strategy – it enables in some ways while constraining in others. Cosmic feminism's quest for attunement tends to render invisible that which does not and will not fit, in both epistemology and politics.

Codes of Bodies and Play

The third alternative perspective challenges the dominance of the speaking subject by calling upon a model of semiotics and play, a deliberately unfocused invocation of bodies-and-pleasures. Countering 'the masculine obsession with classification, systematization, and hierarchization' (Moi, 1985: 111), this code tries to evade binary divisions by opening itself to difference, marginality, and contrast. Julia Kristeva, for example, distinguishes between two moments of language: the symbolic, which functions to represent and define; and the semiotic, where ambiguities, nuances, and multiple possible meanings emerge. Kristeva views the semiotic as innocent of sexual difference; it can thus weaken the dualism of male and female while evoking that which is marginal to power. Luce Irigaray attempts a deconstruction of the subject who loves authority into a fluid and musical semiotic play, calling upon a multiplication of sites of pleasure in female bodies to counter the singleness and propriety of the male. 'Woman', Irigaray states, 'is neither open nor closed. She is indefinite, in-finite, *form is never complete in her*. She is not infinite but neither is she *a* unit(y), such as letter, number, figure in a series, proper noun, unique object (in a) world of the senses, single ideality in an intelligible whole, entity of a foundation, etc. . . . No metaphor completes her' (Irigaray, 1985a: 229). Both writers view Western culture as having repressed the playful and sonorous in language in favour of the rational and representative, in the same way that it represses the body in favour of the mind, and women in the service of men. While Irigaray's project focuses more on the articulation of difference, and Kristeva's on the deconstruction of gender, both share this turn to the semiotic and to bodies-and-pleasures.

This perspective offers a radical challenge to the fixity of juridico-legal discourse by attacking hierarchy and authority where they reside in language. The discourse of the modern subject seeks to pin things down, to specify, to hold them still for examination and judgement. Linguistic feminism loosens the hold of the symbolic and representational, taking language itself as a model of experience, one that is patterned and structured but without a centre, without a beginning or an ending. Language that attends to the semiotic 'moves and twists, starts over again from different perspectives, does not go straight to the point' (Young, 1985: 179). It accepts and plays with the paradox of using language to point to the limits and excessiveness of language, invoking indirect strategies of metonymy and metaphor to indicate its own gaps, doublings, and fissures. Recognizing the incompleteness of our organizations of life in relation to the life being organized, this view takes to heart Foucault's admonition that one 'does not inhabit the whole of his [*sic*] language' (Foucault, 1977: 42). The bounded self-as-subject is rejected in favour of a dislocating and co-mingling of identities, a play of possibilities across undisciplined bodies.

But once again the weaknesses of the position are the underside of its strengths. The insistence on the total maleness of language, and men's successful exclusion of women from thinking and speaking (particularly in Irigaray) leaves one wondering why such a miserable creature as woman, one so fully dominated, should command our attention at all. The very insistence on the category of 'woman' has a totalizing impact that tends to blur articulation of diversities among women and men. Gayatri Spivak suggests with good reason that 'the question of woman in general . . . is *their* question, not *ours*' (Spivak, 1983: 184). Linguistic feminism tends, paradoxically, to cloud our vision of material differences in its effort to bring linguistic difference into focus. Irigaray gives both too much and too little to women: too much, in seeing women's meaning as always already in their bodies; too little, in giving them no territory or words of their own.

Furthermore,the focus on pleasures in bodies can narrow one's notion of embodiment to the specifically sexual, leaving out the arena in which many people experience their bodies on a daily basis – labour. There is more to embodiment than sexual desire, no matter how diffuse and multiple we acknowledge it to be: there is grace, strength, action, exertion, pain. While Irigaray's goal is to multiply our vision of the body, she speaks rather relentlessly about the genitals, ignoring arms, legs, backs, shoulders, the parts of our bodies called upon most by those who do physical labour for a living. The vaginal metaphors, meant to multiply meaning, end up constricting it. Patriarchy too has defined women primarily in terms of their sexuality; where is the line between reclaiming (or claiming in the first place) our sexuality and co-operating with male power?

The focus on language sometimes takes one too far away from the distributive power of structures and from the requirements of political judgements concerning collective life. Consider Irigaray's appeal for connections among women:

> We can do without models, standards, or examples. Let's never give ourselves orders, commands, or prohibitions. Let our imperatives be only appeals to move, to be moved, together. Let's never lay down the law to each other, or moralize, or make war. Let's not claim to be right, or claim the right to criticize one another. If one of us sits in judgement, our existence comes to an end. (Irigaray, 1985b: 217)

This appeal to evade judgement and division in the name of connection is both liberating in its openness and disabling in its lack of distinctions. The world does not oblige us by leaving us alone, and some of those who do the work of power (for whatever reason) are women. If we forfeit the option of opposing those women, we are likely to be their victims. This is not to say that there is no vision of revolt in linguistic feminism. Kristeva appeals to all those marginalized by power to subvert phallogocentrism's hierarchical closure on meaning. Irigaray appeals to women to '*Overthrow syntax* by suspending its eternally teleological order, by snipping the wires, cutting the current, breaking the circuits, switching the connections, by modifying continuity, alternation, frequency, intensity' (Irigaray, 1985a: 142). Seeing the established order as capable of colonizing any clear and straightforward utterance, she urges women 'to speak only in riddles, allusions, hints, parables' (p. 143). Through this confounding and distorting of the representational and the symbolic, 'something of the difference of the sexes would have taken place in language also' (p. 360). There is much that is compelling here. Given the power of discourse to constitute the realities it then claims merely to describe, an indirect approach is often better able to loosen the hold of discursive hegemonies. Inciting the discrepancies and silences within the domain of the already-said is a political act in that it helps us to see, within the language events that make us what we are, the possibilities for being otherwise (Love, 1987: 7). My complaint is not that linguistic feminism lacks politics, but that its politics lacks direction, and that its critique of phallogocentrism gives far too much to men. Theory is not their domain alone, even if they control the main vehicles of legitimation; and our response can invoke play and the loosening of language without degenerating into self-indulgence. Irigaray often writes as though believing that if she is at all clear she has capitulated to patriarchy. There are ways to evade the language strategies of male power without being driven by it into a hostility toward communication. And the move toward deconstructing male power in language need not take place at the expense of the historical and the material.

Connecting the Codes?

It is tempting to end this chapter by calling for a wedding of the strengths of each of the positions, invoking a merger that would call out the 'good' aspects of each set of arguments while divorcing the 'bad'. But this move, however comforting, is not fully available, since in each of the above cases the weaknesses of the codes have been presented as the shadow of their strengths. Following Heidegger, each of these theoretical formations enables a revealing by simultaneously imposing a concealing; that is, in each case the sharpness of vision offered comes at the expense of that which is unnamed or engulfed.

Given this, in what ways can the codes be related to one another? They share a great deal: they all evince a concern with language, with the ways women and men take up and are taken up by language. They all evoke disorder in their struggles against the confinement of patriarchy, urging us to heed the multiple voices within us. They all affirm an anti-dualistic posture, and they all focus on women's bodies – our reproductive experiences, our sexuality, our labour – as central to both knowledge and politics. They all participate to some extent in the deconstruction of rationality, re-reading the claims of reason in light of desire, including the desire for reason itself. They all invoke the capacity to imagine beyond the familiar, and name (some of) the obstacles to the cultivation of that capacity. They all look to women to be resisters to male power.

These and other similarities allow practitioners of the three codes to recognize one another as feminists. A different strategy of inquiry would concentrate on this shared ground, constituting feminism as a unity and celebrating its harmonies. My project instead is to incite the discrepancies among the various codes, not to leave them standing unconnected but to force open a space within feminist discourses for greater acknowledgement of discontinuity, incompleteness, and tension. This effort to incite multiplicity against the somnolent hand of totalization need not weaken feminism as a strategy of political struggle; rather, it may multiply the levels of knowing and doing upon which resistance can act. Nor does it push for a complete divorce among the various interpretive codes, since the ground they share is substantial. For example, the explicit political commitments of the first two codes can strengthen the third by naming the differences most worthy of articulation and struggle – differences that name historically and materially specific dimensions of gender; differences that locate the human within the natural rather than on top of it; differences that let other differences be.

But at the level of epistemology, the three codes (and the discourse of rights and subjects against which they are mobilized) cannot be happily combined. Humanist feminism seeks a universal, that of rights and subjects, under which to demand fair treatment of all individuals. Similarly, cosmic feminism (the second alternative) also seeks a universal, that of nature, spirit, or the divine, to serve as the umbrella of meaning through which human place can be ascertained. The first and third alternatives move more in the direction of the particular: the first focuses on the concrete and historical experiences of women to articulate the values of need and connection (although those values could themselves be viewed as universals); and the third attempts to loosen the hold of universal male discourse in order to let difference be (either the difference of women or the multiple diversities of a differently gendered world). While none of these codes stands without deficits on its ledger, the third seems to me to be the most livable in that it is the most alert to its own dangers. It is a kind of theorizing that is aware (at least some of the time) of the problems of theorizing, that attends to the practices of its discourse through the only tools available – its own discourse. Some feminists have argued against a totalizing strategy for feminist theory, seeing in the totalizing impulse a duplication of the practices of power, and fearing that such practices will force us to hide from ourselves that which does not fit into our schemas. Others have held out hope that feminist universals would be different, that it is only universals wielded by men that shut down the field of meaning around their own defences. I fear the latter position is too quick to duck the power of its own discourse to subdue the dissonances inconvenient to its unities. While linguistic feminism has sometimes capitulated to the totalizing impulse it denounces, the strategies for struggle against that impulse are still available within its own codes. Linguistic feminism best heeds Nietzsche's warning that 'The will to a system is a lack of integrity' (Nietzsche, 1954: 470). It enables us to replace the search for new totalities with the interrogation of limits. And it need not be hostile to the political commitments of its sisters; it can help us to select principles and actions that are worthy of our endorsement even after their ambiguities come to light (Connolly, 1987: 159). It may even help us to name persons, relations, and events in ways that free them, as Irigaray urges, from 'systems, those houses of ill fame for the subject, of fetish-words, sign-objects whose certified truths seek to palliate the risk that values may be recast into/by the other' (Irigaray, 1985a: 143).

Note

My thanks to Tom Dumm, Andy Hoffman, Valerie Wayne, Kathie Kane, and Farideh Farhi for their comments on an earlier version of this essay.

References

Andrews, L. (1981) *Medicine Woman*. New York: Harper and Row.
Barthes, R. (1981) 'Textual Analysis of Poe's "Valdemar"', in R. Young (ed.), *Untying the Text*. Boston: Routledge and Kegan Paul.
Belenky, M.F., B.M. Clinchy, N.R. Goldberg, and J.M. Tarule (1986) *Women's Ways of Knowing*. New York: Basic Books.
Bennett, J. (1987) *Unthinking Faith and Enlightenment*. New York: New York University Press.
Chernin, K. (1981) *The Obsession*. New York: Harper and Row.
Connolly, W.E. (1987) *Politics and Ambiguity*. Madison: University of Wisconsin Press.
Dumm, T. (1986) 'The New Politics of Aesthetics: Habermas versus Foucault on the Postmodern'. Paper delivered at the American Political Science Association Conference, Washington, DC.
Foucault, M. (1977) *Language, Counter-Memory, and Practice*. Ithaca, NY: Cornell University Press.
Foucault, M. (1984) 'Politics and Ethics: An Interview', in P. Rabinow (ed.), *The Foucault Reader*. New York: Pantheon.

Frye, M. (1983) *The Politics of Reality*. Trumansberg, NY: The Crossing Press.

Gilligan, C. (1982) *In a Different Voice*. Cambridge, Mass.: Harvard University Press.

Griffin, S. (1978) *Woman and Nature*. New York: Harper and Row.

Hartsock, N.C.M. (1983) *Money, Sex and Power*. New York: Longman.

Irigaray, L. (1985a) *Speculum of the Other Woman*. Ithaca, NY: Cornell University Press.

Irigaray, L. (1985b) *This Sex Which Is Not One*. Ithaca, NY: Cornell University Press.

Lopez, B. (1986) *Arctic Dreams*. New York: Charles Scribner's Sons.

Love, N. (1987) 'Foucault and Habermas on Discourse and Democracy'. Paper delivered at the American Political Science Association Conference, Washington, DC.

Moi, T. (1985) *Sexual/Textual Politics*. New York: Methuen.

Nietzsche, F. (1954) 'Twilight of the Idols', in W. Kaufman (ed.), *The Portable Nietzsche*. New York: Viking.

Ochs, C. (1983) *Women and Spirituality*. New York: Rowman and Allenheld.

Spivak, G.C. (1983) 'Displacement and the Discourse of Woman', in M. Krupnick (ed.), *Displacement: Derrida and After*. Bloomington, IN: Indiana University Press.

Starhawk (1979) *The Spiral Dance*. New York: Harper and Row.

Wheeler, C.E. and P.L. Chinn (1984) *Peace and Power: A Handbook of Feminist Process*. Buffalo, NY: Margaretdaughters.

Young, I.M. (1985) 'Humanism, Gynocentrism, and Feminist Politics', *Women's Studies International Quarterly* 8: 173–83.

5

Women's Interests in Local Politics

Gun Hedlund

At the end of the eighteenth century the women of France demanded that the goals of the Revolution should apply also to them. During the nineteenth century feminists marched through the streets of many countries demonstrating for women's suffrage. And in the 1960s enraged young women formulated the slogan 'the personal is political'. These events indicate different phases in women's history when women have organized and acted as a gender-based interest group. Regardless of the position one may take about the appropriateness of using interest theory in the analysis of women's conditions,[1] it is an unquestionable fact that during recent centuries women have acted politically on the basis of their gender.

Partly following Kraditor (1965), Helga Hernes (1982: 91) formulates three different lines of reasoning found in discussions concerning women's political participation. The essential point in *the justice reasoning* is women's right to political participation; the contents of political decisions are of less concern. In *the resource reasoning* the claim is made that if women do not participate in politics society is deprived of some particular knowledge and skills that women possess. According to *the interest reasoning* women's interests are different from men's and often in conflict. Women's need to act politically for their own interests is emphasized here while their vocation to act benevolently for other deprived groups is played down. Throughout history women's demands for political rights have been motivated by different aspects of these three types of reasoning. The justice reasoning, based on the ideology of natural law, was used primarily during the earlier phases of the first wave of women's movements to justify women's suffrage.

When their demands for suffrage encountered a strong and forceful opposition women gradually moved to resource reasoning, often emphasizing women's 'feminine' nature. In addition to their particular skills and knowledge, women would bring other special qualities to political decision making: unique feminine and mothering qualities would contribute to a more peaceful world (Evans,

1979; Kraditor, 1965). During the same period reasoning in terms of advantage and interests started to develop. Kraditor (1965: 43–5) mentions different forms of this type of reasoning which she calls expediency, 'women needed the ballot for self-protection'. Thus up until the 1920s women organized on the basis of their gender although the reasoning they used to justify women's political rights changed.

After women became politically eligible and attained the right to vote it seemed less and less necessary to assert their right to political representation as women. Instead, women's political participation was defended by claiming that women as individuals should hold the same political rights as men (Sapiro, 1981: 701–2). The demands for the right to political influence raised by the second wave of women's movements during the 1960s and 1970s may, from an interest perspective, seem like a step backwards to the representation by Estate. In fact it was evidence of a totally new awareness of the existence of social conflicts based upon gender.

In a discussion of the relevance of interest theory for the analysis of women's concerns, Jónasdóttir (chapter 3) proposes that a central point to consider is whether and to what extent present political structures enable women to build, maintain, and control their presence in politics as women. Women's participation is desirable and acceptable in the traditional political system in so far as it is not founded on gender-based interests. The question is, under what conditions can women as women develop a controlling presence in situations of choices in general and in authoritative decision making?

In this chapter I intend to describe the conditions of women politicians, and their views of their role in local politics, based on a case-study I did in a Swedish town in 1981/82.[2]

The position of women in Scandinavian politics is especially interesting when viewed from an international perspective. In the mid-1980s women constitute between 26 and 31 per cent of the political representatives on the national level. In local politics, women representatives constitute between 21 and 31 per cent. In Denmark, Finland, Norway, and Sweden the percentage of women politicians doubled during the 1970s and there has been a further slow increase during the 1980s. In Iceland, however, the Women's Alliance has entered the Parliament during the 1980s and the percentage of women politicians on the national level has increased from 15 to 21 per cent, while on the local level the percentage of women is still low, 12 per cent. The high proportion of women politicians in the Scandinavian countries has been explained by a number of factors (Haavio-Mannila *et al.*, 1985).[3]

Thus, Sweden has one of the leading positions in the world when it comes to the high percentage of women representatives. Twenty-nine is the average percentage in all city councils. The proportion of women elected to office was large in the particular municipality studied: they held 39 per cent of the seats in the town council. On different committees and boards, the total percentage of women representatives was 41 per cent, including the deputy members. Thirty per cent of the leading positions as chairpersons and party group leaders were held by women. Consequently, these women cannot be put into the category of powerless tokens. They constitute what Rosabeth Moss Kanter describes as a minority in a titled group. 'Minority members have potential allies among each other, can form coalitions, and can affect the culture of the group' (1977: 209).

Before describing in more detail the basis for, and methods of, the collection of data as well as the Swedish political system in general, I will present the conceptual framework used in my study. This framework is divided in two different parts, which together constitute a total model of analysis. The first part describes theoretical assumptions about a specific *women's culture* and its implications for women's social situation in politics and society as a whole. The second part is a compound model that aims to categorize the women politicians' views of women's political interests, their strategies for action, and their different roles within the political system.

Women's Culture – a Multidimensional Model of Reality

As an overall theoretical framework for my study I use a version of theorizing about women's situation in terms of the concept of culture. This specific approach has been used in feminist social research in Norway (Ås, 1975, 1976, 1982; Halsaa, 1977; Holter, 1982; Waerness, 1977, 1984), and it provides a multi-dimensional model for empirical research.

Although the concept 'culture' is a notoriously vague one, this approach has been useful as a starting-point for analysing *women's* reality in its entirety.[4] Research done from this approach is directed at the empirical investigation of women as actors where they are not solely compared with men, thus allowing for comparisons between different groups of women. Several studies have introduced new concepts – such as different forms of communality among women, and specific forms of rationality held by women (see Holter, 1982).[5]

Besides serving as an empirical model this approach depends upon some basic hypotheses: that the women's culture is, on the one hand, a suppressed culture but, on the other hand, one which carries a potential for change and liberation that affects the entire society (see Jónasdóttir 1984: 96–7).

It is important to stress this hypothesized doubleness of women's culture. This is a culture of the suppressed, that includes elements such as passivity, dependence on men, and lack of self-confidence. On the other side of the coin are the independent qualities of this culture, positive values and activities borne by women in connection with their care for others' well-being (Halsaa, 1977: 110–13). Jónasdóttir (1984) argues that an important difference between the women's culture perspective and earlier theories of patriarchy is that women's lives are not viewed as being entirely controlled by men, nor are women considered to be totally powerless. By using the theoretical approach of a specific women's culture we can discover those values and contents in women's lives which are independent of the male world and not merely compensatory in relation to it.

One definition of women's culture is: 'an assembled set of values, interpretations and causal connections that are effective for women but difficult to understand or invisible for men' (Ås, 1976: 98). In order to operationalize women's culture Ås (1975) proposes five dimensions as useful for studying men's and women's different views of reality and different activities. These dimensions are: language and communication; organized work and activities; relation toward technology and finances; estimation of self-worth within one's culture; and relation to time and use of time, planning and the future.[6] Empirical research has shown that men and women tend to have different perspectives, rules, and forms of activity in relation to all of these areas.[7]

For some researchers the focal point of women's culture is women's *unpaid* and *invisible* work within the domestic sphere (Ås, 1976) while others concentrate on the *care-giving* responsibilities held by women (Waerness, 1977) and some point to women's identity as objects in relation to the male world (Halsaa, 1977).

Nevertheless, it is an empirical question how the worlds of men and women are in fact organized in different societies (Rosaldo, 1980; Hellevik, 1978; Hedlund-Ruth, 1986). In some societies, such as the Nordic, women live in a situation where their lives are fragmented by conflicting demands from the domestic sphere and the labour market. Today almost 80 per cent of Swedish women work outside the home (Gustavsson, 1986). However, it is still women who have the main responsibility for children, do most of the domestic work, and work part-time (SOU, 1979: 89; SCB, 1985). The labour market in Sweden is very segregated, with women working in medical care, education, child care, office work, and at service jobs, while men mainly work in industry, forestry, and farming (SCB, 1984). The women's culture approach, where women are seen as a social group with specific values and connections, may still be useful even though its locus is no longer the domestic sphere (Hedlund-Ruth, 1986). I concentrate on *women's work*, unpaid and paid, and the constantly conflicting demands from actors within their families and at the work-place that divide and fragment women's lives. These contradictions should not be defined as role conflicts since research results show a strong identification with both the home sphere and the outer sphere among politically active and working women (Bak-Hansen and Lund-Christiansen, 1982; Sørensen, 1982; Togeby, 1985).[8]

In this chapter I analyse the specific dimensions of language and communication; organized work and activities; and estimation of self-worth within one's culture, in order to operationalize women's culture and to study its relation to the political system.

Women's Interests, Strategies, and Roles

My model employs two different perspectives describing the specific interests women politicians are expected to represent. The first perspective addresses itself to *human interests* in general and the second to the fundamental idea of *women's interests*.

In the first perspective women politicians are seen as representatives of human interests in general and also of the interests of certain deprived groups, regardless of gender. This perspective also reflects the complementary viewpoint that women's particular

	Human interest perspective	*Women's specific perspective*
Consensus	(a)	(b)
	Women participate in politics as individuals. Women's interests are common human interests. Men and women work together.	It is in women's interest to organize and articulate women's views of political issues in general. The rules of the political system are accepted.
Conflict	(c)	(d)
	Women represent *care* of both environment and human beings (for example, children, the elderly, and the deprived) as opposed to the technically–economically oriented interests in the political system.	Women represent women's interests. These interests are in conflict with men's interests. The rules of the political system are not accepted.

Figure 5.1   *Perspectives on different interests represented by women politicians*

experiences and knowledge are seen as a political resource. The second perspective includes the idea that women constitute an interest group and the notion that only women can represent women's views in politics, regardless of whether these are specific women's issues or not. In addition both perspectives include two dimensions about whether interests expressed by women are articulated in an atmosphere of consensus or opposition in relation to the male-dominated political system. Figure 5.1 illustrates the resulting bivariate model.

(a) Human interests – consensus. Within this perspective we find both the justice and the resource arguments in relation to women's views of women's political interests. Women are considered to be active politically as individuals, and the solutions to different groups needs and interests are viewed as common human interest solutions, not gender-specific ones. The assumption is that women usually have particular experiences which complement those of their male colleagues and that women and men should work together for the good of all. Harmony between the sexes is the fundamental principle in this perspective.

(b) Women's interests – consensus. Women's right to organize and to articulate their opinions is the focal point of this perspective. It is an open question what results this may lead to in terms of content. Here concern is not with particular interest areas but with women's participation in political decisions in general. The framework of the political system is accepted and women act within its boundaries. This implies that gender-type conflicts are avoided, or suppressed.

(c) Human interests – conflict. More emphasis is placed on the resource argument in this perspective than in perspective (a). As the existing gender-based division of labour gives women care-giving responsibilities they are seen especially as representatives of different deprived groups. Thus women's complementary experiences are considered to be important but they are difficult to assert because of the techno-economic perspective that dominates the political system.

(d) Women's interests – conflict. Representatives of this perspective are, like those of perspective (b), oriented towards organizing women into separate and gender-specific political interest groups. Gender conflict is the point of focus here and it is assumed that in the short run the level of political conflicts will be high. The political system is viewed as one part of the patriarchal system, and it is claimed that male dominance must be broken before women's interests can be asserted in politics.

Placing the representation of women's interests into separate perspectives does not mean that when applied empirically they exclude or stand in contrast to one another. The aim is to illustrate different women representatives' views of their roles in politics.

The Human Interest–Consensus (a) perspective has its roots in the gender-neutral phase of the 1940s and 1950s, while the Gender-specific–Consensus (b) perspective can be found within the women's sections of different parties and among certain moderate women's organizations. Typical representatives of the Human Interest–Conflict (c) perspective are often members of non-feminist peace and environmentalist organizations. The Gender-specific–Conflict (d) perspective is mostly found within the new women's movement where the goal is women's liberation, that is, a claim for equality that does not aim at genderlessness.

Women representatives are caught between these different perspectives and their advocates. In her role as the party representative a woman representative shares the values and ideologies of her male colleagues and is often faced with expectations from the Human Interest–Consensus perspective. On the other hand, she can hardly avoid being influenced by impulses and ideas emanating from discussions outside the political system, where the expectation is that she should represent women as an interest group. Thus she finds herself in a situation abounding in conflicting expectations and demands for support from different quarters. This situation is typical of women representatives and similar to women's ambiguous situation in society in general.

The hypothesis (Jónasdóttir, chapter 3) that it is in women's objective interest to create a real and definite presence in politics based on gender leads us to the question of women's consciousness and women's unity within the political system: in what ways do women in politics perceive themselves, and how do they define their political roles?

Haavind (1982: 410–13) has formulated four prototypes for the premises underlying women's relations to one another and their strategies for action. She assumes that women's relations to one another are determined by their relations to men, and if we apply this assumption to the relation of women politicians to the male-dominated political system then we can describe the premises that lead to different strategies as follows:

1 According to the first premise women compete and work together as men do; they strive toward the same goals and use the same means as those considered appropriate for men. Gender is secondary, and the fundamental line of conflict runs along party lines.

2   The assumption in the second premise is that women compete and co-operate as women, and that they strive to increase their esteem by establishing connections to men. Here different means are considered legitimate; for example, organizing separate women's sections within a party. On the other hand, the political party's goals and its definition of conflict apply to women as well.

3   The third premise holds that women can avoid competing among themselves and with men since they see themselves as outsiders and not as a part of male politics. Here women's communality becomes one of defensive unity, based on goals and means other than those of the political system.

4   The fourth premise can be described as one of offensive solidarity amongst women. Here women do not allow their relations to their male colleagues to determine their goals or the means of achieving them. Because of this they try to change the political system in the interests of women, and they work against male dominance which prevents women from participating actively and articulating their interests.

With the interest perspectives and action strategies described above in mind, it is possible to categorize women's roles into four different role-types. Figure 5.2 illustrates these.

	Defensive as women	*Women's solidarity*
Consensus	(a)	(b)
	Community Worker	*Party Woman*
	This woman is active as an individual. She works well with her male colleagues and accepts the norms of the political system.	This woman is actively engaged in recruiting and supporting other women. She does not oppose the norms of the political system.
Conflict	(c)	(d)
	Outsider	*Oppositionist*
	This woman works in the interest of deprived groups and environmental issues. She experiences estrangement from the political system.	This woman gives priority to women's issues and she also maintains an offensive stance against the political system's male dominance.

Figure 5.2   *Role-types of women in politics*

In the role of the *Community Worker* a woman is active politically as an individual and does not work specifically with women's issues. These women engage in other kinds of issues, work well with their male colleagues and view political set-backs as personal set-backs rather than gender-specific ones (interest perspective (a) and action strategy premise 1).

The *Party Woman* often works for the party's women's section where she actively engages in recruiting women into politics. She understands that women have particular difficulties trying to assert themselves in politics, but at the same time strives to maintain good relationships with her male colleagues. She accepts the norms of the political system and struggles to acquire a political style which is neither conformist nor provocative (interest perspective (b) and action strategy premise 2).

The *Outsider's* experience is one of estrangement from the political system as a whole. She does not actively pursue working relationships with her male colleagues since the existing political culture and language usage is foreign to her. Her commitment to working in the interest of deprived groups or environmental-type issues accentuates her position as an outsider (interest perspective (c) and action strategy premise 3).

The *Oppositionist* woman politician maintains an offensive stance against the political system's male dominance. She views herself as a representative of women's particular interests and her role is a much more controversial one than that of the Party Woman. She actively pursues working relationships with other women within as well as outside the political system. She avoids working with certain men since she considers this to be a waste of time and irrelevant to her goals. She also refuses to adjust her political style to the existing norms (interest perspective (d) and action strategy premise 4).[9]

Some of these perspectives and strategies are evident in previous studies (Diamond, 1977; Eduards *et al.*, 1985) as well as my own research on women in local politics in Sweden. It is to that research that I now turn.

Politics in Sweden

The autonomy of the councils in Sweden is relatively comprehensive, including independent rights of taxation, direct council elections, and limited government control. Hernes (1982) remarks that women's entry into the political world in the Nordic countries can be viewed partly as a result of the development of the welfare state. Many traditional women's tasks – child care, care for the elderly and handicapped, activities for youth – have been transferred to the state, so that women's knowledge in these sectors became important in political decision making. Because the local authorities administer much of the welfare policy, their decisions greatly influence the social conditions of women (Sinkkonen, 1985).

In the Swedish electoral system, people vote for a party and not for individual candidates. Nominations and listing of candidates are mainly controlled by the parties. Party politics dominates the political scene in Sweden, on the national as well as on the local level. The pressure on local politicians to keep to the party line is strong, especially within the Social Democratic Party (Wallin *et al.*, 1981). The dominating line of conflict within Swedish politics is the Left–Right conflict of the parties, even though an increasing gender-gap has become visible among voters (Oskarsson, 1987). In recent years there has been strong pressure from women's organizations and the women's sections of parties to increase women's political representation.

Four out of the five parliamentary parties have specific women's sections that act as pressure groups within their own party. Political co-operation with other women's groups is, however, unusual. Such cross-party alliances would be disloyal to the party and might affect negatively the future career of the women politicians. The basis of political work is therefore the party group. At each level of the decision-making system representatives are organized in specific party groups. At internal meetings the party's line on different issues is decided. Thus, the number of women representatives has to be divided into four to five different party groups, with the result that within each group women may find themselves in a minority, even though taken together they constitute a significant proportion of elected representatives.

If we look at the positions of women in local politics we find that even though women entered the political arena during the 1970s, male dominance is still very noticeable. This is particularly clear if one focuses on the hidden internal recruitment patterns for the higher political positions in the local political system. As the criteria of representativeness loses importance, the qualification criterion used – namely, seniority – is less favourable to women. The compositions of boards and committees are typical examples of senior, male party leaders horse-trading. The gender-based division of labour within the hierarchical structure of politics is evident. It is a division both horizontal and vertical. Men remain in leading positions and have responsibility for economic and technical issues. Women find themselves in lower positions and are often experts on social and cultural issues (Sinkkonen, 1985; Hedlund-Ruth and van der Ros Schive, 1983).

The local decision-making organization in Sweden is arranged on three levels. The *town council* is the municipalities' parliament with direct open elections and public debates. Here the formal decisions about political proposals are made. The *executive committee* is the board where the agenda is prepared and political decisions are proposed before reaching the council. In reality proposals from the executive committee are seldom turned down in the council. Preparations of political issues are undertaken by different *committees* and *boards*. These boards play an important role in the further decision-making process. Being a member of the executive committee, chairperson of a board, or leader of a party group is an important position which gives direct influence over the political decision-making process. The most important power position is however the full-time politician, *kommunalråd*, who controls specific policy areas, such as economics and taxation or social issues. A *kommunalråd* has the double function of being a political representative of the ruling majority, and taking the leading role in the administration's implementation (Gustafsson, 1984: 96).

A Swedish Council

I studied women politicians in a council which, from a structural point of view, is favourable to women.[10] It is a medium-sized town (120,000 inhabitants) with a Social Democratic majority in the city council and a large public sector. Women have access to a favourable labour market, training possibilities, well-developed child-care facilities and public transport. At the time of my study, 1981/1982, female representation was somewhat higher than the national average – 39 per cent in the town council, with ten women out of twenty-four members of the executive board and 30 per cent holding positions as chairpersons in boards and as party group leaders. Three out of six full-time politicians, *kommunalråd*, were women. In this town, therefore, at least in terms of numbers of representatives, women no longer constitute a completely dominated minority. Women's culture may have certain opportunities to express itself in contrast to the male political culture, despite the barriers mentioned above. Which groups and interests do women perceive themselves to represent? Does the presence of women change the political culture in measurable or symbolic ways? Is their presence in politics of a purely formal nature, or the beginning of what Jónasdóttir (chapter 3) mentions as a controlling presence?

Data were collected in 1981/1982 by three different methods. A questionnaire was sent out to all women politicians at all levels in the political organization and to a stratified sample of the men – 380 people, 160 of whom were women. The percentage of response was 85. A directed selection of thirty women was made for extensive interviews. These women had different backgrounds, ages, positions, and party affiliations. When replying to the questionnaire, half of the thirty women had reported being discriminated against, and these were automatically selected for interviews since one of the aims of the investigation was to examine manifestations of male dominance in politics.[11] Other descriptive materials were collected while I attended sixteen political meetings as a non-participant observer, and observed the culture, language, and male–female interaction patterns in internal party group meetings, in the meetings of three different committees and in the full council debates.[12]

Above (page 82), I described a five-dimensional model of women's culture. Of those five dimensions I selected three to study in depth; language and communication, self-worth, and organized work. Against this background I posed the following questions: Are women politicians aware of a women's culture, and if so, how do they describe and estimate its function in politics and how do they act in accordance with its values? How are the specified role-types connected to a sense of being a member of a woman's culture?

My data imply, as other researchers have suggested (Dahlerup, 1986; Hellevik and Skard, 1985) that we are approaching a new role for women in politics in Scandinavia. Diamond's passive 'Housewife/ Benchwarmer' (1977) does not seem to be so common since there now exists a rather large pool of eligible, competent women, at least in urban areas. Two-thirds of the women in the interview sample (n = 21) fell into the categories either of Party Women or Oppositionists, according to the analytical model developed above. They are of different ages and parties and hold different political positions, but they are united by the fact that they acknowledge women as an interest group. These women show an awareness of a women's culture. They acknowledge the need to re-evaluate women's experiences and specific political styles. By far the largest sub-group are *Party Women*, having an identity clearly parallel to what Staines *et al.* (1974) call 'Sisters'. They (n = 18) identify with other women, are conscious of sex differences in politics, and believe that women as a group do face certain gender-based obstacles in society. The Party Women are more loyal than the Oppositionists to the conditions of the political system and try to maintain a good co-operation with male colleagues. The Opposition-ists (n = 3) find it difficult to fit into the patriarchal norms within politics. It is primarily these women who draw attention to the *contradictions* that exist between women's culture and the male-dominated political system. They are disappointed with what they see as other women's passive attitude toward male domination. Two of them have chosen to withdraw from some of their functions.

Five Community Workers and four Outsiders were found as the

supporters of the Human Interest Perspective. Among the *Community Workers*, there is the same loyalty to the political system as with the Party Women. The needs and interests that these women claim should be satisfied through political decisions are of a generally human character, but the awareness of a woman's culture held by this group is different. Four women are conscious of certain differences between men and women concerning political style, but they tone this down in their answers. One woman denies the idea of different genders completely, claiming that humanity should not be divided into different groups. She avoids contact with other women and corresponds to what Staines *et al*. (1974) describe as the 'Queen Bee' role. The *Outsiders* often experience alienation in party politics. These women claim a certain feeling of solidarity with other women from competing parties. This feeling reflects a sense of social community which is defensive. They all oppose the techno-economic values held by their male colleagues.

These role-types are not mutually exclusive. Some of the Party Women may change into Oppositionists as a result of failure within the political system. Some Outsiders may change into Party Women or Oppositionists when they get support, influence from, and contact with other women. A couple of Party Women report that they have been Community Workers but they have recently changed opinion and strategy and become aware of the need for support among women.

Women in Politics

In their answers to the questionnaire (see note 12) a majority of both women and men agreed with the statement that 'Women politicians represent the interests of women voters better than men do' (Table 5.1). The view that women are really needed in politics is constantly repeated in the interviews of the thirty women.

Table 5.1

Do you agree with the following statement?

Women politicians represent the interests of women voters better than men do.

	Men %	Women %
Yes, I agree	66	83
No, I do not agree	33	17
	100	100
	(n = 184)	(n = 131)

One of the interview questions raised was 'Which group in society do you, as a politician, mainly represent?' This question was posed at the beginning of the interview, in order to avoid any influence from the final questions concerning women's interests, attitudes toward the Women's Liberation Movement, and eventual experiences of discrimination against themselves as women. We can therefore presume that the answers describing their own roles as representatives were given spontaneously. The most common answer given by these women (Party Women and Oppositionists) was that they represented women in general and, in particular, women as mothers (n = 10): 'I represent an ordinary, married mother of small children. To be a woman and a mother is in itself important. This group is very badly represented.'

It is evident from the interview answers that the women identify the care of others as in line with their own interests. Besides the mothers of young children mentioned by the younger interviewees, women of the middle generation point out that children and teenagers belong to the 'silent' groups in society which lack representation. As the life-cycle proceeds, the responsibility for care of children and youngsters is displaced by concern for the care for older and handicapped people: 'When I was younger it was child-care facilities and housing. . . . Now I want to have an influence on the situation of the elderly and how they live before my own old age. The younger women can see to child care'. Families with young children, single parents, immigrants, and handicapped people are among the other groups mentioned by Party Women and Outsiders. The Oppositionists see themselves as representatives of women as a group without mentioning women's special caring role. Solidarity among women inside and outside the political system is most important to them: 'I would never manage if I did not have their support. I do this for the sake of all women.' Community workers state that they represent the party or the electorate at large. To say who they represent was a difficult task only for a small group of the Party Women. They state firstly the party's politics, followed by children, youngsters, or the policies of the party's women's section. These women express uncertainty about their roles as representatives: 'No, I think I represent all voters. . . . But as a woman one certainly thinks about women's issues. One does that spontaneously. But at the same time one should consider all categories.'

To summarize, two-thirds of the thirty women politicians interviewed regard themselves as representing women, or are concerned with such social groups as children, elderly people, and teenagers.

Twenty interviewees stress that women have something special to contribute to political discussions, such as unique *knowledge* and *experience*, which male politicians lack. All role-types are represented here. There is an obvious generation gap between the women as regards to what extent the male and female viewpoints can be reconciled in a dialogue. The older women among both the Community Workers and the Party Women think that decisions are made in agreement when men and women listen to each other's opinions. For the older Party Women, a collective articulation of women's experiences via the women's sections in the party is necessary, but they start with the idéa that co-operation with the men is possible: 'The decisions must not be dominated by men. All the factories, like everything else, are built for men. We become worn out, our bodies can't cope with the environment. *We must assist each other here.*'

A Community Worker describes her view of women's complementary role in solving *human problems*: 'Yes, obviously. It is unreasonable that only one side should make the decisions. It is perfectly plain that women's experiences, views, and women's conceptions of reality are important as a basis for meeting our *common needs.*' Among the younger Party Women and the Oppositionists there are several who take the position that it is not just a question of complementing the men, but also of breaking male domination in politics. They differ mostly from the older women over strategies. The Oppositionist women have more clearly demonstrated their displeasure regarding the forms of politics and have refused to accept certain unwritten rules within the political culture. Besides being younger, these women represent only two parties, the Liberal Party and the Social Democrats.

Twenty women have the firm opinion that women present a special way of looking at life. These women describe their women colleagues as more earthbound, concrete, and practical. They regard reality in a different way from their male party colleagues, since they have specific experiences as women and care-takers. For many of the women (n = 12) it is not only a question of women and men having different *experiences* and knowledge as a result of the gender-based division of labour. They think that women's life context has given rise to different *values* and perspectives: 'Yes, because of our appreciation of which things are important, our closeness to life and the care of others, we have a knowledge, a feeling about how we want to build a constructive society. A society that is good for us and our children' – a quotation in which there is a pride in, and a feeling of dignity about, the 'invisible' women's culture which is often seen in descriptions of what the female gender-specific viewpoints contain.

But in the confrontation between the values of the women's culture and the techno-economic culture in politics problems arise. It is especially in the technical committees that male politicians and officials demand that women must transform their experiences into a different language in order for such experiences to be regarded as valid knowledge: 'It is extremely difficult to sell one's ideas . . . because the engineers and architects and the male politicians tell us to formulate our experiences in their terms first, then they will listen. That is why it is difficult for us women politicians to make ourselves understood and to be taken seriously.' These difficulties are seen by Party Women, Outsiders, and Oppositionists. Situations arose in internal party group meetings where on four different occasions I observed how women argued from their concrete experiences in certain discussions. In two cases their experiences, doubts on certain proposals, and suggestions for solutions were not accepted despite a long, intensive debate. The men made use of different tactics of domination, including ridicule, and told the women to come back with figures and diagrams to reinforce their statements.[13]

Those women who have been active during several election periods maintain that it has become easier for women to put forward their ideas. The changes have been partly the result of more women appearing in political circles, and partly a function of a clear generation gap between younger and older male politicians. Those younger men who take active responsibility for children and housework support women's general care arguments. Swedish legislation allows men to take paid parental leave from their work and this seems to change a few men's attitudes: 'During the last few years I think younger men have made a wholehearted contribution. Paid parental leave from work for fathers is very important.'

One of the questions in the interviews asked if there are specific content-oriented areas of special interest for women in politics. The intention of the question was to discover if the women define certain political issues in an interest-group perspective. Eighteen women among the Party Women and Oppositionists answered 'yes' to the question. The answers clearly show that care issues and women's interests are closely linked with each other (n = 10). It is a question here of political issues that directly touch upon women's lives. The women find that these issues would be neglected if they were not brought up by women. But several of the women politicians stress that it is a question of responsibility. Men also can have an interest in areas such as child-care facilities, schools, and issues concerning the handicapped. Other issues defined as of specific interest for women were public transport, labour policy, housing, and environmental policy.

Six of the seven women who answered this question with a definite 'no' belong to the groups I have called Community Workers and older Party Women. They stress that the content of politics should be equally shared by men and women. The seventh woman, an Outsider, refers to her practical experiences and explains that on her board child care is an issue which occupies the younger men. Finally five women, Outsiders and Party Women, are hesitant when answering this question: 'There should not be separate women's issues. I am, of course, a bit hesitant when it comes to Crisis Centres for women.'

When the politicians were asked about their attitudes towards the Women's Liberation Movement of the 1970s it turned out that a majority of the thirty representatives held positive views (n = 20). Among the younger women who are members of the Social Democratic and Liberal parties the attitude is unequivocally positive (n = 10). They also showed an understanding of the fact that the autonomous Women's Liberation Movement in its avant-garde role has shown militancy and forced forward certain issues which have been of interest to marginal groups of women. The language used by these women shows how they have been inspired by the ideas of the Women's Liberation Movement; they talked of 'confrontations' and 'liberation'. These women regarded the movement primarily as a force outside the political system, but stressed that new issues have been introduced on the political agenda and find that the parties' women's sections have been influenced. Some of the younger women, especially the Oppositionist ones, would really like women from the Women's Liberation Movement to come into the political system: 'I wish that these women could be with us. I think they are close to us and that there would be an improvement in quality if they would like to enter politics and join us.' Among the older Party Women and the Outsiders, there are reservations about the militancy of parts of the Women's Liberation Movement. They are partly positive to the movement, but also mention the importance of considering men's role in the struggle for a better society. They stress that within the political system women must keep a dialogue and create alliances with male party colleagues and avoid a polarization between men and women. The Community Workers are sceptical or negative toward the Women's Liberation Movement and demand that men's rights should be considered too: 'Men also have rights. We must fight for man-as-a-person's rights. Men must also be included.'

Conditions in the Political System

Results from the general study indicate that there are clear differences between men and women concerning their opinions on gender differences in style and behaviour. Thirty per cent of the men and 72 per cent of the women agree with the statement that 'An increase of women in politics makes political meetings less formal' (Table 5.2).

Table 5.2

Do you agree with the following statement?

An increase of women in politics makes political meetings less formal.

	Men %	Women %
Yes, I agree	30	72
No, I do not agree	70	18
	100	100
	(n = 187)	(n = 134)

Thirty-nine per cent of the men and 65 per cent of the women agree with the statement 'Women and men do behave differently in politics' (Table 5.3).

Table 5.3

Do you agree with the following statement?

Women and men do behave differently in politics.

	Men %	Women %
Yes, I agree	39	65
No, I do not agree	61	35
	100	100
	(n = 185)	(n = 132)

In previous sections we established how women experience differences and confrontations between female culture's values and the techno-economic thinking among both male politicians and officials. It is plausible to assume that the political language and forms of debate, as well as the structure and atmosphere of the meetings are important factors that affect women politicians' feelings of satisfaction with the political culture. It comes out clearly from the interviews that most of the women representatives experience a feeling of alienation from the political culture and its working conditions. Both beginners and more experienced politicians describe how difficult it is to accustom themselves to the political culture. There is no difference between the role-types concerning this feeling. Even the Community Workers agree with the criticism of the political culture, but they do not do so in a perspective of gender differences. They describe the atmosphere as 'hard' or 'non-personal'. The interviews also indicate how women want things to be; they have visions of a political culture where women can develop an alternative role as politicians and feel comfortable.

In the interviews the women were asked to describe the atmosphere on different boards and committees as well as on the city council. They were also asked to compare different situations and election periods. The higher up in the hierarchy the women find themselves the more usual it is that they are critical of the political culture. This is especially true of one Oppositionist and some Party Women who have made a quick career in politics and who, despite their high positions, still have not become adapted to the political culture. The meetings of the executive committee and the town council are described in very negative terms. The women object particularly to the hostile atmosphere which characterizes the debates there. The men assume most of the leading positions, and a Community Worker describes the situation with regard to the executive committee as follows: 'I knew there was a hostile atmosphere when I joined the executive. . . . It is extremely ugly sometimes; a sarcastic, patronizing attitude in which they provoke each other. And a hostility is in the air which everyone is sensitive to. I think that we should be able to discuss things in a calm, sensible manner.'

The meetings of the town council are public but those of the executive and the boards are not. Ten out of twelve women with a seat on the town council dissociate themselves from the existing style of debate; they describe it as 'unbearable', 'spiteful', and 'without respect toward opponents'. They would like to replace this aggressive political atmosphere with a debate including shorter contributions, fewer repetitions, and more informed arguments. The forms of discussion developed within the private sphere of the women's culture are based on dialogue and the need to listen to the other side (Minnich, 1981; Lakoff, 1973). This way of talking is difficult to practise in political debate. A Party Woman describes her entry into the public debate like this:

> When I first requested leave to speak the men rose and walked out of the chamber. Oh, yes, I learnt something then. I then became determined that I would get them to listen. So the next time, I was categorical and a bit nasty and then they began to listen. My way of speaking was not good at first. It was impossible to speak as women do speak to each other. For a period I sat and thought all the time about what I would say and I tried to adapt to the game. Now I'm tired of it and don't usually take part in the debates of the town council.

She does not take part in the broad, general debates any more where the men dominate. At the meetings which I observed, however, she was active on one board and in the town council's debates on women's issues.

Concerning the board meetings, the atmosphere and the working conditions are described as varying greatly between different boards and different periods. Negative features are described as follows: the meetings are formal, boring, and impersonal; political language is abstract, far removed from reality, and often incomprehensible; and the political game is marked by unnecessary 'prestige confrontations' which are not justified. Positive features include: an open and pleasant atmosphere; humour – people joke with each other; dialogues where representatives of different parties have scope in the discussions; a non-hierarchical form of discussion when others besides the party leaders have a chance to express themselves.

The women describe the absence of unnecessary conflicts and an unpleasant impersonal atmosphere as something positive, and by unnecessary conflicts they do not mean those ideological conflicts which distinguish the parties; they stress that there is a difference between party differences and party prestige, and it is primarily conflict about the latter that they derogate. There are some women among the Oppositionists and the Outsiders, however, who do not want to subordinate themselves to the party line (n = 3). Others accept the strong demand for party loyalty but dissociate themselves from conflicts which they describe as the 'men's game'.

The women's descriptions of differences in atmosphere and how the meetings were organized in committees were noticeable during the observations I made (see note 11). Data from the interviews and observations indicate that the activity strategies the women use depend on their roles, their positions, and whether they are tokens. Two Outsiders are single women in their party groups and feel helpless, for they are not able to introduce any alternative political roles or oppose the male dominance. One Oppositionist, despite being a token, is breaking the invisible values of the political culture and playing an active role in both the party group and board. Those Party Women who are chairpersons try to promote an alternative political role: 'I said at the start that I was glad if we had no confrontation politics in our committee. I made it clear to the members that I wanted to avoid that.' One Party Woman observes how the vice-chairperson, a woman, differs in style when directing the otherwise hostile executive meetings: 'I have been participating when —— has been chair, then it is a completely different atmosphere. You can feel how different it is, but it is difficult to describe. When she gives the word she may give us a little smile, she has another way of treating us. She sees us, meets our eyes, we seem to exist even though we belong to different parties.'

Data from my observations show that in one technical, male-dominated committee with a man as chairperson there existed a non-flexible, formal atmosphere with very strict role divisions between the male politicians and officials. The women were tokens (n = 3), but one Oppositionist secretly supported other women later as she said in the interviews. It was only the Oppositionist who openly opposed the proceedings, and the male officials and the chairperson used several tactics of domination such as ridicule, hiding information, and making her invisible (see note 13) to control her. In a committee concerned with social policy the women were in the majority, politicians and officials taken together. The chairperson was an experienced woman holding one of the political power positions, *kommunalråd*. In this committee I noticed how the atmosphere was considerably more open and personal. Not only the party leaders but also other members of the committee were given the opportunity to express themselves. Tactics of domination were rare, and when it once occurred the chairperson immediately interrupted the male politician who tried to ridicule a female colleague. In the city council debates the atmosphere was aggressive, as described in the interviews. All women except one Community Worker avoided personal attacks and long and repetitive speeches. On one occasion a woman who was a vice-chairperson served as the chairperson and she used her position to interrupt the men several times, demanding that they keep to the subject during their speeches. They changed their behaviour to some extent but this change did not last since the male chairperson at the next meeting let the debate go on as usual.

Antolini (1984: 34) mentions *realpolitik*, tokenism, and institutional sexism as institutional pressures which affect behaviour patterns. Dahlerup (1985) suggests that 'barriers' is a concept more usable than discrimination concerning Scandinavian politics. Data from my general survey show that 16 per cent of all women have experienced some kind of discrimination as women. Twenty-three per cent mention that they have observed discrimination against other women. When asked to describe this in the interviews there are mostly descriptions of partly hidden, psychological techniques of domination. In two cases, one Party Woman and one Oppositionist have faced open sexist treatment. They both reacted very strongly against this treatment. One of these women is a token in her party group. The other women who are not tokens seem to meet a more subtle form of discrimination. The Community Workers claim that they have no experience of discrimination, and some women within all the other groups describe this kind of experience. The fact the only one-fifth of the women who responded to the survey mention experience of sexism does not necessarily mean that they are not conscious of this form of suppression. As Dahlerup stresses (1985) it may also be a sign that increasing the number of women in politics has improved the conditions and treatment of women as a whole during the last few years.

Conclusion

In this chapter I have analysed data from a study done in a Swedish city where women politicians constitute what Kanter (1977: 209) has denoted 'a minority in a titled group'. In what way are these women's views about women's interests and their relation to the political culture influenced by the fact that they no longer are tokens in the political system? Drude Dahlerup (1986) claims that feminist attitudes among women in Scandinavian politics is not something that has developed recently. Women's organizations and the parties' women's sections have for decades acted in the interests of women. As a result of interviewing women in Scandinavian politics she points to the difficulty of dividing the legislators into a simple typology of roles such as 'the feminist, the traditional care/social issue politician and the politician who consciously avoids women's issues' (1985: 23). There seem to exist roles which belong somewhere between the outspoken feminist and the traditional care/social issue politician.

I have analysed my data by using a compound model of roles and interests which include different views about women's interests and different strategies of activity related to those opinions. I find, as Dahlerup (1985) suggests, that most women interviewed do perceive women as an interest group even if most of them do not belong to the category of radical and outspoken feminists. Surveys made in the USA also show that most women in local government are supporters of women's issues (CAWP, 1978; Mezey, 1978; Carroll, 1979; Merrit, 1980; Flammang, 1985). As Antolini (1984) remarks when discussing the conclusions of Mezey (1978) and Bers (1978), questions raised where a single point of view measures a feminist orientation may give a biased result concerning the women politicians' views on women's interests.

By posing broad questions on the topic of women's concerns and interests I find that a majority of the women interviewed define themselves as representing issues of special interest to women. When they mention certain issues concerning care of others they do not define those areas as something women *should* be caring for.

However, these women stress that as long as the existing gender-based division of labour remains those issues affect women's lives in a special way. In a few cases coalitions are made with younger men who have personal experiences of housework and care for children.

As an overall conceptual framework I use the theoretical approach of a woman's culture, described as an invisible sphere, suppressed in the world of men, as an explanatory model. Among the respondents to the survey questionnaire, women are more aware of gender differences in political style and behaviour. In the open-ended interviews several women politicians describe their difficulty to adapt their language and way of thinking to the male-dominated political culture. Recognizing they are no longer tokens, seen as a total group, several women expressed pride in their own values, experiences, and priorities as opposed to the techno-economical thinking which dominates mainstream political culture. Several senior women stressed that their arguments are given more status since more women have entered the political arena and argued along the same lines.

The women studied claimed awareness of gender differences when acting in the political system, but they mostly try a less aggressive role as politicians. The observation data from sixteen meetings in three different committees and the town council show that only one woman adapted to the dominating style of her male colleagues. The men, however, do not become affected necessarily by the alternative ways of debate and co-operation of these women. Two different cultures seem to exist side by side and most women are conscious of this. It is when some women use their power positions to introduce values from the women's culture that the pattern in the male-dominated culture may change. Thus, when women as chairpersons declare that they expect a non-hostile atmosphere on their boards, the men do change their behaviour.

This case-study indicates that having more women in politics does affect the political culture. However, the strong demand on party loyalty still prevents Swedish women politicians from acting as an organized interest group concerning specific policy issues.

Notes

I wish to thank Anna G. Jónasdóttir, Kathleen Jones, Janneke van der Ros, and Ingrid Pincus for their contributions and comments to this text. I am also thankful to the Bank of Sweden Tercentenary Foundation which gave a grant to the project 'Women in local politics'.

1. Jónasdóttir (chapter 3) explores some of the theoretical discussions of the problem 'women's interests'.

2. 'View' is used here as a rather wide concept. It includes opinions about particular issues as well as evaluations of the political system. It also includes perceptions of women's possibilities of acting politically.

'Condition' is a part of the total life conditions which are defined as a set of dimensions affecting each other reciprocally: an objective, a subjective, and an activity dimension constitute a whole (Büchert, 1979).

3. Factors explaining the high percentage of women in politics are the level of education, women's entrance into the labour market, the strong pressure from the women's sections towards the parties, and women's social conditions in general in the Scandinavian welfare systems (see chapter 7 in Haavio-Mannila *et al.*, 1985).

4. The concept of culture has been used especially in feminist anthropology. See Rosaldo (1980).

5. Jónasdóttir (1984) suggests that the women's culture studies in Norway correspond to what Geertz (1983) denotes as 'thick description' where theory and detailed empirical research interact.

6. These dimensions are suggested by Myrdal (1968) in his analysis of the Western master culture syndrome and its lack of ability to understand other cultures. The same phenomena can be seen in the relation male master culture/women's culture, according to Ås (1975).

7. Differences between men and women on these dimensions have been described in several studies: language and communication (Lakoff, 1973), relation to finances and capital (Asplund, 1984), self-worth within one's culture (Gilligan, 1982), relation to time and use of time (Hernes, 1982), and a number of time studies in several countries.

8. By using the concept outer sphere and home sphere Halsaa (1977: 24) wants to point to the fact that parts of the private sphere are public and parts of the public sphere are private. I find these concepts useful in my study.

9. Diamond (1977) uses self-image and attitude towards women's role in society as variables when defining her role-types. This distinguishes her role-types from the ones used in this study, as some Outsiders show strong self-image and one Community Worker does not.

10. Eduards (1980) finds that several structural variables indicate why some communalities seem more 'women-friendly' concerning women's political representation; these are size, urban area, and socialist majority.

11. These directly selected women may show a higher awareness of gender differences and may be more feminist than the total population. Results from the general survey show however that a majority of the women in the total population agree to statements that women represent female voters better than men do and that men and women behave differently in politics.

12. Strata used in the randomized selection of men were position and party. Half of the men in the lower positions were selected within each party. The general survey included questions on personal background, family situation, estimation of domestic work done by different family members, support from wife/husband, experienced difficulties in the political work, and attitudes towards gender differences. The women got some additional questions on sexism, political initiatives in women's issues, and relations to women's organizations. The questions in the survey were both closed and open-ended. I made observations as a direct, non-participant observer. I made quantitative and qualitative notes on behaviour, content of arguments, frequency and length of arguments. The interviews were made as the last step and they were structured and open-ended. They lasted between 1½ and 4 hours.

The same topics were covered as in the survey. I conducted all interviews and designed the questionnaires.

13. Tactics of domination described by Ås (1981) consist of ridiculing somebody, making somebody invisible, hiding information, giving feelings of guilt and double punishment (damned if you do and damned if you don't).

References

Antolini, Denise (1984) 'Women in local government: An overview', in Janet A. Flammang (ed.), *Political Woman*. Beverly Hills, CA: Sage.

Asplund, Gisèle (1984) *Karriären villkor (The Conditions of Making a Career)*. Stockholm: Trevi.

Bak-Hansen, Anne and Birgitte Lund-Christiansen (1982) *Hug en hael og klip en tå – eller skaf et par nye sko. En undersøgelse av sammenhangen mellom kvinders politiske aktivitet, kvinders levevilkår og politikens form og inhold (Cut a heel or a toe – or get yourself another pair of shoes. A study on the relation between women's political participation, women's life conditions and the forms and content of politics)*. Århus: Institut for statskunskap. Special publication.

Bers, Trudy H. (1978) 'Local political elites: Men and women on boards of education'. *Western Political Quarterly* (Sept.): 381–91.

Büchert, Erik (1979) *Velfaerd, levevilkår, livskvalitet. . . . (Welfare, life conditions, quality of life . . .)*, Band 1. Århus: NordREFO.

Carroll, Susan (1979) 'Women candidates and support for women's issues: Closet Feminists'. Paper presented at the annual meeting of the Midwest Political Science Association, Chicago, IL.

Center for the American Women and Politics (CAWP) (1978) *Women in Public Office: A Bibliographical Directory and Statistical Analysis*. Metuchen, NJ: Scarecrow Press.

Dahlerup, Drude (1985) *Blomster og Spark. Samtaler med kvindelige politiker i Norden (Flowers and Kicks. Talks with women politicians in the Nordic countries)*. Stockholm: Nordiska Ministerrådet.

Dahlerup, Drude (1986) 'From a small to a large minority. A theory of a "critical mass" applied to the case of women in Scandinavian politics.' Unpublished paper, prepared for the International Seminar of the IPSA Research Committee on Sex Roles and Politics, New Delhi, India, 14–17 Aug. 1986.

Diamond, Irene (1977) *Sex roles in the State House*. New Haven, CT: Yale University Press.

Eduards, Maud (1980) *Kvinnorepresentation och kvinnomakt (Representation of women and power of women)*. Forskningsrapporter, Statsvetenskapliga institutionen, Stockholms Universitet 1980: 2. Research report.

Eduards, Maud, Beatrice Halsaa, and Hege Skjeie (1985) 'Equality: How Equal' in E. Haavio-Mannila, D. Dahlerup, M. Eduards, *et al. Unfinished Democracy. Women in Nordic Politics*. Oxford: Pergamon Press.

Evans, Richard J. (1979) *The Feminists: Women's emancipation movements in Europe, America and Australia 1840–1920*. London: Croom Helm.

Flammang, Janet (1985) 'Female Officials in the Feminist Capital: The Case of Santa Clara County', *Western Political Quarterly* 38: 94–118.

Geertz, Clifford (1983) *Local Knowledge: further essays in interpretive anthropology*. New York: Basic Books.

Gilligan, Carol (1982) *In a different voice: Psychological theory on women's development*. Cambridge, MA: Harvard University Press.

Gustafsson, Agne (1984) *Kommunal självstyrelse (Local self-government)*. Lund: Liberförlag.

Gustavsson, Siv (1986) *Familjepolitik, arbetskraftsdeltagande och barnafödande. Projektbeskrivning av en jämförelse mellan Sverige, Västtyskland och USA (Family policy, participation in labour and birth of children. Description of a study comparing Sweden, West Germany and USA)*. Stockholm: Arbetslivscentrum.

Haavio-Mannila, Elina *et al.* (1985) *Unfinished Democracy, Women in Nordic Politics*. Oxford: Pergamon Press.

Haavind, Hanne (1982) 'Premisser for personlige forhold mellom kvinner' ('Premises of personal relations between women'), p. 403–15 in Harriet Holter (ed.) *Kvinner i felleskap (Women Together)*. Olso: Universitetsforlaget.

Halsaa, Beatrice (1977) *Kvinner og politisk deltakkelse (Women and political participation)*. Oslo: Pax.

Hedlund-Ruth, Gun (1986) 'The public or the private sphere – a biased way of thinking?' Paper prepared for the ECPR joint sessions, Gothenburg, 1986.

Hedlund-Ruth, Gun and Janneke van der Ros Schive (1983) 'The impact of the new women's movement on local politics'. Paper prepared for the ECPR joint sessions, Freiburg, 1983.

Hellevik, Ottar (1978) 'Kjønsforskeller i politisk deltakkelse' ('Gender differences in political participation'). *Tidskrift for Samnfunnsforskning*, 5–6: 527–47.

Hellevik, Ottar and Torild Skard (1985) *Norske kommunestyrer – plass for kvinner? (Norwegian city councils – a place for women?)* Oslo: Universitetsforlaget.

Hernes, Helga Maria (1982) *Staten – kvinner ingen adgang? (The State – women no entrance?)* Oslo: Universitetsforlaget.

Hernes, Helga Maria (1986) 'Interests and values affected by time reforms'. Paper prepared for the ECPR joint sessions, Gothenburg, 1986.

Holter, Harriet (ed.) (1982) *Kvinner i felleskap (Women Together)*. Oslo: Universitetsforlaget.

Jónasdóttir, Anna G. (1984) *Kvinnoteori – några perspektiv och problem inom kvinnoforskningens teoribildning (Feminist theory – some perspectives and problems within feminist theory in development)*. Högskolan i Örebro, Skriftserien 32.

Kanter, Rosabeth Moss (1977) *Men and Women of the Corporation*, New York: Basic Books.

Kraditor, Aileen (1965) *The Ideas of the Woman Suffrage Movement 1890–1920*. New York: Anchor Books.

Lakoff, Robin (1973) 'Language and woman's place', *Language in Society* 2: 45, 47–8.

Merrit, Sharyn (1980) *Women in Local Politics*. Metuchen, NJ: Scarecrow Press.

Mezey, Susan Gluck (1978) 'Support for women's rights policy: An analysis of local politicians', in *American Politics Quarterly* (Oct.): 485–97.

Minnich, Elisabeth Kamarch (1981) 'A Feminist Critique of the Liberal Arts', pp. 22–37 in *Liberal Education and the New Scholarship on Women. Issues and Constraints in Institutional Change*. A Report of the Wingspread Conference, Wisconsin, 1981.

Myrdal, Gunnar (1968) *An Asian Drama. The Poverty of Nations*, vols 1–3. New York: Allen Lane.

Oskarsson, Maria (1987) 'Gender, Social Structure and Party Choice in Sweden'. Paper prepared for the ECPR joint sessions, Amsterdam, 1987.

Rosaldo, Michelle Zimbalist (1980) 'The Use and Abuse of Anthropology: Reflections on Feminism and Crosscultural Understanding', in *Signs* 3: 389–417.

Sapiro, Virginia (1981) 'Research Frontier Essay: When are Interests interesting? The problem of Political Representation of Women', *American Political Science Review* 75(3): 701–16.

SCB (1984) *På tal om kvinnor och män (Talking about women and men)*. Stockholm: Statistiska Centralbyrån.

SCB (1985) *Kvinno- och mansvärlden (The worlds of women and men)*. Stockholm Statistiska Centralbyrån.

Sinkkonen, Sirkka (1985) 'Women in local politics', chapter 4 in Haavio-Mannila, Elina et al. *Unfinished Democracy*.

SOU (1979) *Kvinnors arbete. Hur jämställda är vi? (Women's work. How equal are we?)* Stockholm: Statistiska Centralbyrån.

Staines, Grahame, Toby E. Jayartne, and Carol Tavris (1974) 'The Queen Bee Syndrome', *Psychology Today* (Jan.): 55–60.

Sørensen, Bjørg Åse (1982) 'Ansvarsrationalitet: Om mål-medel-tenkning blant kvinner' ('Rationality of responsibility: On goal-means-thinking among women'), p. 392–402 in Holter, Harriet (1982).

Togeby, Lise (1985) 'Starka, aktive, arga kvinnor' ('Strong, active and angry women'), in *Kvinnovetenskaplig tidskrift*, 3: 3–16.

Waerness, Kari (1977) *Kvinnors omsorgsarbeid i den ulønnete produksjon (Women's care work in the non-paid production)*. NAVF, Arbeidsnotat nr 5/77.

Waerness, Kari (1984) 'Women's work in the Welfare State', pp. 67–101 in Holter, Harriet (ed.), *Patriarchy in the Welfare State*. Oslo: Universitetsforlaget.

Wallin, Gunnar, Henry Bäck, and Merrick Tabor (1981) *Kommunalpolitikerna (Local politicians)*. Rapport 8 från kommunaldemokratiska forskningsgruppen. Stockholm DsKn 1981: 18.

Ås, Berit (1975) 'On Female Culture; An Attempt to Formulate a Theory of Women's Solidarity and Action', in *Acta Sociologica* 18(2–3): 142–61.

Ås, Berit (1976) 'Førsørgerrolle, kvinnekultur og kvinners utdannelse og yrke-sønsker' ('Breadwinner role, women's culture and women's education and wishes of education'), in Erik Grønset (ed.), *Familie og kjønsroller. Arbeid-forsørgelse-likestilling (Family and gender roles. Work-breadwinning-equality)*. Oslo: Cappelens forlag.

Ås, Berit (1981) *Kvinner i alle land (Women in all countries)*. Oslo: Aschehoug.

Ås, Berit (1982) 'Tillbakeblikk og sideblikk på begreppet kvinnekultur' ('Looking back and from the side on the concept women's culture'), p. 74–100 in Haukka, Runa et al. *Kvinneforskning bidrag till samfunnsteori (Women's studies a contribution to social theory)*. Oslo: Universitetsforlaget.

6
The Mobilization of Gender Group Consciousness

Arthur H. Miller, Anne Hildreth, and Grace L. Simmons

The Substantive Debate

Did gender become increasingly politicized in the United States during the decade of the 1970s and 1980s? The emergence of a statistically significant gender gap in all the national elections between 1980 and 1986 (Lake, 1982; Miller, 1983; Kenski, 1986; Heideprien and Lake, 1987), the shrinking participation difference between men and women (Baxter and Lansing, 1980), increased institutional strength of women's organizations and the appearance of the first female vice-presidential candidate in 1984, all suggest an increased political integration (Sapiro, 1983) of women. Available attitudinal evidence also appears consistent with these trends. For example, Gurin (1985) demonstrated that gender identification among women increased during the seventies. Over that same period women increasingly questioned the legitimacy of the lower status and relative lack of influence that women in general have in society. This evidence presumably indicates that women have established a strong presence in national politics and it raises the possibility that women as a group are increasingly viewing their social situation in political terms.

Yet, other evidence appears to contradict this conclusion. The relatively poor showing of women candidates generally in the 1984 and 1986 elections, the inability of Ferraro to mobilize a majority of women to support her ticket in 1984, the failure of women's organizations to gain passage of the Equal Rights Amendment (ERA), and the absence of any significant impact of ERA on the 1980 vote (Mansbridge, 1985) all appear to suggest that women did not become more politicized and that gender has a minimal effect in the political arena.

In addition, some scholars dismiss the recent gender gap as a short-term reaction to the warmongering image of the early Reagan administration (Zeigler and Poole, 1985). When Reagan moved toward reconciliation with the Soviets the gender gap closed in

1984. Even Gurin (1985) points out that men and women alike have come to endorse pro-feminist attitudes of equality for women. These parallel shifts among men and women presumably imply that little political conflict surrounds concerns about the role of women in society. Indeed, at least some political observers (see for example Plissner, 1983) have dismissed gender, arguing that it is an irrelevant dimension in American politics.

Our purpose in this chapter is to examine this controversy more closely. At the outset some clarification is in order, since part of the controversy appears to arise out of a failure to differentiate political cleavage between men and women from the question of whether or not women view the social situation of their group in political terms. The latter is what we refer to as gender politicization. The two are interrelated in the sense that gender cleavage may be the result of gender politicization. The absence of gender politicization, however, does not necessarily follow from the lack of gender cleavage.

The gender gap literature often considers women as a whole. It thereby assumes that women are a cohesive group and that female solidarity implies polarization with men. But women are not a homogeneous group. It is also a fallacy to conclude, as does some research (Zeigler and Poole, 1985; Plissner, 1983), that because women do not form a homogeneous bloc of political actors, gender is not politicized or relevant to the understanding of politics. How an individual woman feels about other women and the place of women in society more generally may be very important for her political behaviour. Therefore, to conclude that gender is irrelevant to politics because the gender gap is not larger totally ignores the relevance that gender may have for the political behaviour of women.

The focus of this chapter will be gender politicization, not gender cleavage. We directly address the extent to which gender identification has become increasingly politicized among women. Then, drawing upon social psychological theories of intergroup behaviour, we formulate and test alternative empirical explanations for recent trends in gender group consciousness.

The work of Gurin (1985) is an excellent starting-point. Her research demonstrated overall shifts in gender group awareness and the attitudes of women toward the status of women in society. She presented trends showing that both men and women had become more favourable towards increasing the influence of women in society. Clearly, increased political conflict is not implied if everyone in the population is becoming more concerned about the subordinate position of women, as that would simply reflect consensus. Conflict is implied, however, when it is primarily those women who are becoming increasingly identified with women as a group who are politicized by their perception that women lack power and influence in society. But Gurin's research did not directly determine if shifts in gender identification were associated with assessments of women's relative status. Nor did she correlate gender identification with political attitudes or behaviours to determine if gender awareness was indeed politicized. The analysis presented here, therefore, will attempt to determine explicitly the extent to which gender identification has become associated with both perceived inequities in women's status and with political behaviour.

Major Concepts and Trends

The first step in the development of group consciousness is a psychological awareness of shared interests among the categorical members (Jackman and Jackman, 1973; Gurin *et al.*, 1980; Miller *et al.*, 1981). To speak of individual behaviour in terms of groups requires that the individuals have a sense of group identification; that is, they think of themselves and others as members of certain groups or categories (Tajfel, 1981). In addition, this explicit acceptance of membership in a category must go beyond simply acknowledging that one is a member of the category to an expression of shared solidarity, a feeling of being close or similar to others of the category.

Much of the work on the gender gap (for example, Zeigler and Poole, 1985), and on political group cleavages in general, is limited because it focuses solely on demographically defined groups. The problem with this type of approach is that it fails to measure directly the underlying theoretical reasons often assumed to be the basis of the cleavage – perceived deprivation and intergroup competition for scarce resources. This approach also fails to recognize the fact that individuals can and often do deny the reality of their situation, or that they fail to make comparisons between their situation and that of others.

The demographic approach is further limited because it does not draw a distinction between the person who makes social comparisons in individual terms (I make less than my co-worker) and one who makes comparisons in terms of groups (blue-collar workers make less than white-collar workers). The latter comparison indicates that the individuals think of themselves in terms of their own group and differentiates that group from other groups in society.

This social identity, that is, thinking of oneself in terms of categorical groups, implies that identification with a group is a positive attribute for the individual. After all, no one would set out to devalue their self-image (Tajfel, 1981: 137, 256). Studies of subordinate groups that are negatively evaluated by the majority in society do, however, frequently reveal a low sense of self-esteem among the group's members. But, one psychological means frequently employed by individuals to escape a negative group image is to de-emphasize or deny membership in the social category. For example, an elderly person for whom growing old carries negative connotations will be more likely to deny their age and think of themselves in terms of other categories. Strength of identification with a group, therefore, represents not only solidarity or a sense of shared interests among objectively defined group members but also the degree to which the group contributes to the self-definition of the individual.[1]

Trends in Gender Identification
Empirical evidence on gender identification among women demonstrates that the trend found by Gurin (1985) for the seventies has persisted into the mid-eighties (see Table 6.1). The largest increase in gender identification occurred between 1972 and 1976 when the percentage of women in the University of Michigan National Election Study (NES) survey who were *not* 'close' to other women in terms of shared interests dropped from 57 to 40 per cent.[2]

Table 6.1   *Group identification among women and blacks*

	1972 %	1976 %	1980 %	1984 %
Women				
Closest identifiers	9	11	10	8
Close identifiers	34	49	47	60
Not identified	57	40	43	32
	100	100	100	100
(N)	(1238)	(1064)	(783)	(1044)
PDI*	−48	−29	−33	−24
Blacks				
Closest identifiers	33	32	36	32
Close identifiers	51	49	51	56
Not identified	16	19	13	12
	100	100	100	100
(N)	(211)	(163)	(160)	(192)
PDI*	+17	+13	+23	+20

*The PDI was computed by subtracting the percentage not identified from the percentage closest.

Source: NES

Gender identification, however, failed to rise any further during the period from the mid-seventies to the early eighties, probably because of the conflict facing the women's movement during these years. In early 1972 the Equal Rights Amendment was passed with overwhelming support in the US Senate and sent to the states for ratification. Within the first year of the seven-year period specified by Congress for ratification 30 state legislatures had voted to ratify the Amendment (Steiner, 1985). Yet, despite this successful start it was not long before opposition to ERA was mobilized and began to be effective (see Boles, 1979, for a detailed discussion of the conflict surrounding the ratification attempt). Even after a three-year extension was granted in 1978 the Amendment failed to be ratified by the required 38 states, thus providing a visible defeat for the women's movement.

Another setback for the movement occurred at the 1980 Republican national convention, where Phyllis Schafly and others were successful in promoting a platform that was opposed to the ratification of the ERA. No doubt the group conflict occurring around these issues contributed to the decline in gender identification that appeared in 1980 (see Table 6.1). Nevertheless, this setback was temporary, and in 1984 there was again a noticeable decline in the percentage of women who did not identify at all with the category 'women'.

Although gender identification increased markedly between 1972 and 1984, the percentage of women indicating the strongest sense of identification with women failed to grow. When asked to select from a list of 16–19 categorical groups that group to which they felt *closest*, the percentage of women who said they felt 'closest' to 'women' hovered around 10 per cent from 1972 to 1980, and then fell to 8 per cent in 1984. The consistently small percentage of females who were strongly identified with women suggests that this was never a very intensely held identification and that the intensity appears to have peaked in the late seventies.[3]

Despite the recent decline in the percentage of strongest identifiers, the overall level of gender identification, as summarized by a Percentage Difference Index (PDI), attained a new high in 1984. In comparison with group identification among blacks, however, it is apparent that group solidarity among women has not yet reached the level that blacks have consistently exhibited for some time (compare the PDI for blacks and women in Table 6.1). Relative to blacks, a much higher proportion of women fail to identify at all with their gender group. Moreover, the percentage of blacks that are most strongly identified with their group is roughly three times that found among women.

The Political Effect of Group Identification

The high level of group identification evident for blacks is presumably one of the reasons why blacks act as a solid political group (Verba and Nie, 1972, chapter 10). The relatively lower incidence and strength of identification for women implies that we

Table 6.2 *Political attitudes and behaviour by gender identification*[a]

	1972	1984
Party identification for:		
Closest identifiers	19.8	18.4
Close identifiers	16.2	12.0
Not identified	17.3	6.4
	r = 0.02	r = 0.12*
Presidential vote for:		
Closest identifiers	−13.6	5.6
Close identifiers	−22.4	−6.0
Not identified	−27.4	−26.2
	r = 0.09*	r = 0.18*
Party best on important problems:		
Closest identifiers	0.0	4.3
Close identifiers	−4.1	−0.5
Not identified	−1.1	−5.5
	r = 0.01	r = 0.08*
Which party avoids war:		
Closest identifiers	−5.8	14.8
Close identifiers	13.1	4.3
Not identified	16.9	−7.7
	r = 0.08	r = 0.15*
Interest in campaign:		
Closest identifiers	3.5	10.3
Close identifiers	10.6	4.2
Not identified	−6.9	−7.4
	r = 0.10*	r = 0.14*

*p < 0.01

[a] Table entries are percentage difference values calculated for the first four variables by subtracting the Republican proportion from the Democratic proportion. Negative values thus indicate a predominance of Republican over Democratic partisanship, voting or party assessment. The interest in the campaign entries reflects the percentage interested minus the percentage not interested. Correlations are Pearson r.

Source: NES

cannot expect women to act as cohesively in the political arena as blacks. Nevertheless, the rise in overall gender identification among women suggests the potential for increased participation and political solidarity among women, that is, greater politicization.

If gender identification does indeed spill over into the political arena, as does race identification for blacks, we would expect significant correlations between gender identification and politically relevant variables such as participation, partisanship, and vote choice. Furthermore, if increased politicization of the identification has accompanied the increase in level of identification, we would expect the correlations to be even stronger in 1984 than they were in 1972. Empirical evidence does indeed support these expectations. In both 1972 and 1984 gender identification was significantly related with most of the political variables examined in Table 6.2. More importantly, in 1984 gender identity was always more strongly related with political attitudes and behaviours than in 1972 (see Table 6.2). For example, in 1972 there was virtually no difference in the partisan orientation of women identified with their gender group and those who were not at all identified. By 1984, on the other hand, those expressing the strongest gender identification were significantly more Democratic in their partisanship than non-identified women.

Distinguishing Group Identification and Consciousness
Nevertheless, the increased politicization of gender identification suggested by Table 6.2 is at best only modest. Although there is a statistically significant relationship between the political variables and gender identification in 1984, the correlations are quite weak. There are, however, good theoretical reasons why we might not expect much higher correlations when investigating only group identification. Particularly relevant here is the conceptual distinction that has been made between identification and group consciousness (Gurin, Miller, and Gurin, 1980). Identification, as indicated above, refers to a person's awareness of themselves in relation to others within a particular group or category. It implies that the person believes that he has ideas, feelings, interests, and character-istics in common with others who are members of the same category, and that they are distinct from members of other groups. Group consciousness goes beyond group identification and reflects cognitions that arise out of comparing the social status of one group with another (Tajfel, 1981). Group consciousness develops when individuals believe that their own group is unfairly lacking political and social influence, and that collective action in the political arena is a legitimate and necessary avenue for redressing the situation.

Because group identification and consciousness are conceptually distinct, it is possible that an individual may identify with a group, even a subordinate group, without seeing the group's relative lack of power in society as unjust or believing that political action is necessary for changing this status. Individuals may accept their relatively lower status for a variety of reasons (see Tajfel, 1981, for a discussion of these) and believe that individual rather than collective or political action is the best way to improve either their own situation or that of the group.

The results presented earlier in Table 6.1 do not differentiate group identification and group consciousness. In a study of blacks this distinction may not be necessary, as their group identification and consciousness may have empirically converged because of historical circumstances. In contrast, recent history suggests that women have not uniformly adopted a political action orientation as part of their increased gender identification. Some women, those generally thought of as feminists, might approve of a collective approach. Whereas other, more traditional women, those vocally represented by Phyllis Schafly in recent years, might identify very closely with 'women', but not endorse the political approach of the movement.

Operationalizing Gender Consciousness
Operationally group consciousness could be indicated by how strongly an individual endorsed various politically active organizations that represent the group's interests.[4] For example, among blacks it may be represented by support for civil rights leaders or activist black organizations such as PUSH, for the elderly by an endorsement of the 'gray panthers', and for women by support for NOW or the women's liberation movement more generally.

Available survey evidence is rather limited in the number of items that could be used to measure gender consciousness. The one questionnaire item consistently asked between 1972 and 1984 was the feeling thermometer rating of the women's liberation movement. Over that period the average rating of the movement among women rose from 45 to 59 degrees. In 1972 only four out of ten women rated the movement positively (that is, above 50 degrees), by 1984 that figure had risen to almost six out of ten. Yet, women as a whole exhibited far less group consciousness than blacks. In both 1972 and 1984 somewhat more than 80 per cent of blacks were equally as positive about civil rights leaders.

In both 1972 and 1984 gender identification and ratings of the women's movement were correlated. However, in both years a significant proportion of identified women gave the movement a negative rating (in 1984 roughly 40 and 26 per cent of close and closest identifiers respectively rated the movement 50 degrees or lower). Thus, as suggested above, identification and endorsement of a collective orientation are not one and the same for women. For this very reason we would expect the combination of identification and collective orientation to produce a more valid measure of politicized identification (that is, gender consciousness) than would identification alone.

It should be noted that combining gender identification and support for the women's liberation movement into a single measure is more than merely a methodological exercise. We are not saying that the NES gender identification measure is a weak or invalid indicator of the underlying concept, and that the only way to improve it is by combining it with another indicator. Rather, we contend that substantively the measurement model underlying the concept of group consciousness can be fit *only* by combining these two components into one. If previous research and social psychological theories on intergroup relations are correct, the result should be a substantively more relevant and empirically more powerful measure of politicized group identification.

Trend and Political Effects of Gender Consciousness
The resulting distribution of gender consciousness among women as determined by the combined measure for the period 1972–1984 is presented in Table 6.3. The measure was constructed by dichotomizing the 'women's liberation' thermometer ratings at the median and then using this split to divide identified women into the two top categories of consciousness displayed in Table 6.3. Included in the high category of gender consciousness are the women who were

Table 6.3   *Gender consciousness among women 1972–1984*

	1972 %	1976 %	1980 %	1984 %
Consciousness				
High	19	32	26	30
Low	23	26	30	38
Not identified	58	42	44	33
	—	—	—	—
	100	100	100	100
	(1201)	(1022)	(770)	(1027)
PDI	−39	−10	−18	−3
mean[a]	2.39	2.10	2.18	2.05

[a] The mean was computed with High equal to 1 and Not identified equal to 3.

Source: NES

the closest and close gender identifiers in Table 6.1, those who rated the movement positively; the low category incorporates closest and close identifiers who rated the movement negatively; and those women who were not identified at all comprise the third category.

The across-time trend in Table 6.3, summarized by either the mean or PDI, suggests an increase in gender consciousness during the past decade and a half. A good deal of growth, however, has occurred among the category of women who are less than enamoured with the women's movement (those labelled 'low' consciousness) – in other words, those respondents who thought of themselves as women, but who did not feel warmly toward the women's movement. Indeed, the growth in the low consciousness category suggests the possibility of a women's backlash and increased polarization among women.

Initial evidence supporting this possibility can be found in the association between gender consciousness and the across-time change in the thermometer ratings of 'women'. Between 1976 and 1984 the average thermometer rating of women as a group fell from 78.8 to 74.2. The decline occurred for both women (79.5 to 76.0) and men (78.0 to 71.9). This shift runs counter to expectations because gender identification had increased during this period, and identification has generally been correlated with positive effect towards the in-group. But as we shall see, the decline in positive feelings toward 'women' did not occur equally for all women. In fact, the ratings fell only among those women who were not identified or did not support the women's movement, with the sharpest decline evident for the low consciousness group (see Table 6.4). Among women with a strong sense of gender consciousness, the ratings actually increased over time. These divergent trends suggest that between 1972 and 1984 the category 'women,' or gender more generally, had become increasingly politicized and conflictual.

Table 6.4 *Affective ratings of 'women' by gender consciousness*[a]

	1976	1984
Total Women	79.5	76.0
Gender consciousness		
High	82.0	85.2
Low	79.0	73.1
Not identified	75.3	72.5

[a]Table entries are mean thermometer ratings of 'women'.

Source: NES

The most telling evidence of this increased politicization appears in Table 6.5. As hypothesized above, the gender consciousness measures were more strongly correlated with partisan attitudes and political behaviours than was identification alone.[5] But far more important is the fact that the correlations with political variables got markedly stronger across time. Furthermore, the stronger correlations have appeared at the very same time that the percentage of

Table 6.5   *Political attitudes and behaviour by gender consciousness*[a]

	1972	1984
Party identification for:		
High consciousness	13.2	33.4
Low consciousness	18.3	−0.2
Not identified	17.3	6.4
	r = 0.03*	r = 0.18*
Presidential vote for:		
High consciousness	−2.8	31.2
Low consciousness	−38.0	−30.4
Not identified	−27.4	−26.2
	r = 0.12*	r = 0.34*
Party best on important problems:		
High consciousness	2.0	26.7
Low consciousness	−8.1	−18.3
Not identified	−1.1	−5.5
	r = 0.06*	r = 0.19*
Which party avoids war:		
High consciousness	−1.7	23.6
Low consciousness	20.9	−9.5
Not identified	16.9	−7.7
	r = −0.11*	r = 0.23*
Interest in campaign:		
High consciousness	19.6	24.1
Low consciousness	4.8	1.6
Not identified	−6.9	−7.4
	r = 0.15*	r = 0.28*

*$p < 0.01$

[a] Table entries are percentage difference values calculated for the first four variables by subtracting the Republican proportion from the Democratic partisanship, voting or party assessment. The interest in the campaign entries reflects the percentage interested minus the percentage not interested. Correlations are Pearson r.

Source: NES

women sharing a sense of gender consciousness has increased. The difference in the partisan attitudes and political behaviour for women who most strongly express a sense of gender consciousness and those who do not is quite substantial. For example, in 1984 strongly identified women voted overwhelmingly for Walter Mondale while those lower in gender consciousness heavily supported Ronald Reagan (the actual percentage voting Republican was 34.4 and 65.2 for the highest and lowest consciousness categories respectively).

As can be seen from the percentage difference score in Table 6.5, women classified as 'low consciousness' are generally somewhat more Republican than 'not identified' women. This further supports the suggestion that there are two types of traditional women, those for whom gender is more politicized but in an anti-feminist direction ('low' consciousness), and those for whom gender is not even a salient category influencing their social identity ('not identified').[6]

In summary, the gender consciousness measure provides a more relevant and meaningful political classification of women than was obtained with identification alone. Both the across-time trends and the stronger correlations with political variables in 1984 support the conclusion that there has been an increase in politicized gender identification – that is, thinking about one's gender (consciousness) has become more connected with political beliefs and behaviours. Whether or not this trend will continue into the future, however, depends on the durability of the factors correlated with gender consciousness.

Explanations of Politicized Gender Identification

The literature suggests a number of alternative correlates of gender consciousness. Some researchers have suggested that fundamental changes in the social and economic situation of contemporary women have led to the rise of gender consciousness. Entry into the work-place for an ever-increasing number of women has been given particular emphasis (Klein, 1984; Anderson and Cook, 1985). Others have argued that marital status is a particularly important discriminating demographic variable among women: Sapiro, 1983; Zeigler and Poole, 1985, and Gurin (1985) argued that during the 1970s four demographic characteristics (marital and work status, age and education) were significant correlates of gender identification.

Demographic Correlates

The relationship between gender consciousness and these background variables can be readily seen from Figures 6.1–6.4. Clearly, single, working, younger, and better-educated women are much more likely to express a strong sense of gender consciousness than are older, married, less well-educated and non-working women. Taken together these demographic correlates of gender consciousness appear very similar to the popular stereotype of the contemporary feminist: young, single, college educated, career oriented, and white. There is good theoretical reason why gender consciousness would be most prevalent among these types of women. According to Sapiro (1983) and Klein (1984) these women were most likely to have had socialization experiences that deviated from those associated with traditional sex roles, thus they should be more open to the politicization of their gender awareness.

Yet, in certain other respects the data of Figures 6.1–6.4 run contrary to the popular notion of feminists. For example, gender consciousness has increased somewhat among even the most traditional women, thereby implying that demographic differences and shifts in life experiences or early socialization cannot alone account for the increased politicization of gender identification. In

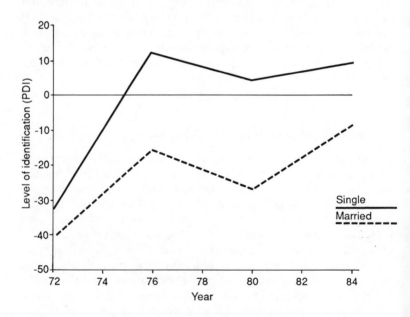

Figure 6.1   *Politicized gender identification by marital status*

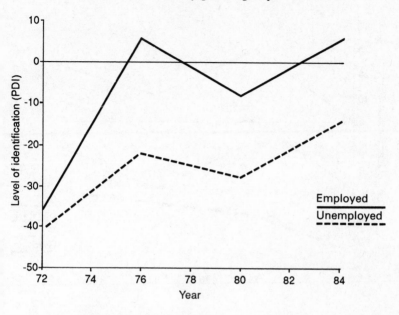

Figure 6.2   *Politicized gender identification by work status*

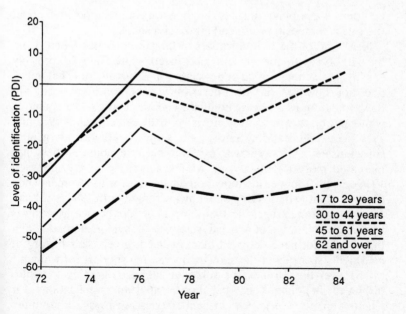

Figure 6.3   *Politicized gender identification by age*

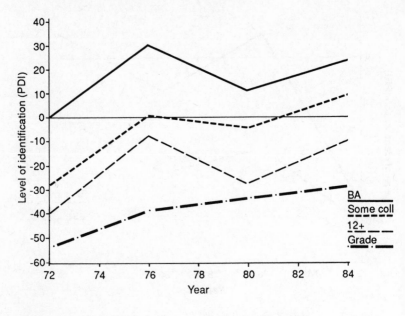

Figure 6.4   *Politicized gender identification by education*

addition, the popular image is simply wrong in its supposition about the racial composition of gender consciousness.

Nearly all of the visible leaders in the women's movement from the late 1960s to the present have been white, thereby possibly conveying the image of an upper-class white movement. That image does not, however, fit with a description of gender identification in the population as a whole. Politicized gender consciousness among white and black women was virtually at the same level in 1972 and 1976 (see Figure 6.5). Since 1980 some divergence in gender consciousness has occurred, but not because consciousness has increased more rapidly among whites. On the contrary, between 1976 and 1980 gender identification declined for white women while blacks exhibited increased gender awareness in both 1980 and 1984. If, as suggested earlier, the 1980 drop in gender consciousness was motivated by a wave of anti-ERA activity, it is understandable that this would not have deterred black women, given their history of civil rights struggles, from showing increasing support for women.[7]

The over-time trends for some of the demographic variables displayed in Figures 6.1–6.5 hold important implications for whether or not the growth in gender consciousness will continue into the future. Although some increase in gender consciousness has occurred across all these demographic categories, the youngest and

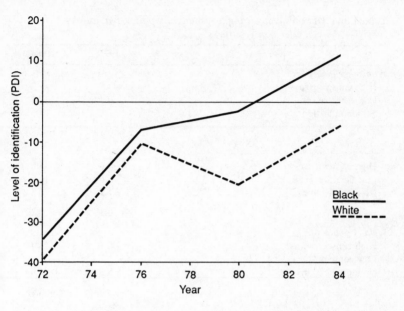

Figure 6.5 *Politicized gender identification by race*

oldest women continue to diverge and the differences across education levels have remained fairly stable over time. As women on the whole continue to become better educated and younger women replace older women through generational turnover, we can expect a continuation in the trend toward increased gender consciousness.

Perceived Social Inequities

In addition to demographic shifts, certain social psychological and political factors can be entertained as theoretical explanations for the rise in gender consciousness. Tajfel (1981), for example, has proposed a theory of intergroup relations that is relevant for understanding the process by which group identification becomes politicized. His theory specifies a convergence in the processes of social categorization, social identity, and social comparison which result in a psychological sense of group distinctiveness and a motivation for changing the social status of the group. According to the theory, an individual's social identity, that aspect of the self-concept which is determined through an awareness of membership in various social categories and the status attached to these groups, acquires meaning only by comparison with other groups. Hence, individuals who are members of a group that has an inferior social

Table 6.6 *Attitudes concerning inequities and policy evaluations*
by gender consciousness[a]

	1972	1984
Women's equality for:		
High consciousness	43.1	49.2
Low consciousness	−0.4	23.5
No identification	7.8	13.6
	r = 0.19*	r =·0.30*
Self/system blame for:		
High consciousness	20.6	35.8
Low consciousness	5.6	−10.2
No identification	−1.2	−8.2
	r = 0.18*	r = 0.28*
Welfare policy for:		
High consciousness	6.1	12.4
Low consciousness	−17.7	6.4
No identification	−5.8	−3.9
	r = 0.06*	r = 0.25*
Concerns about war for:		
High consciousness	9.1	19.2
Low consciousness	−33.6	0.6
No identification	−30.8	−1.4
	r = 0.12*	r = 0.16*
Personal financial evaluations for:		
High consciousness	29.7	15.7
Low consciousness	34.8	30.1
No identification	28.0	18.2
	r = −0.00	r = 0.04
National economic evaluations for:		
High consciousness	38.8	10.0
Low consciousness	47.9	15.2
No identification	39.5	13.8
	r = 0.05*	r = 0.03*

*p <0.01
[a] Table entries are percentage difference values calculated for the first four variables by subtracting the 'low' value of the variable (women in the home, blame self, individual responsibility, low concern) from the higher value. For the two economic entries a scale was used that combined retrospective and prospective evaluations, with the low value being equivalent to a 'worse' assessment. See the Appendix for the exact wording of the items used. Correlations are Pearson r.

Source: NES

status are said to possess an inadequate social identity. The group identification among those historically lacking power, such as women, becomes politicized, however, when group members begin to perceive the status inequities of their group as unjust and subsequently attribute the cause for these status differentials to barriers in the social structure rather than to their own individual failings. This combination of beliefs produces the motivation to act collectively with other group members to change the social situation of women as a whole. A similar mobilizing process among élites was suggested by Gelb and Palley (1982) in their study of women's lobby organization efforts on legislative initiatives designed to establish role equity for women.

Extending Tajfel's theory to the study of gender suggests the hypothesis that, in a cross-sectional analysis, gender consciousness should be with items reflecting issues of equality for men and women and perceptions of the individual versus the system as the locus of responsibility for these inequities are reported in Table 6.6. Indeed, the first entry in Table 6.6 provides ample support for the argument that the perception of inequities is very strong among women who express the highest level of gender consciousness. The change in these attitudes across time indicates that while traditional women have come to be more opposed to inequities between men and women, they remain substantially more accepting of these status inequities in 1984 than do the most politicized women.

A slightly different pattern emerges with the measure tapping blame. Women with higher gender consciousness are much more likely to identify society as perpetuating gender-related status inequities. In 1984 the divergence of women at different levels of gender consciousness widens. What this suggests is that while women as a whole are coming to recognize the prevalence of status inequities, only some women, those with a higher level of politicization, locate responsibility for women's subordinate status at the societal level. Although both concerns about status inequities and the attribution of gender inequality to social barriers are strongly associated with gender consciousness, the relationships are not so strong as to suggest that these are the sole explanations for the increased politicization of women.

Policy Preferences
One alternative explanation evident in the literature suggests that the recent growth in gender consciousness may reflect the policy concerns of contemporary women (Frankovic, 1982; Miller, 1983; Klein, 1984; Deitch, 1986). Pomper's (1975) analysis of the relationship between women and their attitudes toward war reveals that women are consistently less likely to favour policies that advocate the use of force. Pomper and others have generalized this to apply in the domestic policy sphere by characterizing women as

more humanitarian than men and less likely to endorse hard positions on civil rights issues and welfare programmes. The recent assault on welfare programmes under the Reagan administration has served to widen further the gender gap on domestic policy issues. Through an earlier expansion of government programmes relevant to the needs of women, and more recently through an attack on those programmes, the state itself has played an active role in politicizing gender. Deitch (1986), however, suggests that the expansion of the welfare state in the 1960s and 1970s benefited certain classes of women more than others. Both women in marginal economic positions, who constitute the bulk of recipients of welfare programmes, and the organized feminist movement have benefited from the expansion of benefits and career opportunities that have come with the growth of the state.

The correlations between gender consciousness and policy preferences provide support for the contention that, where policy concerns are involved, women fail to coalesce around a uniform point of view. In general women may be more humanitarian in their policy preferences than men, but it is quite clear from Table 6.6 that those with the strongest gender consciousness are more supportive of domestic welfare programmes and more opposed to the use of military force than those less strongly identified with women.

Economic Self-interest

The correlation between gender consciousness and domestic policy preferences suggests an alternative explanation which potentially contradicts the altruism and caring often assumed to underlie these attitudes among women. Some women, particularly single heads of families, are in a situation characterized by economic uncertainty and anxiety. These women may feel that it is important for government to provide economic security for needy groups. In part this preference may arise out of a generic concern for all underprivileged groups, including women. On the other hand, the policy preference may reflect only personal economic uncertainty and narrow self-interest.

Some of the demographic differences revealed by Figures 6.1–6.5, particularly the high level of gender politicization among younger and unmarried women, suggest that perhaps economic self-interest might account for the growth in gender consciousness. Two-adult families should be economically more secure than single-member households. Moreover, divorced women are frequently the heads of single-parent households. In addition, working women in general, regardless of marital status, earn less money than men and frequently enjoy less job security. The possibility arises, therefore, that growing economic pessimism and discontent among some women produced the rise in gender politicization.

The last two entries in Table 6.6 provide evidence supporting the assumption of increased economic distress among women in general between 1972 and 1984. During that period there was a significant rise in the percentage of women expressing a pessimistic assessment of both their own personal financial situation and the economic conditions of the nation (this change is indicated in Table 6.6 by lower positive PDI values for the economic attitude measures in 1984 relative to 1972). Contrary to what Heideprien and Lake (1987) have argued, however, gender politicization does not appear to have been correlated with economic pessimism in either 1972 or 1984. In both years women with a low degree of gender consciousness were more optimistic about the economy than either those who lacked any gender identification or those for whom gender had become highly politicized. But the differences are quite small, thus providing little support for the argument that gender politicization was the direct result of personal economic distress.

A Multivariate Analysis of Gender Politicization

While economic self-interest appears to be eliminated as a direct explanation for gender politicization, we are still left with a number of competing theories, thus suggesting the need for a multivariate analysis.[8] The results of such an analysis demonstrate that age and education were the only demographic variables that consistently influenced gender consciousness between 1972 and 1984 (see Table 6.7).[9] Among the social-psychological explanations, concerns about equality for women and self/system blame stand out as most important. Perceptions of inequity in the influence and status of women, as well as the belief that social barriers rather than individual limitations account for the subordinate position of women, both contributed substantially to an expression of gender consciousness. The relatively strong impact of these variables on gender consciousness, even after controlling for competing explanations, provides substantial support for Tajfel's theory of intergroup relations.

These regression results imply that thinking about gender in political terms involves certain critical elements: the realization that women as a group unjustly occupy a disadvantaged position in society, that this status is unacceptable, and that this perceived discrimination is connected with current social and political arrangements. If women either failed to perceive any status differential between the sexes, or accepted the situation of subordinate status as legitimate, or attributed the status discrepancy to some limitation

Table 6.7   *Multivariate analysis of gender consciousness*[a]

	1972	1984
Predictors[a]		
Demographics:		
Age	0.09	0.12**
Education	−0.13*	−0.13**
Marital status	0.01	0.01
Work status	0.03	−0.10*
Blue collar	−0.09	−0.01
White collar	−0.07	−0.05
Other workers	0.00	−0.04
Income	−0.06	0.01
Race	0.03	−0.02
Political:		
Women's equality	0.12**	0.16**
Self/system blame	0.11**	0.12**
Welfare policy	0.04	−0.15**
Concerns about war	−0.08*	−0.06
Personal finances	−0.05	0.05
National economy	−0.03	−0.03
r	0.30	0.45
Explained variance	0.09	0.20

* $p < 0.05$ ** $p < 0.01$

[a] See the Appendix for a definition of the political predictors.

Source: NES

assumed to be innate to women rather than social arrangements, there would be little motivation to seek redress in the political arena. Indeed, the regression results suggest that traditional women accept these status differences as legitimate, whereas feminists do not.

Although concerns about equity and system blame were strongly related with gender consciousness in both 1972 and 1984, the impact of both domestic and foreign policy considerations, contrary to the hypotheses raised earlier, were at best inconsistent. Preferences regarding welfare assistance for the needy were significantly related with consciousness only in 1984, whereas concerns about the use of force in international relations were significant only in 1972. These inconsistent relationships call into question previous explanations for gender differences in policy preferences.

Over the years women, relative to men, have been more sympathetic towards welfare programmes and more peace oriented in their preferences on international relations. Generally, the explanation given for this substantive difference between men and women has been socialization into gender roles. Women, in their private role as mothers, are supposed to be more nurturant, protective of the children, and the guardian of domestic harmony, thus in the public domain they are more concerned with peace issues and more supportive of policies that aid disadvantaged groups (Sapiro, 1983).

While such an explanation helps us understand the policy differences between men and women, it is less applicable to the study of women only. Indeed, the logical extension of the theory would lead to the hypothesis that traditional women should be more nurturant, hence more favourable towards welfare programmes and more peace-minded than feminists. Yet, the empirical evidence shows that those women for whom gender identification is most politicized are the ones who express the greatest support for welfare and the strongest opposition to the military. Surely some theoretical argument other than nurturance is needed to account for these empirical results.

A more general interpretation may be found in the differential attentiveness of various women to certain issues. In 1972 and 1980 attitudes toward the military, and foreign relations generally, were important issues on the public agenda. In 1980, the ongoing embarrassment of the Iranian hostage crisis and fears raised by Reagan's warmongering image increased the relative salience of foreign issues. By 1984, however, Reagan had attempted to soften his foreign policy image, and domestic issues, spurred by the cuts in welfare programmes, regained visibility. Women expressing a politicized sense of gender identification were more attentive to these issues than women were traditionally. They were also more dissatisfied with Nixon's and Reagan's positions on the issues, thus supporting the anti-military, pro-welfare position advocated by the leadership of the women's movement from which they may have been picking up cues. In short, the relationship between gender consciousness and either foreign or domestic policy preferences among women may be a function of information processing and ideology rather than nurturance.

Finally, the larger degree of explained variance found for the 1984 equation adds support to the broader conclusion that gender identity had become more politicized across time. The political predictors also account for a noticeably larger proportion of the explained variance in 1984 than in 1972. These results provide a quantitative measure of the extent to which gender has become infused with political significance during the past two decades in contemporary America.

Conclusion

The research reported here indicates that gender is more than a dichotomous demographic variable for describing differences between men and women. On the contrary, it is a continuous cultural variable that takes on different meanings at different points in time, with social-psychological implications for how individuals perceive themselves and their relative status in society. Such a theoretical view moves our thinking about gender and politics beyond looking only at the differences between men and women as a whole or as subdivided by demographic descriptions. The gender identification approach provides a theoretical framework for exploring and explaining both political differences between the sexes and among women. It shifts the substantive focus to a concern with those factors that promote or limit the development of group solidarity, and the political implications of group identification, including the impact of group consciousness on intergroup competition for political resources.

The empirical evidence presented above strongly suggests that women are increasingly viewing their social situation in political terms. This increased politicization has occurred primarily among younger and better-educated women. As these women are gradually replacing older, more traditional women we can expect a continued future growth in gender consciousness. Holter (1970) has suggested that as these well-educated women, with their newly acquired intellectual skills, seek a more active role in society they will increasingly come to question existing social arrangements because they will find that their skills are at odds with the traditional role and expectations that they will so frequently encounter. Because the average educational level of women is still rising we would expect the resulting growth in gender consciousness to extend into the foreseeable future.

But change in education is not the sole source of either past or potential future growth in gender politicization. The policy actions of government may also influence the politicization of gender by addressing issues of importance to certain women (or more generally to all women). Surely the development of women's consciousness is not simply a short-term response to the actions of the Reagan administration. Yet, it would be false to conclude that Reagan and his policies have had no effect on the politicization of gender identity. On the contrary, a measure of Reagan approval is statistically significant (0.05 level) when added to the 1984 equation in Table 6.7. Moreover, Reagan's attack on welfare policies was surely a major catalyst behind the increased impact of welfare policy preferences on gender consciousness in 1984.

Similarly, it would be a mistake to conclude that the increased politicization has moved women uniformly in a liberal, pro-feminist direction. Over the long term this has been the principle thrust of politicization, but the outcomes associated with rising gender consciousness have not been confined to this. The stronger correlations in 1984 between consciousness and some political variables show that women have also become more polarized on various questions of public policy. Clearly, group identification among women as a whole is not at the same level of solidarity, nor does it hold the same implications for policy cohesiveness, that is found for some other subordinate groups, such as blacks.

The more enduring and most important element in the development of gender consciousness, however, involves perceptions of the relative status of women in society. An increasing proportion of women are coming to view the lower status of women in society as unjust and requiring change gained through political action. As long as women earn less than men for comparable work; as long as women occupy fewer positions of influence despite comparable levels of competence; and as long as the predominant male ideology maintains that their position of privilege is legitimate, gender consciousness will continue to rise and become increasingly politicized.

Appendix

The six substantive indices used in the multivariate analysis were selected by performing a factor analysis on relevant variables. Those items loading above 0.5 were included; in some cases special exception was made to make the indices compatible across the survey years. What follows is a list of the items used in each index. Those items denoted with an * were also used to construct the percentage difference indices reported in Table 6. Variables used in scale construction were recoded when necessary so that the scales represent low positions consistent with substantive meanings discussed in the text.

1972

EQROLE   Men are born with more drive to be ambitious and successful than women. (A/D)

By nature women are happiest when they are making a home and caring for children. (A/D)

In general, men are more qualified than women for jobs that have a great deal of responsibility. (A/D)

Recently there has been a lot of talk about women's rights. Some people feel that women should have an equal role with men in running business, industry, and government. Others feel that women's place is in the home. Where would you place yourself on this scale? (7-point scale)*

BLAME   Our schools teach women to want the less important jobs. (A/D)

Our society discriminates against women. (A/D)*

WELFARE   Should the government in Washington see to it that black* people get fair treatment in jobs or leave these matters to the states and local communities? (7-point scale)

1984

Men are just better cut out than women for important positions in society. (A/D)

Most men are better suited emotionally for politics than are most women. (A/D)

This country would be better off if we worried less about how equal people are. (A/D)

Most people who don't get ahead should not blame the system; they have only themselves to blame. (A/D)

We have gone too far in pushing equal rights in this country. (A/D)

Some people feel that the government in Washington should make every effort to improve the social and economic position of women. Others feel that the government should not make any special effort to help women because they should help themselves. (7-point scale)

1972

Some people feel that the government in Washington should make every effort to improve the social and economic position of blacks and other minority groups. Others feel that the government should not make any special effort to help minorities because they should help themselves. (7-point scale)

Some people feel the government in Washington should see to it that every person has a job and a good standard of living. Others think that the government should just let each person get ahead on his own. (7-point scale)*

1984

Some people think the government should provide fewer services, even in areas such as health and education, in order to reduce spending . . . . Other people feel it is important for government to provide many more services even if it means an increase in spending . . . . (7-point scale)

WAR

With regard to Vietnam, some people think we should do everything necessary to win a complete military victory, no matter what results. Some people think we should withdraw completely from Vietnam right now, no matter what results. (7-point scale)

How about the chances of our country getting into a bigger war? Compared to a few years ago, do you think we are more likely, less likely, or have about the same chances to get into a bigger war?

Some people believe we should spend much less money on defence. Others feel that defence spending should be greatly increased. (7-point scale)*

How worried are you about our country getting into a conventional war at this time, one in which nuclear weapons are not used? Are you very worried, somewhat worried, or not worried at all?

How worried are you about our country getting into a nuclear war at this time? Are you very worried, somewhat worried, or not worried at all?

ECONPERS

Would you say you (and your family) are better off or worse off financially than you were a year ago?

Now, looking ahead, do you think that a year from now you and your family will be better off financially, or worse off, or just about the same as now?

ECONNATL

Would you say at the present time business conditions are better or worse than they were a year ago?

And how about a year from now, do you expect that in the country as a whole business conditions will be better or worse than they are at present or just about the same?

Notes

1. Another distinction of importance is that between the identification of an in-group member and the sympathetic identification of someone who is not a member of the objectively defined categorical group. A wealthy person, for example, may identify with poor people and may express a sense of shared interest with the poor and be politically supportive of poor people as a group. Nevertheless, there are important differences between this sympathetic identification and the group identification expressed by a poor person. The potentially negative impact on one's self-image that can accompany identification with a subordinate group is clearly absent for the rich sympathizer. Also, others will not treat or act toward the rich person as if they are poor just because they identify sympathetically with the poor. Because of these differences our substantive focus is identification among objectively defined group members, not sympathetic identification.

2. The actual survey question used to measure a minimal degree of identification was: 'Here is a list of some of the groups we just asked you about. Please read over this list and tell me the letter for those groups you feel particularly close to – people who are most like you in their ideas, interests and feelings about things.'

3. In 1984 'feminists' was added to the list of groups from which the respondent was asked to select the one group to which they felt 'closest'. Only 1.1% of women selected feminists as their closest groups. When constructing the gender identification measure those women who selected 'feminists' were combined with those who chose 'women' as their closest group.

4. Subordinate groups are usually liberal or change oriented; dominant or traditional groups are status quo oriented. We are interested here in subordinate groups.

5. The increased correlation is not simply an artefact of increasing the variance on the independent variable (identification versus consciousness) nor is it all due to using the women's liberation thermometer. In a regression analysis with each of the five different political variables of Table 6.5 as the dependent measure and two independent variables (identification and the women's liberation thermometer), identification remains significant. In short, both identification and collective orientation add to the explanation for political behaviour. In addition, when gender consciousness II is added to this analysis it is significant in two-thirds of the equations. Thus, consciousness adds some explanatory power over and above the individual components from which it is constructed.

Although consciousness II is used for the data presentation in Table 6.5 the results with consciousness I are very similar. The correlations are slightly weaker with consciousness I but in every case they are still stronger than with identification alone, and across-time increase in the correlation is evident for both measures.

6. This is an important substantive distinction that invites further analysis aimed at differentiating the 'not identified' and 'low' categories, and comparing each of them separately with the 'high' consciousness group. Such a task, however, goes beyond the scope of this paper. In short, our analysis, for lack of space, ignores the slightly non-monotonic patterns that appear in the PDI values of Table 6.5. The curvilinear relationships in Table 6.5, however, are primarily evident when partisanship is involved. Given that our goal is to test for increased relationships between gender consciousness and political behaviours and attitudes more generally, the combination of PDIs and Pearson correlations in Table 6.5 are adequate for our research purpose.

7. At the same time the data of Figure 6.5 should not be misunderstood to mean that black women are increasingly identifying with the women's movement while showing less support for blacks as a group. Race consciousness among black women has remained relatively stable and at a high level for the entire period from 1972 to 1984, just as suggested by Table 6.1. In short, race rather than gender remains the primary focus of social identity for black women.

8. The hypotheses and theories discussed above propose a number of alternative explanations for individual variation in gender consciousness. These theories treat the explanatory variables as exogenous, but we realize that consciousness may in turn influence certain of these explanatory factors. Although the combination of data in Tables 6.6 and 6.7 provides evidence from which inferences about causality might be drawn, our task here is a more modest one. We are primarily interested in sorting out the direct effects that consistently influence an expression of gender consciousness at more than one point in time. We would have preferred to perform the same analysis in additional years, but comparable measures were available only in 1972 and 1984.

9. Marital status, contrary to what some have argued (Plissner, 1983; Zeigler and Poole, 1985), played no significant role in either promoting or deterring the development of gender consciousness. Similarly, working outside the home was not consistently related with the politicization of gender identity, although it did have some impact in 1984. In part, the weak influence of work status may arise from the fact that some women work outside the home because of economic necessity rather than free choice. The interpretation of the work status variable is also complicated because self-selection into the work-place is confounded with change in attitudes that may take place after a woman enters the work situation. In addition, as Sapiro (1983, 1986) has noted, women generally work in sex-segregated occupations that tend to maintain traditional norms. The politicization of gender does not simply occur because women enter the work-place. Rather, they must still come to the realization that they are in positions that lead to discrimination against women as a group before we can theoretically expect any political ramifications to develop.

References

Anderson, Kristi and Elizabeth A. Cook (1985) 'Women, Work, and Political Attitudes', *American Journal of Political Science* 29: 606–25.

Baxter, Sandra and Marjorie Lansing (1980) *Women and Politics: The Invisible Majority*. Ann Arbor, Mich.: University of Michigan Press.

Boles, Janet K. (1979) *The Politics of the Equal Rights Amendment: Conflict and the Decision Process*. New York: Longman.

Deitch, Cynthia H. (1986) 'The Gender Gap and the Backlash Against the Welfare State', in Carol Mueller (ed.), *The Politics of the Gender Gap*. Beverly Hills, CA: Sage.

Frankovic, Kathleen A. (1982) 'Sex and Politics – New Alignments, Old Politics', *PS* 115: 438–48.

Gelb, Joyce and Marian Leif Palley (1982) *Women and Public Policies*. Princeton, NJ: Princeton University Press.

Gurin, Patricia (1985) 'Women's Gender Consciousness', *Public Opinion Quarterly* 49: 143–63.

Gurin, Patricia, Arthur H. Miller, and Gerald Gurin (1980) 'Stratum Identification and Consciousness', *Social Psychology Quarterly* 43: 30–47.

Heideprien, Nikki and Celinda C. Lake (1987) 'The Women's Vote: The Winning Edge', *The Policy Report* 3(7): 1, 6–7.

Holter, Harriet (1970) *Sex Roles and Social Structure*. Oslo: Universitetsforlaget.

Jackman, Mary R. and Robert W. Jackman (1973) 'An Interpretation of the Relation Between Objective and Subjective Social Systems', *American Sociological Review* 38: 569–82.

Kenski, Henry (1986) 'The Gender Factor in the Changing Electorate', in Carol Mueller (ed.), *The Politics of the Gender Gap*. Beverly Hills, CA: Sage.

Klein, Ethel (1984) *Gender Politics*. Cambridge, MA: Harvard University Press.

Lake, Celinda (1982) 'Guns, Butter, and Equality: The Women's Vote in 1980'. Paper presented at the Annual Meeting of the Midwest Political Science Association, 28 April–1 May, Milwaukee, Wisconsin.

Mansbridge, Jane (1985) 'Myth and Reality: The ERA and the Gender Gap in the 1980 Election', *Public Opinion Quarterly* 49: 164–78.

Miller, Arthur H. (1983) 'The Emerging Gender Gap in American Elections', *Election Politics* 1: 7–12.

Miller, Arthur H., Patricia Gurin, Gerald Gurin, and Oksana Malanchuk (1981) 'Group Consciousness and Political Participation', *American Journal of Political Science* 25: 494–511.

Plissner, Martin (1983) 'The Marriage Gap', *Public Opinion* 6(1): 53.

Pomper, Gerald (1975) *Voter's Choice: Varieties of Electoral Behavior*. New York: Dodd, Mead and Co.

Sapiro, Virginia (1983) *The Political Integration of Women: Roles, Socialization and Politics*. Urbana, IL: University of Illinois Press.

Sapiro, Virginia (1986) 'The Effects of Gender Segregation of Work on Political Orientations and Behaviour'. Presented at the Annual Meeting of the International Society for Political Psychology, July, Amsterdam.

Steiner, Gilbert Y. (1985) *Constitutional Inequality: The Political Fortunes of the Equal Rights Amendment*. Washington, DC: Brookings Institution.

Tajfel, Henri (1981) *Human Groups and Social Categories: Studies in Social Psychology*. Cambridge: Cambridge University Press.

Verba, Sidney and Norman H. Nie (1972) *Participation in America: Political Democracy and Social Equality*. New York: Harper and Row.

Zeigler, Harmon and Keith Poole (1985) 'Political Women: Gender Indifference', *Public Opinion* 8(4): 54–6.

7

Under Permanent Guardianship: Women's Condition under Modern Civil Law

Ursula Vogel

Introduction

In contemporary feminist theory a legal understanding of women's oppression – often associated with the dominance of liberal values and modes of analysis – has been subjected to much criticism. Its focal point is perhaps no longer the gap between the official egalitarian ideology that supplies the normative frame of legislation in liberal democracies, on the one hand, and women's concrete experience of overt and covert discrimination, on the other. Rather, disillusionment seems to have enveloped the very core of the belief that equality before the law – the goal envisaged by nineteenth-century feminists – could ever bring about those fundamental social and cultural changes that would enable women – as women – to exercise the rights and duties of citizenship. Although socialist and radical feminists will differ as to whether the primary causes of women's oppression should be sought in the sphere of economic production or in the power mechanisms operating on the level of personal relationships, they are in agreement that a legalistic approach, with its concentration on the formal guarantees and opportunities of individual independence, is inadequate both as a tool of analysis and as a strategy for emancipation (Jaggar, 1983: 173–206; Smart, 1984; 3–23; Brown, 1986; Rhode, 1986). For such an approach cannot but conceal the ubiquitous and unique forms of power which men exercise over women within the patriarchal structures of marriage and the work-place. Moreover, the demands that arise from women's role as mothers and home-makers and, in particular, from their lack of access to the basic resources of personal independence tend to fall outside the claims which liberal legal systems – with their rigid distinction between rights and needs – will recognize as legitimate.

It is the distinct feature of modern law that it applies uniform standards to different individuals in different situations. Thus, in order to fit women and men into the same uniform category of legal persona and right-holder the law must altogether abstract from the separate identities that they may have as members of a particular sexual group. This abstract universalism has also informed the notion of citizenship in classical political theory. It leaves little space for reflecting upon the particular claims that women, as citizens, might be entitled to make on the democratic welfare state, nor conversely on their specific contributions to the affairs of the community (Hernes, 1986). If we believe that women have interests and needs significantly different from those of men and, furthermore, that these constitute not disabilities but sources of identity and strength, then the construction of a uniform genderless agent and, with it, the central premise of modern legal thinking must become problematic.

This does not mean, however, that the law should be written out of the feminist critique and reconstruction of the dominant paradigms of political analysis. For if we want to explore the full dimensions of gender as a social relation, we cannot bypass the legal determinations of power and dependence that shape the lives of women and men through the institutions of marriage and family. In using concepts like 'male domination' and 'female oppression' we do not, as in the case of parent and child, refer to relationships born of, and bounded by, natural disparities. We confront a complex web of social roles, the demands of which extend far beyond any given biological characteristics. The law has played a major part in determining these roles and thus the social significance that we attribute to natural differences (O'Donovan, 1982: 344–6). Such a claim does not necessarily imply that relations of patriarchal power are *created* by legislation and judicial practice. But it does draw attention to the ideological and institutional mechanisms through which they have been sustained (Smart, 1984: 22).

There are then compelling reasons why the law should remain a major concern of feminists and, furthermore, why feminist political theory should seek closer links with legal theory and legal history. In so far as the law operates through a system of normative principles and values capable of generating social consensus, it has always shaped the general intellectual context within which political thinkers have conceptualized problems of power, authority, justice, and citizenship. The fact that the institutional models supplied by positive law (for example, marriage) are typically not reflected upon by normative political theory makes it all the more necessary that we lay bare this 'silent' incorporation of traditional gender roles into an allegedly universalist and abstract philosophical argument. Liberal thinkers like Locke and Kant – and with them the major exponents of egalitarian Natural Law – offer a good example of how the application of the universalist postulate of equal natural rights is disrupted by the implicit acceptance of women's permanently inferior status – as defined by contemporary legal institutions (Brennan and Pateman, 1979; Okin, 1982; Eisenstein, 1981).

It is the aim of this book to unravel the conceptual distinctions between the general attributes by which we commonly identify individuals as legal persons and citizens – without regard, that is, to their special circumstances, interests, and needs – and the unique characteristics that those individuals share as members of a particular sex. An historical reconstruction of the different phases in the process of women's emancipation will emphasize that such distinctions must be understood in their historically specific and changing meanings. Thus, for the contemporaries of Mary Wollstonecraft and Condorcet the inclusion of women in the universalist idea of equal right stood in a closer relation to their true identity, and had greater relevance as the indispensable condition of their liberation, than is the case for many feminists today (Vogel, 1986).

In this chapter I want to show in some detail why at this earlier stage in the evolution of modern society – a period whose intellectual horizons derived from the Enlightenment and the democratic revolutions in America and France – the exclusion of women both from the entitlements and the obligations of civil law could be perceived as the primary cause of their oppression. For this purpose I shall examine the new codifications of civil law that were enacted in the period of the French Revolution. My main point of reference will be the Prussian Civil Code of 1794. In order to obtain a clearer profile of the underlying general assumptions common to many European legal systems of the time, I shall occasionally draw upon corresponding provisions of the Code Napoléon (1804) as well as on English Common Law. It is hoped that the analysis of legal institutions and of the general norms from which they derive legitimation will allow us to place the concepts central to feminist discourse – patriarchy, oppression, emancipation – in a context of concrete and precise meaning. There is no doubt that the legal construction of women's particular identity, that is, the nature and extent of their legal disabilities, presents us with tangible evidence of a unique form of power – although it is less clear where we should look for a conclusive explanation of its cause.

The first section attempts to establish the fact of women's 'oppression' by the extent of their rightlessness. Two qualifications are necessary at the outset. In speaking of 'women' we have to bear in mind a crucial distinction: all the legal codes under discussion here treated the single woman differently from the wife and mother. Only on the latter did the law impose conditions which deprived her, in principle, of personal independence. The distinction was most sharply drawn by the English Common Law under which single women, whether spinsters or widows, enjoyed by and large the same civil rights as men. Even in Continental legal systems where for a long time all women had been subordinated to the institution of sex-guardianship, this dependency was gradually relaxed for the single woman. At the beginning of the nineteenth century, it survived only in the requirement that in any court dealings she had to be represented by a male curator (whom she could choose herself and who possessed no power to interfere with her property and business arrangements). For the defenders of the status quo this difference in legal status between the unmarried and the married woman was bound to produce considerable problems of legitimation. Given the capacity for personal independence that the law accorded to the single woman it was impossible to base the subordination of the wife upon an assumption of the *natural* disabilities of the female sex as a whole. In her case inequality of right could be justified only by reference to the special *political* functions of marriage (and the family). Yet, recourse to the immutable imperatives of sexual nature remained indispensable if one wanted to place the separation of private and public spheres on firmer ground than mere political expediency and, most importantly if one wanted to sustain the exclusion of all women from the rights of political participation, irrespective of whether they possessed, as many single women did, all the assets required for the vote.

Moreover, in what follows my argument will most often refer to the legal conditions of married women because I want to look at civil, not political, rights as the primary site of women's oppression. Following T.H. Marshall's distinction between different conceptual and historical meanings of 'citizenship' (Marshall, 1976) the term 'civil rights' will focus on the rights to personal freedom (including those to one's body and labour), to the acquisition and disposal of property, and further on the rights of contract and of access to the courts. It was this set of rights, which before the struggle for political enfranchisement in the nineteenth century, conferred upon an individual the status of a 'citizen'. It is sometimes forgotten that until then the most conspicuous proof of women's inferior position in society did not lie in their exclusion from the vote. The rights of active citizenship were denied to many other groups. But women alone – at least in countries where slavery and serfdom had been abolished – stood outside the boundaries not only of the political community but also of civil society itself. Their position in relation to men was in some respects analogous to that of children, in others to that of slaves and serfs. Since the very concept of civil society refers to an association whose members are bound together by common laws, women were, in this sense, not properly 'persons'. In the eyes of the law they did not exist, being dependent upon others to represent them in court, to administer their property, to make decisions for their children.

The second section will explore the peculiar normative context of women's legal subordination. It will examine the persistent legacy of older moral and religious beliefs such as those embodied in the medieval institution of sex-guardianship, as well as the impact of new ideas that had been developed in eighteenth-century Natural Law. Its major innovation lay in the postulate of men's universal capacity for rights (*allgemeine Rechtsfähigkeit*) as the basis of positive law. Yet this postulate which transformed the very foundations of modern civil law hardly affected the position of women. What could justify their continued legal disabilities at a time when the members of other hitherto disadvantaged groups (such as Jews, serfs, aliens) were gradually admitted to the rights of citizenship? If, for example, the ideas of the Enlightenment sparked off a heightened public awareness of the 'Jewish Question', what blocked the similar perception of a 'woman's question'?

The concluding section will suggest that in the domain of modern ideological developments women's delayed emancipation can be related to the emergence of a new – bourgeois – patriarchalism. It gradually obliterated the emancipatory potential that could have been derived from Natural Law and its contractual, 'legalistic' understanding of all social relationships, private as well as public. The most potent device of this new ideology was to refurbish, and thus to lend new credence to, older notions of women's distinct sexual nature. The conception of their separate identity lost the cruder connotations of biological inferiority and became amalgamated with the ideal of the family as an organic community whose superior ethical life and special political mission in modern society elevated it to a sphere outside and above the law.

Woman's Rights and Rightlessness under Civil Law: the Example of the Prussian Civil Code

'There remain no legal slaves, except the mistress of every house' (Mill, 1984: 323). That the legal condition of women in modern society was virtually indistinguishable from the institution of slavery was a common phrase in the political vocabulary of nineteenth-century feminism. Like the members of other oppressed groups, the advocates of women's equal rights made use of this analogy in order to uproot deeply entrenched prejudices. The task was to change the perception of familiar practices by assimilating them to the most extreme form of unfreedom.

How accurately does a concept that conveys a sense of total rightlessness describe the status of women as defined by the new legal codes of the Enlightenment period (Conrad, 1957)? The laws themselves did not, of course, speak the language of slavery, subjugation, inferiority, or even inequality. Legislators did not overtly discriminate against women by excluding them from rights granted to all subjects. The Prussian Code, for example, seemed to place them in the same category of legal persons as all other subjects: '(Man (*der Mensch*) is called a person in so far as he/she enjoys certain rights in civil society' (*Landrecht*, 1794: I, 1, §1). Moreover, it explicitly proclaimed the equality of women and men: 'The rights of both sexes are equal, unless exceptions are stated by special laws or valid declarations of will' (*Landrecht*: I, 1, §24). This general egalitarian norm is reflected in the definition, new in German law, of marriage as a civil contract valid only because of the 'free consent of both parts', as well as in the emphasis placed upon the reciprocal character of conjugal rights and obligations. As regards common residence, mutual assistance and the performance of 'the conjugal duty' (*Landrecht*: II, 1, §§173–83) husband and wife were held to have the same obligations towards each other. In return for her special duty to supervise the household according to her husband's social standing, a wife received, together with the name, all the rights associated with his social rank. She had a claim to be adequately provided for and to be protected and defended by him in all juridical and non-juridical matters in the outside world.

However, while in these general formulations marriage could appear as a partnership based upon equal exchange and mutual benefit, the principle of equality was soon revoked in the unequivocal affirmation of marital power within a hierarchical relationship: 'The husband is the head of the conjugal association and his decision prevails in all common affairs' (*Landrecht*, II, 1, §184). This ultimate power of decision was still accorded to the husband in the Civil Code of the German Empire, enacted in 1900. With regard to all those rights which together ensure the practical reality of personal independence women were treated as if they were children – human beings in need of special protection and supervision. Thus, women were deemed incapable of engaging in litigation in their own right (they could not sue, or be sued, in court). They could not make valid contracts in their own name, and without the permission of husbands or fathers they were not free to set up their own business, for example, or to take up a job. Barring certain exceptions, which will be cited below, a woman would, at no point in her life, emerge from this state of guardianship. Its powers passed from father to husband or to another male relative. Unlike sons, unmarried daughters could remain subject to paternal control even after they had reached the age of majority (Twellman, 1972: 199; Evans, 1976: 11–19).

Women's rights did not fare much better in relation to their children. Although the law commanded respect and obedience towards both parents, and although it recognized the mother's special responsibility for the physical well-being of infants – all decisions affecting their education and future life prospects rested in the last instance with the father: children stood 'primarily under paternal power' (*Landrecht*, II, 2, §74).

'A person unable to acquire property is a slave' (Otto-Peters, 1866: 103). This statement of a leading German feminist reflects the priority accorded by the nineteenth-century women's movement to woman's economic independence, to her right to work and freely to dispose of her own goods. It also points to the centrality of property in the liberal conception of citizenship: a person's standing in civil society is predicated upon, and co-extensive with, the rights of ownership. Because of the conceptual interchangeability of individual freedom and proprietary rights, and because property alone is thought to confer that independence which secures each individual against the arbitrary power of others, legal disabilities in this domain would most convincingly affirm the analogy between women and slaves.

In none of the legal systems under consideration did the regulation of marital property conform to the idea of marriage as a freely contracted partnership. In different forms – the complexity of which cannot detain us here – they all placed a wife's property under the administration and control of her husband (Weber, 1907: 217–55, 318–41; Huebner, 1918: 621–56; Basch, 1982: 15–69; Holcombe, 1983). His powers extended not only to the goods which she brought into marriage or which she might acquire, through gift and inheritance, afterwards. Most significantly as regards the increasing number of working women, the law regarded him as the sole owner of what she had earned by her own labour: 'What a wife acquires, she acquires, as a rule, for her husband' (*Landrecht*, II, 1, §211). The law allowed, on the other hand, for certain exceptions (mainly to the benefit of daughters from wealthy families), which did assume that a woman was entitled to hold property in her own name and which by implication acknowledged her status as a legal agent. One such exemption concerned the special status of landed estates which a husband could not alienate without his wife's consent. In addition, the Prussian Code made provisions for her to acquire undiminished property rights to all her goods under the legal form of a 'reserved estate' (*Vorbehaltsgut*), depending on special contractual arrangements between the spouses. It was, above all, this innovation of granting to women separate property and, with it, the condition of personal independence which the conservative critics of the Code denounced as a threat to the very nature of the marriage relation: 'If a wife has to entrust her husband with her body, her honour, her children and, indeed, her whole happiness, it would seem to follow – and is surely only a trivial matter – that she should also entrust him with her property' (quoted in Gerhard, 1978: 87).

What does this catalogue of denied rights – of particular privileges and obligations, complemented by special provisions for exceptional cases – tell us about the nature and extent of women's oppression? As their most conspicuous feature the new civil law codifications of the Enlightenment betray a fundamental ambiguity rather than the unified and single-minded determination to suppress women. Different categories of women were treated differently. Thus women (often widows) who carried out a business or trade in their own name enjoyed considerable contractual and litigational powers. Single women in general – this was especially true of the English case – had a more independent standing in law than wives. Even the latter, as we have seen, might in some instances be considered as legal persons in their own right (that is, as property owners) while in others they remained part of, and an appendage to, the *persona* of fathers or husbands. Egalitarian principles found their clearest expression in the contractual definition of marriage and, if we consider the innovations of the Prussian Code, in the relatively liberal and non-discriminatory provisions for divorce (Buchholz, 1981a; Frevert, 1986: 54–6). Yet given the numerous incidents of sovereign power placed at the disposal of the husband, there can be little doubt that legislators had no intention of subverting the traditional hierarchical structure of the family.

We must evaluate the attitude of the law towards women from two perspectives. The dominant ideology of the time – rendered explicit in the voices of those who drafted, enacted, and commented upon, the new legal codes – would suggest that the subordination of woman to the will of man was devised mainly for her own benefit. The most self-confident assertion of this view can be found in Blackstone's well-known phrase: '. . . we may observe, that even the disabilities which the wife lies under, are for the most part intended for her protection and benefit. So great a favourite is the female sex of the laws of England' (Blackstone, 1765: I, 433). If, on the other hand, we refer to the idea of personal autonomy as the self-proclaimed normative centre of modern civil law and if on that basis we deny any comparability between the condition of women and that of children, we will describe the legally constructed relation between the sexes in terms of domination and subjugation, of force in the guise of benevolence, of rights claimed by masters over their servants.

This last point raises an issue of wider significance on which feminists have always been sharply divided. The reasons for which the law has in the past withheld from women the recognition of their full entitlement to equal rights have typically been cast in the language of their special needs and particular sexual identity. Legal disabilities of the kind that we have analysed above entailed both the restriction of individual freedom *and* the exemption from ordinary obligations. In other words, the privileges and powers granted to men could be justified as but the corollary of their special duties and liabilities. This blurred distinction between the dimensions of power and protection in the law's discriminatory treatment of women must be taken as the characteristic and unique feature of their 'oppression', compared to the condition of other underprivileged groups.

For feminists who argue from a liberal position there is of course no ambiguity. They have always categorically rejected women's privileges under the law, whether as mere embellishment of a fundamental injustice or as the posture of paternalist solicitude equally incompatible with the status of an autonomous agent (Wollstonecraft, 1975: 153; Mill, 1984: 284). Yet many women have, in past and present, been reluctant to give up the benefits of protective legislation and have been suspicious of the language of equal rights precisely because such equality, it would seem, can be purchased only at the price of exposed vulnerability (Banks, 1981: 106–16; Rhode, 1986: 56; Shanley, 1986: 67–77). Moreover, where feminists assume that the special needs of women are an essential, rather than a contingent, attribute of their identity as human beings, they might want to see this particularity recognized in the differential treatment of women and men under the law. The question is, however, whether we can at all conceive of a legal system in which such differentiation would not carry the connotation of strength and weakness and would not, as a consequence, become entrenched in relations of power and dependence.

A reflection on the entrenchment of patriarchal power in the historical foundations of modern civil law will elucidate some general problems that would have to be overcome in reconciling the demands of justice to an endorsement of women's and men's separate identity.

**Natural Dependence and Voluntary Submission:
the Normative Foundations in the Legal Definition of Women**

Mundium and Sex-guardianship

The recognition of all human beings as legal persons and right-holders is of relatively recent origin – the constitutive mark only of modern legal systems (Huebner, 1918: 42–4; Thieme, 1962). By contrast, older traditions distinguished between the legal worth of individuals: whether, as in primitive law, primarily on grounds of natural, biological differences (sex, age, health) or according to a divinely sanctioned hierarchy of ascribed status, as in the medieval and feudal ordering of society. To stand outside the law, that is, to be incorporated in the legal *persona* of another individual, defined not only the condition of women and children but of many other groups and categories of people (slaves, serfs, apprentices, domestic servants). It was only in the eighteenth century that the beliefs which legitimated such exclusions gradually lost credibility: 'Nowadays we no longer presume that there are human beings (*Menschen*) who are not persons in law (*Rechtssubjekte*)' (quoted in Conrad, 1956, from a legal commentary of 1800).

In common with legal practices that prevailed in the earliest history of most civilized peoples, ancient Germanic law assumed a fundamental difference between the sexes. The high esteem accorded to women's moral standing in the community and their important role in its economic organization stood in stark contrast to their total legal subordination. Like the other members of the extended kinship network they existed in society's legal and political life solely through the mediacy of the houselord (patriarch). The character of his rule is conveyed in the term *mundium* (Germanic 'munt') which refers to the hand as a symbol of absolute power. For our present purpose of ascertaining the nature of women's dependence the salient feature in this early form of male domination lies not only in its brutality but in its 'political' character. That is, as fathers and husbands men possessed towards women rights and responsibilities – sovereign powers of command, control, and punishment – which in our modern understanding of the law are assigned to the public authority (Maine, 1863, ch. 5). A husband could with impunity kill a wife guilty of adultery; he had the unquestioned right to chastise her, lock her up, deprive her of food. Primitive law barely distinguished between the attributes pertaining to the ownership of things and the quasi-proprietory power over other persons. Conversely, the houselord bore full responsibility for all damages claimed against those included in his *dominium* (on the same grounds that he was held liable for damages caused by his domestic animals).

In its earliest manifestations – in the Roman *patria potestas* as well as in the Germanic *munt* – patriarchal domination thus presented itself as the undivided unity of personal and political power. It did not allow for the distinction between a man's will and his right to make and enforce laws, barring any appeal to a superior judge outside the domain of the house. Although folk custom and, later, Christian religion mitigated the harsher elements of brute force, patriarchal power retained, for centuries to come, its essentially political character – as a quasi-public authority interposed between women and the state. For notwithstanding the fact that women became liable for criminal offences, that they acquired the right to inherit property, and could in certain circumstances seek protection and redress at court – they remained outside the public sphere. Unlike other categories of people previously bonded to private power they were not, as subjects and citizens, placed under the direct authority of the sovereign state. In the medieval institution of sex-guardianship which transmitted the structure of the Germanic *munt* into modern times, their legal existence continued to be enclosed in that of men.

What were the normative ideas that sustained this seemingly unbroken continuity of male power? On what grounds did the law discriminate between women and men? Here, in the changing historical forms of legal ideology, we can discern a significant shift in emphasis. It highlights a fundamental ambivalence in patriarchal power which we have already observed in a different context and which may account for its often-observed capacity for self-mystification. Initially, it was women's alleged bodily weakness that justified her complete dependence on men. Since membership in the Germanic community required the capacity to bear arms and since legal disputes were of a kind that procedural contests could at any time turn into active combat, women's 'natural' inability to perform military duties seemed to place them in a separate category of human beings – incapable of legal self-representation. Under the influence of Christianity (institutionalized in the prescriptions of the Canon Law) the right of force gave way to the duty of protection and guidance. To be sure, neither Catholic doctrine nor the teachings of the Protestant church lessened woman's duty of total submission nor her narrow confinement to the domestic sphere. Yet the reasons invoked for her inferior social status shifted to 'natural' defects of moral and intellectual character, to her lack of experience in civil affairs and consequent vulnerability to deception. It could be claimed that the law placed women under male guardianship solely for their own good. In the language of a sixteenth-century decree:

> Certain provisions have been made for female persons (*Weibspersonen*) in order that they may not, due to lack of wise council and prudence, be cheated and defrauded. Be it therefore decreed that from now on also widows and spinsters [i.e. in addition to married women], regardless of age, are unable to perform valid actions in court . . . without a guardian. Whatever obligations women may have contracted . . . without prior knowledge and authority of their marital stewards or other legal guardians – these shall be deemed invalid in cases where they would disadvantage or damage them. (Quoted in Gerhard, 1978: 465)

The notion of women's permanent, separate identity as a 'natural' group proved capable of ever new formulations and rationalizations. It has served, until our own time, to mask the social causes and the historically specific character of their subordination to men. Moreover, the emphasis on protection as a response to special needs has been able to conceal the coercive core in the power granted to men in their role as guardians. That the ascribed traits of women's sexual nature were derived from, and in turn reinforced, a special nexus of domination could perhaps not become transparent as long as, in the hierarchical cosmos of medieval law, there existed numerous other relationships within which persons of ascribed superior status held power over their 'natural' inferiors.

We have to ask, then, why the oppressive legal consequences of the medieval institution of sex-guardianship could survive virtually intact as an enclave in modern legal codes built upon egalitarian norms. The transformative ideas that inspired the legal codifications of the Enlightenment period derived to a large extent from modern Natural Law and its rational construction of civil society from the premise of men's equal moral status. Here, if anywhere, would we expect to find a decisive break with all traditional arguments that elevated the natural differences between human beings into legitimate reasons for subjugating some to the rule of others.

*The Contractual Definition of Marriage and Family
in the Natural Law of the Enlightenment*
The legal customs that eighteenth-century European society had inherited from the medieval and feudal past still preserved basic elements of an order in which rights and obligations were distributed unequally. The law addressed individuals not as separate, self-sufficient units but as members of particular groups to which they belonged by birth. The rights which they enjoyed thus depended upon a variety of natural and conventional determinations – upon their nationality and religion, their place within the

family, their occupational status and inherited social rank; to these manifold differentiations must be added the fundamental divisions according to age, sex, and health. The family mirrored the hierarchical status-based order of society at large. It was conceived as a natural, divinely ordained community that served a wide range of moral, political, and economic functions. With the exception of the father who represented the household in the world outside and who alone stood in a direct relation to the law, the rights and obligations of all other members – wife, children, servants, and other dependants – were defined and confined by their particular place and tasks *within* this community (Schwab, 1975: 270–81).

By the end of the century the traditional justifications that sustained this system of differential and particularistic rights no longer enjoyed unquestioned allegiance. They were challenged, on the one hand, by the trend towards administrative uniformity that marked the rise of the modern absolutist state and, on the other, by the secular and egalitarian ideas that had come to dominance in the development of Natural Law since the sixteenth century. As the conception of man's natural and moral state became dissociated from its affiliation with an immutable hierarchical order, individuals emerged as 'persons', divorced from the particular attributes of unequal status and defined by general, abstract qualities which they all had in common (Conrad, 1956). In attributing to all human beings indiscriminately (that is, as members of the human species) the same capacity to hold and exercise rights, modern Natural Law demolished the presuppositions of any natural or pre-ordained authority. *All* social and political arrangements derived legitimacy solely from the voluntary agreement of individuals: *all* forms of power were reduced to contractual origins (Schwab, 1972: 364f).

This shift in the foundations of legitimate power affected both the state and the family. The attack upon the divine right of rulers also eroded the unassailable position of fathers and husbands. The challenge could either take the form of altogether freeing the understanding of political power from the traditional analogy with paternal power (Locke). Or, if the familial analogy was kept intact (Pufendorf, Thomasius, Wolff) it had the effect of placing not only the state but the family, too, on a contractual basis.

In the writings of eighteenth-century German philosophers, whose influence can be traced in the programmatic statements of the Prussian Code, marriage has lost the character as an institution ordained by divine law; it is conceived purely as a contractual association. Not only does it come into being through the voluntary agreement of woman and man (both of whom enter into it with the same rights and obligations). It retains the nature of a social contract – with the implication that its purpose and duration as well as the specific character of the conjugal relationship must at all times be subject to the free will of the partners. Construed on this basis, neither the indissolubility of marriage nor even the exclusiveness of the sexual bond (monogamy) are made imperative by Natural Law:

> The purpose of marriage must be left to the free will of each of the partners; each of them may enter into marriage on whatever conditions he/she likes . . . they may conclude the marriage for as long a period as they wish and may also, given the consent of the other partner, suspend it before this time. (Pörschke, 1795, quoted in Schwab, 1972: 368)

How radically a doctrine postulating the universal capacity for rights might transform traditional notions of familial authority is shown by the fact that it also extends to children. Parental power, too, admits of no other justification than that it *could* be considered – in the presumption of a *conventio ficta* – as based upon the voluntary consent of children. It is legitimate only in so far as a child would submit to it if it were in full possession of its rational capacities:

> There is as little inequality between parents and children as between other citizens. For the parents can impose upon the child – in its own name – only those commands that the child if it were in full possession of reason, would impose upon itself. (Schwab, 1972: 373)

However, with regard to women, the end-result of such radical legitimation procedures was, again, their total subjection to the power of men. Most striking in this respect is the deceptive ease with which the general postulate of equal human rights could be compromised in order to reinstate patriarchal power within a framework of free agency and purely contractual obligations. The most common argument used to this effect subordinates the freedom of woman (not of man) to the end of marriage. Its unity and the effective pursuit of the common purposes of the household require that power be concentrated in the hands of one person. In the words of Kant:

> Hence the question may be raised as to whether it is not contrary to the equality of married persons when the law says in any way of the husband in relation to the wife, 'he shall be thy master', so that he is represented as the one who commands and she as the one who obeys. This, however, cannot be regarded as contrary to the natural equality of a human pair, if such legal supremacy is based only upon the natural superiority of the faculties of the husband compared with the wife, in the effectuation of the common interest of the household; and if the right to command is based merely upon this fact. For this right may thus be deduced from the

very duty of unity and equality in relation to the *end* involved. (Kant, 1887: 112)

This 'sovereignty-requirement' on which virtually all Natural Law theorists agree (Conrad, 1957; Rousseau, 1973: 118) rests on the premise that in the family – as in the state – there must be an unquestionable authority for issuing final decisions. Yet given the contractual basis of marriage there should, in principle, be several options for solving the problem: to make either the husband *or* the wife head of the household, or to set up a joint rule of both spouses. However, what should be an open question – to be left to the free will of the partners – is solved by the simple and virtually unanimous presumption that it is the woman who has voluntarily concluded a pact of submission renouncing her rights to her husband. But why should this outcome be taken for granted? It is argued that the continued existence and universal acceptance of a practice as widespread as the husband's commanding role in civil affairs allows us to infer the wife's tacit consent. Unchallenged tradition, it seems, implies approval. This claim is supported by the further – and equally tenacious – assertion that supreme power belongs naturally to man because of his superior strength and ability.

Neither of these reasons is, of course, compatible with the basic premises of Natural Law theorizing. The first has no legitimate place in deductive procedures which derive moral and political rules from *a priori* principles. Any appeal to the normative power of facts – that is, to mere experience, however widely registered – is thus ruled out. The second argument rehabilitates, for the relationship between men and women, the very presumption that modern Natural Law categorically bans from even a serious discussion of legitimate authority – *that might is right!* Moreover, if, as Rousseau and Kant insist, voluntary enslavement falls outside the scope of a legitimate renunciation of rights, why should this prohibition be waived in the case of women? Why should they be assumed to have surrendered their freedom to the will of another person? And why should their voluntary submission go so far as to leave them, in the eyes of the law, without any attributes of independent agency?

How are we to explain this blatant inconsistency between the universalism inherent in the postulate of equal natural rights and the continued affirmation of women's particularity? An answer that takes the strength and all-pervasiveness of patriarchal bias for granted would be unsatisfactory. It remains too unspecific to count as an explanation. For it does not confront the question why philosophers, who in many other respects broke new ground and freed themselves from commonly accepted views, should in this particular case unthinkingly affirm the prevalent prejudices of their time? Kant, for instance, rejected any claims in support of aristocratic privilege and hereditary servitude because the mere accident of birth could never be accepted as the legitimate basis of right. Why did he not even recognize a problem when he relegated women to a condition of 'natural', that is, permanent civil incompetence (Kant, 1887: 167f)?

This is obviously the core question that needs to be pursued further: why was women's exclusion from civil rights not *perceived* as an anomaly and injustice? Why was their rightlessness not judged by the same criteria as that of other oppressed groups? Women in eighteenth-century German society were by no means the only group to be deprived of civil rights, but they were the largest group to be so treated. They shared this condition with Jews, dependent peasants (who in some parts of Prussia still lived under a regime of personal servitude), domestic servants, and aliens. The impact of Enlightenment ideas, on the one hand, and the challenge posed by the French Revolution and by Prussia's defeat against Napoleon's armies, on the other, led in the first decades of the nineteenth century to a series of reforms which aimed at removing the legal disabilities of these groups in order to integrate them, as equal citizens, into the national community (Conrad, 1956; Koselleck, 1967; Rürup, 1975: 11–36).

The same arguments that lent support to the civil emancipation of Jews and serfs could have been used for the purpose of analysing and improving the condition of women. Why was hardly any voice raised on their behalf? The answer must be sought, I believe, in certain widely held assumptions which helped to consolidate women's position in, as it were, an enclave of rationalist thought. In the last section of the paper I shall examine some of the beliefs which neutralized the emancipatory impact of universalist legal norms – by blocking the comparability between the condition of women and that of other oppressed groups and, as a consequence, exempting the former from the category of unjustly treated persons. This new 'bourgeois' patriarchalism which, from the late eighteenth century onwards, developed in response to the individualistic and egalitarian presumptions of Enlightenment rationalism, and which gathered further strength from the experience of crisis and social instability engendered by the French Revolution, was not a preserve of conservative thinking alone. It transcended the common political and ideological divides of the time. Indeed, it was a characteristic phenomenon, in Germany as elsewhere, that a 'progressive' stance in the public sphere – exemplified in the commitment to a democratic franchise or in the pressure for representative institutions and an extension of civil rights – did in most cases not include a sympathetic attitude towards the issue of women's rights. More pointedly, the latter did not even appear on the political agenda of those who fought for the liberalization and democratization of public life (Dubois, 1978: 44–7; Kerber, 1980: 119–55; Rendall, 1985: 41–54).

To take the German case in the first decades of the nineteenth century: liberals differed from conservatives on such politically divisive issues as the introduction of civil marriage and the conditions of divorce. Such disagreement did not, however, affect the general consensus that the inner space of marriage should retain its traditionally hierarchical structure (Schwab, 1975: 284–99; Buchholz, 1981a: 7–16). Yet, given the hostility which bourgeois liberalism displayed towards the 'unjust' privileges of birth claimed by the aristocracy this view on women's proper role in society could not legitimate itself by an outright attack upon the principle of equal right. Women's continued subordination had therefore to be argued within an altogether different intellectual framework which would render the perception of their condition immune to considerations of justice and right.

The New Patriarchalism

Already the last decades of the eighteenth century saw a proliferation of popular treatises devoted to the study of 'sexual character' (*Geschlechts character*) (Gerhard, 1978: 124–52; Hausen, 1981; Frevert, 1986: 21–5, 63–5). They are good indications of the apprehension and disquietude engendered by the apparent determination of upper- and middle-class women to establish a place for themselves outside the circle of domestic duties. (It must be remembered, however, that in this period in Germany the threat arose not from a demand for political rights but rather from the desire to join men as equals in the domains of education, literature, and, in general, sociability). In order to counter this threat effectively, woman's special role in modern society had to be re-connected to the immutable imperatives of her biological nature. It was however a distinctly new element in these legitimations that they no longer presented the differences between the sexes in terms of superiority and inferiority. The focus on the *complementarity* of sexual character ensured that the corresponding differentiations of rights and duties would not appear as instances of inequality and injustice.

Whether the arguments deployed for this purpose claimed a specious scientific validity for psychological speculations, whether they appealed to the allegedly unanimous testimony of history or simply to common-sense judgements of proper conduct – the conclusion invariably confirmed woman's natural dependence on man, albeit in the guise of paying tribute to the special excellencies of her sex. It is unnecessary here to deal at length with the tedious catalogues of sexual stereotype which juxtapose, in a highly predictable manner, dominant female attributes – such as gentleness, delicate feeling, intuitive understanding, refined taste, passivity – to the male disposition of vigour, strength, courage, self-determination, analytical reasoning (together with every writer's pet ideas about the different forms and degrees of female sexual passion). The unquestioned acceptance of such beliefs may be judged from the fact that a philosopher like Kant rose, in this respect, hardly above the common run of conservative moralists who repeated *ad nauseam* the ideas of Rousseau's *Émile*. The political significance of this obsession to determine the unchangeable core of sexual character lay in the claim that nature has so equipped women as to direct their whole existence towards that of other people. Their very excellences are inextricably bound up with this essential instrumentality: a woman becomes a person only through marriage and only through her husband. To stand in a direct and independent relationship to the laws, that is, to exist as a person in civil society, is thus neither necessary nor, indeed, possible: 'A man belongs to his city, his fatherland, to all mankind. Not so woman. . . . Woman can give proof of her virtues only within the most intimately personal relationships. If she lacks these, she lacks everything' (Brandes, 1802: 97).

Drafts for the – extremely conservative – family law of the Code Napoléon show how Rousseau's doctrine of the complementary nature of the sexes could be used not only to justify the restoration of a near-absolute *puissance maritale*, but to do so by reference to the requirements of republican citizenship (Schwartz, 1984: 41–73). Women's seclusion in the patriarchal family appears here not as a contradiction to, but as the necessary complement and the moral basis of the democratically ordered polity: it is the mark of despotism that in order to reduce all subjects to slaves it must aim at weakening all other powers in society. Republics by contrast will use the strength of domestic rule as a means to mitigate, without danger, the power of the magistrate over the citizen. Marital *dominium* is thus understood as an essentially republican institution: 'Among free people this power has always been particularly extended and respected' (Portalis, quoted in Conrad, 1957).

It is the salient point in this argumentation that it defines the nature of women and their particular duties (exclusively as wives

and mothers) in a manner that attributes highest political significance to their non-political status. In these terms, their position
outside the law would not be recognized as an injustice but, on the
contrary, as the condition on which alone the good society could
flourish.

In nineteenth-century Germany the new patriarchalism asserted
itself in a political context divorced from any connotations with
democratic citizenship. In the repressive climate of the Restoration
period the family came to be looked upon as the most effective
instrument to contain the egalitarian tendencies of a revolutionary
age. Conservatives were most concerned to reverse the liberal
provisions for divorce secured in the Prussian Code. To counter the
corrosive idea of marriage as a contractual association founded
upon mutual interest they elevated the conjugal bond to the higher
plane of the nation's ethical life. As an organic community,
marriage stood above the contractual arrangements of the market-
place and was not at the disposal of the individual's momentary and
arbitrary desires (Buchholz, 1979). From the pronouncements of
conservative philosophers and jurists (among them Hegel and Carl
Friedrich von Savigny, the founder of the Historical School of Law)
it is evident that the organic ideal of the family was in the first
instance addressed to women and was anchored in the notion of
their separate sexual nature. While man, in Hegel's words, secured
his true identity in that real, substantive life which was to be found
only in the realm of the state and of academic scholarship, woman,
as the guardian of pure morality, could find fulfilment only in the
inner sanctuary of domestic life.

Unlike the older, pre-bourgeois world view for which the family
was but the microcosm of a hierarchically ordered polity and the
power exercised by men on behalf of women only one instance in the
general pattern of rule and submission, the new patriarchalism
rested upon a sharp segmentation of social life. The exalted view of
woman's moral mission and the association of her nature with
higher-than-political values should not blind us to the political
effects of this ideological construction. It has been a powerful device
to secure her permanent dependence. For the organic ideal of the
family – notwithstanding the emphasis given to the harmonious
integration of *all* individual members in a greater whole – tied in fact
only women, not men. Moreover, the organicist metaphor suggested
that by their very nature familial bonds are not susceptible to, and
are indeed wholly incommensurable with, notions of individual
right and separate entitlements. To claim the essentially non-
juridical nature of the family was to sanction the traditional power
of men over women and children (Schwab, 1975: 293–7). Removed

from the arena of public scrutiny and public debate, personal relationships could not reveal their political character.

Liberal ideology, too, assumed a structural polarity between society and the family, and of the principles that operated in the segregated domains of men and women. Individual independence of man as a rational being – to be guaranteed by equality before the law – was contrasted with loving subordination, service, and natural harmony. The liberal-bourgeois project of social progress and political emancipation (for men) was parasitic upon the traditional family to ensure stability against the potentially disruptive dynamic of a liberated society. The complementarity of male and female nature, and the insistence on woman's special identity, had thus the function to provide an enclave of stable roles and value orientations amidst a rapidly changing world dominated by self-interest, competition and conflict – the very world for which freedom was thought to require the guarantee of equal rights.

This dualistic model of civil society which placed women and men in permanently segregated spheres of different purposes and activities had a profound impact not least upon the nascent women's movement itself. Women fought for the improvement of their condition primarily in terms of educational and employment opportunities. They were adamant that they did not aspire to a false equality which might subvert the attributes of femininity. Defined in the ideal of motherliness, woman's singular destiny lay in the care for children, husband, and home. Political aims did not extend beyond the hope that once women could freely develop their own potential feminine values would – spontaneously and without support of legal mechanisms – permeate and ennoble the whole of social life. Only hesitantly and belatedly, towards the end of the nineteenth century, did the women's organizations in Germany raise the demand for equal civil and political rights (Twellmann, 1972; Frevert, 1986).

Conclusion

Against the background of these new legitimations of the patriarchal family we are in a better position to assess the condition of women in the civil law codes of the Enlightenment period and to consider, in general, the importance of legal categories for the analysis of their oppression. We have seen how the Prussian Civil Code still defined women's place in civil society by reference to the institute of sex-guardianship which entailed the denial of basic civil rights. However, alongside, and in contradiction to, these traditional notions of patriarchal rule the Code asserted, as a general norm, women's claim to equal rights. Eighteenth-century Natural Law to which these egalitarian intentions were largely owed exhibited a similar ambivalence. It affirmed the general practice of women's subordination to men. But it legitimized this condition as the outcome of a voluntary pact of submission. It thus built reactionary conclusions upon premises which acknowledged woman's original equality and her capacity for independent agency. Moreover, in considering the nature of marriage and family as if they were contractual associations Natural Law stressed the formal, legal conditions of freedom even in the domain of personal relationships.

By contrast, the new patriarchalism of the early nineteenth century, which arose as a reaction against these individualistic and egalitarian tendencies in the development of modern civil law, obliterated women's individuality – by re-integrating them into the family and by placing the latter outside and above the law. Woman's biological nature, her superior moral character, and the importance of the family as the natural foundation of the state were woven together in such a way as to render her condition immune to the language of individual rights, contractual obligations, legal emancipation.

In conclusion it might be suggested that the isolation of women in a sphere to which legal definitions of freedom seemed not to apply was one of the major factors that in the past contributed to their continued oppression. This is not to claim that the goal of emancipation should be confined within the boundaries of equal civil and political rights, or that changes in the law alone would be sufficient to achieve it. But it follows from the argument presented in this chapter that the legal dimension is of great importance for the analysis of women's condition in modern society. This implies for feminist political theory that it must acknowledge, and make use of, the dual nature of the law – as an agent of emancipation as well as oppression. In other words, law is located at the intersection of force and liberation (Gerhard, 1978: 15). From the Married Women's Property Acts in the nineteenth century to the equal-treatment directives issued by the European Community in our own time the law has played a vital role in securing for women the prerequisites of citizenship. This process is far from complete as we discover ever new layers of discrimination that contradict the assurance of equal rights.

From a different perspective, however, the lessons to be learnt from this history might appear much more ambiguous than is suggested here (Smart, 1984: 46–9). Changes such as the Married Women's Property Acts, which established the principle of separate ownership and which once could be seen as a landmark in the struggle to gain for women the same rights as those already possessed by men, have subsequently turned out to the disadvantage of a large number of women, especially of non-working wives. Since, due to their different familial roles, women and men occupy structurally different positions in society and thus have unequal access to the resources necessary to acquire property, an impartial, gender-neutral law which treats them *as if* they were equal will do little to diminish women's dependence on men. As long as their particular contributions to the assets and the well-being of the household do not give them a formal entitlement, they will not be able to meet the strict criteria of legal ownership. As a consequence they will be considerably more vulnerable in the case of separation or divorce (despite the discretionary powers now commonly applied by the courts to redistribute family assets – above all, in order to safeguard the interests of children). Property rights might thus serve as a paradigmatic case to demonstrate the apparent incapacity of a formal principle of equal rights to come to terms with qualitatively different situations and needs.

But we should note that very different conclusions can be drawn from this analysis. To correct a situation where the opportunities for acquiring rights are fundamentally unequal could itself be considered a demand of the equality principle. The latter would, however, retain its claim to universal (that is, not gender-specific) validity in that the same considerations would apply to men if they were to undertake the tasks of housekeeping and child-rearing vis-à-vis a working wife. The same holds true for the arguments associated with a recent decision of the United States Supreme Court (*Los Angeles Times*, 14 January 1987) which upheld the legality of discrimination in favour of pregnant women, that is, their right to a four-month maternity leave coupled with the guarantee of getting their jobs back. The ruling confirmed the special conditions that might be required to achieve genuine equality of opportunity. But such special provisions are not in principle confined to women. They would also come into operation if, under the scheme of parental leave, men would choose to stay at home.

A more radical critique would turn against the equal rights model itself as a wholly inadequate device for the theoretical and historical analysis of gender (Rhode, 1986). Its inadequacy is owed not only to its individualistic premises which abstract from the concrete social nexus of individual lives but, more specifically within the context of this book's concerns, to the inability to account for qualitative differences that distinguish and separate the interests of women and men.

In my view this is a highly problematic claim – not least for its obvious historical connotations. The argument that the principle of equal rights – with its focus upon abstract, universal categories such as human agency, autonomy, citizenship – cannot do justice to the unique, incommensurable attributes of gender has in the past always been used to legitimize women's enforced dependence in the form of a tribute to their particular 'nature' and to their particular needs as mothers. On what grounds could a critical analysis reveal the underlying pattern of domination even in the benevolent features of sex-guardianship if one were to dismiss the applicability of those universal concepts associated with the principle of equal rights? Its emancipatory potential – and that applies not only to the specific historical context investigated in this chapter – cannot be disconnected from the claim to universality. It is difficult to imagine that one could graft upon it substantive assumptions about particularity without rendering it meaningless for political theory and ineffective for political practice.

References

Atkins, Susan and Brenda Hoggett (1984) *Women and the Law*. Oxford: Basil Blackwell.

Banks, Olive (1981) *Faces of Feminism. A Study of Feminism as a Social Movement*. Oxford: Martin Robertson.

Basch, Norma (1982) *In the Eyes of the Law: Women, Marriage and Property in Nineteenth-Century New York*. Ithaca, NY: Cornell University Press.

Blackstone, William (1765) *Commentaries on the Laws of England, I*. Oxford: Clarendon Press.

Brandes, Ernst (1802) *Betrachtungen über das weibliche Geschlecht und dessen Ausbildung in dem geselligen Leben*. Hannover: Gebrüder Hahn.

Brennan, Teresa and Carole Pateman (1979) '"Mere Auxiliaries to the Commonwealth": Women and the Origins of Liberalism', *Political Studies* 27: 183–200.

Buchholz, Stephan (1979) 'Savigny's Stellungnahme zum Ehe- und Familienrecht. Eine Skizze seiner rechtssystematischen und rechtspolitischen Überlegungen', *Ius Commune* 8: 148–91.

Buchholz, Stephan (1981a) 'Eherecht zwischen Staat und Kirche. Preussische Reformversuche in den Jahren 1854–1861', *Ius Commune*, Sonderheft 13: 1–122.

Buchholz, Stephan (1981b) 'Preussische Eherechtsreform im Vormärz (1830–1844)', *Ius Commune*, Sonderheft 15: 150–88.

Bussemer, Herrad-Ulrike (1985) *Frauenemanzipation und Bildungsbürgertum. Sozialgeschichte der Frauenbewegung in der Reichsgründungszeit*. Weinheim; Basel.

Conrad, Hermann (1956) *Individuum und Gemeinschaft in der Privatrechtsordnung des 18. und beginnenden 19. Jahrhunderts*. Bonn: Verlag C.F. Müller.

Conrad, Hermann (1957) 'Die Rechtsstellung der Ehefrau in der Privatrechtsgesetzgebung der Aufklärungszeit', pp. 253–70 in J. Engel and H.M. Klinkenberg (eds), *Aus Mittelalter und Neuzeit: Gerhard Kallen zum 70. Geburtstag*. Bonn: P. Hanstein.

Dann, Otto (1980) *Gleichheit und Gleichberechtigung. Das Gleichheitspostulat in der alteuropäischen Tradition und in Deutschland bis zum ausgehenden 19. Jahrhundert*. Berlin.

Dicey, A.V. (1905) *Lectures on the Relation between Law and Public Opinion in England during the Nineteenth Century*. London: Macmillan.

Dubois, Ellen Carol (1978) *Feminism and Suffrage. The Emergence of an Independent Women's Movement in America 1848–1869*. Ithaca, NY: Cornell University Press.

Eisenstein, Zillah (1981) *The Radical Future of Liberal Feminism*. Boston: Northeastern University Press.

Evans, Richard J. (1976) *The Feminist Movement in Germany 1894–1933*. London: Sage.

Frevert, Ute (1986) *Frauen-Geschichte. Zwischen bürgerlicher Verbesserung und neuer Weiblichkeit*. Frankfurt: Suhrkamp.

Gerhard, Ute (1978) *Verhältnisse und Verhinderungen. Frauenarbeit, Familie und Rechte der Frauen im 19. Jahrhundert. Mit Dokumenten*. Frankfurt: Suhrkamp.

Gerhard, Ute (1986) 'Die Frau als Rechtsperson. Über die Voreingenommenheit der Jurisprudenz als dogmatischer Wissenschaft', pp. 108–26 in Karin Hausen und Helga Nowotny (eds), *Wie männlich ist die Wissenschaft*? Frankfurt: Suhrkamp.

Grimm, Dieter (1987) 'Bürgerlichkeit im Recht', in D. Grimm, *Recht und Staat in der bürgerlichen Gesellschaft*. Frankfurt.

Hattenhauer, D. (ed.) (1970) *Allgemeines Landrecht für die Preussischen Staaten von 1794*. Frankfurt a.M.; Berlin: Alfred Metzner Verlag.

Hausen, Karin (1981) 'Family and Role-Division: The Polarisation of Sexual Stereotypes in the Nineteenth Century – an Aspect of the Dissociation of Work and Family Life', pp. 51–83 in R.J. Evans and W.R. Lee (eds), *The German Family. Essays on the Social History of the Family in Nineteenth and Twentieth Century Germany*. London: Croom Helm (first published 1976).

Hecker, Eugene A. (1914) *A Short History of Women's Rights*. Westport, Conn.: Greenwood Press.

Hernes, Helga Maria (1986) 'Die zweigeteilte Sozialpolitik: Eine Polemik', pp. 163–78 in Karin Hausen und Helga Nowotny (eds), *Wie männlich ist die Wissenschaft*? Frankfurt: Suhrkamp.

Holcombe, Lee (1983) *Wives and Property. Reform of the Married Women's Property Law in Nineteenth-Century England*. Toronto: Toronto University Press.

Huebner, Rudolf (1918) *A History of Germanic Private Law*. London.

Jaggar, Alison M. (1983) *Feminist Politics and Human Nature*. Sussex: Harvester Press.

Kant, Immanuel (1887) *The Philosophy of Law*. W. Hastie (ed.). Edinburgh: T. and T. Clark.

Kant, Immanuel (1971) *Kant's Political Writings*. H. Reiss (ed.). Cambridge: Cambridge University Press.

Kerber, Linda (1980) *Women of the Republic: Intellect and Ideology in the American Revolution*. Chapel Hill, NC.

Koselleck, Reinhart (1967) *Preussen zwischen Reform und Revolution. Allgemeines Landrecht, Verwaltung und soziale Bewegung von 1791 bis 1848*. Stuttgart: Klett.

Maine, Henry S. (1863) *Ancient Law: Its Connection with the early History of Society and its Relation to Modern Ideas*. London.

Marshall, T.H. (1976) 'Citizenship and Social Class', pp. 65–122, in T.H. Marshall,

Class, Citizenship and Social Development. Westport, Conn.: Greenwood Press (first published 1964).

Mill, John Stuart (1984) 'The Subjection of Women', pp. 261–340 in J.M. Robson (ed.), *The Collected Works of John Stuart Mill*, vol. 21, Toronto; London: University of Toronto Press; Routledge and Kegan Paul.

O'Donovan, Katherine (1982) 'The Male Appendage: Legal Definitions of Women', pp. 344–62 in Mary Evans (ed.), *The Woman Question. Readings on the Subordination of Women*. London: Fontana.

Okin, Susan M. (1982) 'Women and the Making of the Sentimental Family', *Philosophy and Public Affairs* 11(1): 65–88.

Okin, Susan M. (1983–84) 'Patriarchy and Married Women's Property in England. Questions on Some Current Views', *Eighteenth Century Studies* 17: 121–38.

Otto-Peters, Louise (1866) *Das Recht der Frauen auf Erwerb*. Hamburg.

Pollock, Frederick and F.W. Maitland (1968) *The History of English Law before the Time of Edward I*, vol. 2. Cambridge.

Rendall, Jane (1985) *The Origins of Modern Feminism. Women in Britain, France and the United States*. London: Macmillan.

Rhode, Deborah L. (1986) 'Feminist Perspectives on Legal Ideology', pp. 151–60 in J. Mitchell and A. Oakley (eds), *What is Feminism?* Oxford: Basil Blackwell.

Rousseau, Jean-Jacques (1973) 'A Discourse on Political Economy', pp. 117–53 in G.D.H. Cole (ed.), *Jean-Jacques Rousseau. The Social Contract and Discourses*. London: J.M. Dent and Sons.

Rürup, Reinhard (1975) *Emanzipation und Antisemitismus. Studien zur 'Judenfrage' der bürgerlichen Gesellschaft*. Göttingen: Vandenhoeck and Ruprecht.

Schwab, Dieter (1972) 'Die Familie als Vertragsgesellschaft im Naturrecht der Aufklärung', *Quaderni Fiorentini per la Storia del Pensiero Giuridico Moderno*, 1: 357–76.

Schwab, Dieter (1975) 'Familie', pp. 253–301 in O. Brunner, W. Conze, R. Koselleck (eds), *Geschichtliche Grundbegriffe. Historisches Lexikon zur politisch-sozialen Sprache in Deutschland*, vol. 2. Stuttgart: Ernst Klett Verlag.

Schwartz, Joel (1984) *The Sexual Politics of Jean-Jacques Rousseau*. Chicago; London: University of Chicago Press.

Shanley, Mary L. (1986) 'Suffrage, Protective Labour Legislation and Married Women's Property Laws', *Signs: Journal of Women in Culture* 12(1): 62–77.

Smart, Carol (1984) *The Ties that Bind. Law, Marriage and the Reproduction of Patriarchal Relations*. London: Routledge and Kegan Paul.

Thieme, Hans (1962) 'Die Rechtsstellung der Frau in Deutschland', *Recueils de la Société Jean Bodin* 12: 351–76.

Twellmann, Margrit (1972) *Die Deutsche Frauenbewegung im Spiegel repräsentativer Zeitschriften. Ihre Anfänge und erste Entwicklung 1843–1889*. Meisenheim am Glan: Anton Hain.

Vogel, Ursula (1986) 'Rationalism and Romanticism: Two Strategies for Women's Liberation', pp. 17–46 in J. Evans, J. Hills, K. Hunt *et al.*, *Feminism and Political Theory*. London: Sage.

Weber, Marianne (1971) *Ehefrau und Mutter in der Rechtsentwicklung*. Aalen: Scientia Verlag (first published 1907).

Wollstonecraft, Mary (1975) *A Vindication of the Rights of Woman*. London: Penguin.

8
Towards a Feminist Rethinking of the Welfare State

Birte Siim

In this chapter the focus is upon the feminist perspective on the welfare state and the ways it inspires us to rethink some of our basic conceptions of and general beliefs about the welfare state. The feminist perspective has challenged the dominant theoretical frameworks for understanding the welfare state, which have been built either primarily on the relationship between the state and the economy or the separation of the private from the public sphere. Feminism has challenged the Marxist paradigm by focusing on the relationship between the state and the family, and the liberal paradigm by focusing on the interrelation between the public and the private sphere. It has also challenged the general belief that the welfare state has moved towards a greater equality between men and women and towards a gradual abolition of the sexual division of labour and male dominance.

There is not yet any agreement among feminist scholars about women's relation to the state, about the nature of the state, or about strategies towards the present welfare state. In my comparative work on women and the welfare state in Denmark, Britain, and the United States I have found that the state today has come to play a crucial role determining the position of women in society as workers, mothers, and citizens.[1] With mass unemployment and attempts to restructure the welfare state from the political Right the practical problems of developing a feminist strategy towards the welfare state, including strategies to empower women, have become more urgent than ever.

On the basis of my comparative studies, I have concluded that the state has nowhere been neutral to women (Borchorst and Siim, 1987; Siim, 1987). The state has either actively helped to facilitate the integration of women into the public sphere of work by creating a network of social services in relation to human reproduction, as in the Scandinavian countries, or it has, as in Britain and the United States, made the integration of women a very difficult process by failing to build a network of social services. The gender neutrality of the Scandinavian countries in relation to social policies conceals a transformation of the power structure where sex no longer appears to be a legitimate source of power, but where there is still a sharp sexual division of labour and a distinct sexual power hierarchy both in the institutions of the welfare state and in society (Hernes, chapter 9).

Feminists working within a critical Marxist and liberal framework of analysis have in different ways developed our understanding of the welfare state by the questions they have raised and the problems they have analysed. Feminist analyses from a liberal perspective are important, because they have focused on fundamental values in Western political culture, emphasized the importance of women's political activity and values, and raised questions about the relationship between the private and the public sphere, and about the meaning of a democratic citizenship for women. Feminist analyses from a Marxist perspective are important, because they have focused on the structural interrelation between the state, the economy, and human reproduction, emphasized the importance of sexual power relations and power structures, and raised important questions about the relationship between gender and class.

In this chapter I focus on the theoretical contributions towards a feminist rethinking of the state that in different ways has attempted to transcend the liberal and Marxist paradigms. I look at the strengths and weaknesses of the different approaches, the kind of problems they have analysed and the kind of conclusions they have reached. Later I analyse the new problems raised by the integration of women in the advanced welfare state, using research from the Scandinavian welfare states as examples. I look at what the transition from private to public dependence mean for women, and at the nature of the sexual power relations in the advanced welfare state. Has the patriarchal power structure been transformed, or does the modern welfare state represent a new kind of patriarchy? I argue that the modern welfare state has a double meaning for women: on the one hand women have gained power as workers, mothers, and citizens, but on the other hand they have been subsumed under a new public power hierarchy. In this perspective the Scandinavian welfare states represent at the same time a form of a social patriarchy and a new form of social citizenship in relation to motherhood and care work. Finally, I discuss new research strategies for a feminist rethinking of the welfare state, focusing on sexual power relations and on women's collective interests as social and political agents.

The Relationship between the Private and the Public Sphere

The classical liberal thinkers like John Locke broke with the old patriarchal assumption of a continuity between the family and the state. The ownership of property was taken to establish a sphere of autonomy around the individual and the family into which the state should not intrude. Liberalism was built on a strong belief in the separation of the political from the economic sphere, and on the separation of the public sphere from the private sphere of the family.

Feminist scholars in political theory have developed a critique of the classical liberal thinkers and of the modern liberal conception of democracy and citizenship (Eisenstein, 1981; Hernes, 1982; Evans *et al.*, 1986). Carole Pateman, who has been one of the most radical critics of liberalism, has extended her critique to include new dimensions of life besides work. In her recent work she argues that feminism provides democracy in all forms with its most important challenge and most comprehensive critique (Pateman, 1983; 1985a; 1985b). She argues that liberalism has built into itself a contradiction between the ideals of individual freedom and equality in the public sphere and the assumption that women are naturally subject to men in the family. It is this contradiction that lies at the heart of its democratic theory and practice:

> When women gain access to civil life they do not magically become transformed into examples of 'the' individual citizen. Public laws, policies and practices also work against the development of the social context necessary for democratic citizenship, although this has been less discussed in recent feminist scholarship than the manner in which women's status as wives and mothers works against their involvement in public life. (Pateman, 1985a: 192)

Feminist scholars have documented that the so-called 'universal' categories of liberalism, like the individual and the citizen, are not universal but are sex/gender specific, or masculine. On this basis it becomes both a theoretical and a practical problem to determine how both sexes can become integrated into the category of the individual, and to understand what is the political relevance of sexual and gender differences.

They have also argued that the critique of liberalism must be extended to a critique of sexual and familial relations and have begun to analyse the relationship between the public and the private sphere (Pateman, 1985b; Elshtain, 1981; 1982). The feminist critique of marriage and personal life has challenged the liberal theories which never questioned the apparently natural sexual division of labour within the home. Their main point is that it becomes necessary to abandon the assumption that the personal lives of women and men can be separated from political life, in order to integrate women as citizens on equal terms with men; the public world of politics can be understood only in connection with the private world of the family. For the liberal, the two worlds are governed by different rules: the private sphere is the world of particularism, of subjection, inequality, natural emotions, love and partiality, whereas the public sphere is the world of 'universalism, independence, equality, reason, rationality and impartiality'. Feminists have pointed to the contradiction between the rules of the public sphere built on consent and voluntary associations, and the rules of the private sphere built on oppression and natural subjugation, and they have argued that this division prevents women from realizing a full democratic citizenship. It is symptomatic that in marriage consent has played a very limited role, making rape and violence towards women part of the husband's rights under the law in most countries.

While liberalism has largely ignored the political relevance of the private world of emotions, the classical critics of liberalism have recognized the important differences between public and private lives and have been aware of the differences between the lives of men and women, but they have reached conclusions that differ radically from feminism:

> The great critics of liberal theory, Rousseau and Hegel, insisted that sexual difference was important for political life, but both argued in some detail that, because of women's passions, citizenship must be sexually particular. The enormous task facing anyone who wishes to develop a genuine democratic theory of political obligation is to formulate a universal theory, including civil equality, that also embodies a social conception of individuality as feminine and masculine, that gives due weight to the unity and differentiation of humankind. (Pateman, 1985a: 193)

Pateman argues that in order to integrate women into a full democratic citizenship it is not possible just to extend the concepts and arguments to women as well as to men. Instead it becomes necessary to rethink both the concept of citizenship and the concept of the individual.

Pateman has herself been one of the leading theorists behind the ideas of 'participatory democracy', and on this basis she has criticized the advocates of work-place democracy who want to extend democracy from the state to society for having so far ignored the family and the feminist conception and critique of 'private' life. Contrary to her own expectations, women's integration into the workforce has not solved the problems of citizenship and has in some ways even exacerbated women's problems, because women often have a secondary status as workers and have to do two shifts, as mothers and as workers. She concludes that 'neither the opportunities of liberalism nor the active, participatory democratic citizenship of all people can be achieved without radical changes in personal and domestic life'. In this perspective the integration of the private sphere of the family in the public sphere becomes another way to extend democracy beyond the state to the organization of society that includes the family, the factory, and all dimensions of personal life.

The feminist critique of liberalism has attacked the separation of the public from the private sphere and has analysed the different ways that the two spheres are interrelated. There is, however, no agreement about how the integration between the private and the public sphere can be achieved. What exactly does it mean when feminists claim that 'the personal is political', and how can we define the political sphere when it is no longer separated from the private sphere? The different feminist scholars each have their own answers to those problems. Some want to abolish the distinction altogether, others want keep the distinction as a useful analytical tool. I tend to agree with Carole Pateman that the slogan 'the personal is political' does not mean that the two should be identical: 'The essential feature of a democratic revision of the "political" is that it is no longer conceived as separate from everyday life. The political sphere is one dimension, the collective dimension of social life as a whole. It is an arena of social existence in which citizens voluntarily cooperate together and sustain their common life and common undertaking' (Pateman, 1985a: 174). From this perspective, the aim of a critical feminist theory is not to make the political dimension of life disappear, but to make it part of everyday life, and to change the power relations in the private and public world in away that makes possible women's participation in political life as social and political agents.

Public Man, Private Woman

In the controversial and influential book *Public Man, Private Woman* (1981) and in her later work (1983), J.B. Elshtain has criticized the liberal paradigm and the public–private split from a rather different perspective.[2] She challenges the dualistic understanding of the private sphere in contrast to the public sphere, but contrary to most feminists she focuses primarily on the positive ideals of the family. Her mode of critique is to see the world through women's eyes, that is, from the point of view of the female subject located within her everyday reality within a world that is 'particular, concrete and social'. She attempts to reclaim the family as a social sphere that is different from the public sphere, 'interrelated but truly and importantly autonomous'. To that purpose she puts forward a communitarian ideal that would transform the category of 'the social' but at the same time would preserve the distinctive characteristics between the public and the private sphere: 'A social world, then, features fully public activities at one end of a range of possibilities – writing a manifesto, organizing a protest, framing a law – and intensely private activities at the other – human sexual intimacy, a parent's caress of a child's sleeping face, a young woman's or a young man's dreams, the solitude necessary to reflect or meditate or pray or cry' (Elshtain, 1983: 308). Methodologically, her main point is to use this ideal type of the social, and especially the values connected with the family based on 'maternal thinking', as the main basis for criticizing bureaucratic power and technological politics. The family is described almost exclusively as at least potentially 'a haven in a heartless world' and not as a place of oppression and subjugation, whereas the state, in contrast, is described as a place at least historically dominated by powerful bureaucracies that aim at efficiency and control. On these grounds she is strongly critical of the feminist critique of the family and of the dominating liberal-feminist strategy of women 'going public'. She argues that women's complete integration in the public sphere would mean the final suppression of what she calls the traditional female social worlds.

Elshtain's critique of a strategy of women 'going public' built on women's total identification with the dominant public values of efficiency, rationality, and control has a special relevance in an American context, where going public often means an individual strategy to fight for power and influence on equal terms with men without changing 'the rules of the game'. I find, however, that there are a number of problems with her strategy from a feminist perspective. One problem is related to her mode of critique, where the family is used as an ideal type. By focusing exclusively on the positive values of 'maternal thinking' she fails to analyse the everyday life of concrete families as institutions full of contradictions and inequalities. It is difficult to analyse the world exclusively through the private sphere of the family without simultaneously accepting a traditional definition of femininity. And it is problematic whether the traditional female sphere can serve as the basis for rebellion against the dominant public sphere. How can an idealized version of the family governed only by love and care ever come about in a world dominated by a political, economic, and bureaucratic force? It seems to be a rather idealistic approach to base a strategy on the 'separate but equal spheres', when reality is apparently determined by a structural hierarchy of the family, the state, and the market-place (Jones, forthcoming).

Another problem is related to Elshtain's understanding of women's everyday reality. For the majority of women everyday reality is no longer exclusively related to the values of 'maternal' thinking. Women's lives today are dominated by a contradiction between their public and private lives – between their roles as mothers and workers. Furthermore, there is no empirical evidence that women who speak exclusively as mothers will be the basis of rebellion in the modern welfare state. On the contrary, it has been documented that women who define themselves primarily as mothers usually advocate conservative values and principles of organization for the public sphere (Stacey, 1983). The form of maternal thinking transformed by feminist (or socialist) conscious-ness that Elshtain envisages is not rooted exclusively in the private sphere, but rather in the contradictions between women's public and private lives. For these reasons it seems to me that Elshtain falls victim to the very dualism between the private and the public world that she is attacking. With her approach and her strategy there seem to be few chances for any serious transformation of either the private sphere of the family or the public sphere of work and politics, and it becomes impossible to envisage her own ideal of a transformed citizenship devoted to public, moral responsibility.

Both Pateman and Elshtain want to transform the relationship between the public and the private sphere, but in different ways. In contrast to Pateman, Elshtain seems to agree with Rousseau and Hegel that it is necessary to uphold a distinction between the social and the political spheres, in the sense that passions and emotions are too dangerous – or too private – to be let loose in the public sphere dominated by rationality. The consequences for women of Elshtain's strategy are at best ambiguous: it is hard to imagine any positive changes in women's private and political life, if they are not encouraged to enter the public sphere and fight for a more democratic citizenship, where women would be social and political agents, and where motherhood would become part of a reformed citizenship.

The Relationship between Production and Human Reproduction

According to Marxism, the state cannot be analysed separately from society. In the capitalist mode of production the state is a relatively autonomous institution, but it is still a capitalist state, which must in the last instance support and help to reproduce the capitalist relations of production. The Marxist feminists have rediscovered one dimension of the state – society relation (which for many years was an almost forgotten area for Marxists) or the relationship between the state and the family. Conceptualizing the family has reopened the questions about *the relationship between the production of goods and services and the reproduction of human beings.*[3]

The early Marxist-feminist analysis of women's relation to the welfare state focused on the inherent contradictions between the needs of capitalist production and the needs of reproducing the labour force. The welfare state was understood as one response to these contradictions, securing the reproduction of labour power through state intervention in the family. Both the state and the family were conceptualized as institutions which were predominantly oppressive towards women, because both institutions helped to foster a sexual division of labour in the family and society, one of the cornerstones being women's economic dependency upon their individual husbands. The state helped secure the economic dependency of women on their individual husbands through its ideologies, its legislation, and its public policies; the open or hidden assumptions were that women were first and foremost mothers and housewives. The family, then, came to be seen as a primary site of oppression and the family wage system as a primary means of reproducing women's economic dependency. These Marxist-feminist analyses were important, because they helped to reopen questions about the relations in Marxist thinking between the state and the reproduction of labour and human beings, and about the role of the family and of ideology. Theoretically, however, they represented a tendency to understand all activities and policies of the state as functional for capitalism. As a consequence there was an emphasis on the state as the 'oppressor' and on women as 'victims' of oppression. Empirically, there was also a strong Anglo-Saxon bias in the analysis of state, which was not openly acknowledged. This led to an emphasis on the oppression of women in the family as mothers and carers and an underestimation of the new forms of integration and oppression of women in the public sphere.

Women as Workers and Mothers

In *The State and Working Women* Mary Ruggie has compared women's position in the Swedish and the British welfare state from a structuralist Marxist approach, concentrating on women's economic position as workers (Ruggie, 1984). Ruggie's approach and her interpretations of reality are both stimulating and provoking. On the one hand, she is arguing that the state has an important role in relation to the economy as 'an intervening and independent variable'; on the other hand she is arguing that the different role of the state vis-à-vis women workers is 'a sole reflection' of the different status of labour in society. The conclusion of her comparative study of the state and working women in Britain and Sweden is that it is the strength of organized labour that has improved women's position in Sweden and not what she calls 'women specific' factors like gender-based policies. She is very critical of Marxist-feminist analyses emphasizing the role of sexual power relations in shaping policies and, contrary to most feminists, she has argued that progress for women must be achieved as a by-product of the broader configuration of state–society relations, and cannot be interpreted as an expression of the prevailing conception of the role of women.

Ruggie's approach is illustrative in the sense that she focuses almost exclusively on *women's economic position and on the state–economy relation*. The *state–family relation and sexual power relations* are absent from her analysis. Her framework of analysis is very consistent but can be questioned in several ways. First of all, it could be argued that the 'state–society' relation in Marxist thinking must include the organization of the family/households as an independent sphere of society next to the market economy. The development of the Scandinavian welfare state, with a division of work between the family and the state in relation to human reproduction has today made it even more important to explore the relation between the state and the family. Secondly, it can be argued that the organization of social care work and the prevailing conception of the role of women – and the family – is an important part of the dominant political culture, and therefore it can be seen to be part of exactly those 'state–society' relations that, according to Ruggie, determine progress for women. In contrast, Ruggie argues that the essence of the state–society nexus is state intervention in the functioning of the market sphere. The corporatist welfare model, then, is defined exclusively by the fact that the proper sphere of market forces is circumscribed by the state. The scope of state intervention in the market sphere is undoubtedly one important factor explaining women's economic position in society, but I would argue that *the form and character of the state intervention in the sphere of human reproduction* is equally important for determining women's position in society as mothers, as workers, and as citizens. The main problem with Ruggie's structural framework of analysis is that it makes it impossible to understand either the close interrelations between the state, the family and the economy, or the close connection between women's different positions as workers, mothers, and citizens. The focus on women's economic position as workers makes it blind to the sexual power relations and the sexual power hierarchies in the family and society.

The Patriarchal Capitalist State

Zillah Eisenstein's analysis of the state also grew out of a Marxist-feminist understanding, but in contrast to many Marxist feminists she has maintained and transformed the *concept of patriarchy* (Eisenstein, 1979; 1981; 1983). Her main thesis is that capitalism did not, as claimed by the classical Marxist texts, abolish patriarchy as a system of sexual hierarchical relations that differentiate male from female. She acknowledges that patriarchy has been transformed by the capitalist mode of production and that male privileges are no longer protected by the legal rights of the father, but she argues that this redefinition of male power in the family and society is exactly an expression of the changing nature of male supremacy, not its demise. Eisenstein understands capitalism and patriarchy as two relatively autonomous but dialectically related systems of oppression. She argues that capitalism must ultimately regulate economic life, whereas patriarchy must regulate sexual life. The dynamic power of patriarchy is centred on the controls developed to limit women's options in relation to motherhood and mothering in such a way as to give primary emphasis to their role as child-bearer and rearer (Eisenstein, 1983).

Eisenstein's approach is influenced by the structuralist understanding of the state that focuses on the state as a mediator of the different conflicts and contradictions in society, in this case between the two systems of power capitalism and patriarchy. In the advanced capitalist economy there are three series of conflicts between the two systems: between the relations of patriarchy vs. the ideology of liberalism; between the relations of advanced capitalism and the ideology of patriarchy; and between the ideology of patriarchy and the ideology of liberalism. This focus on conflicts makes possible a more dynamic understanding of the state as an active participant in the struggles within society. It also opens up the possibility of an understanding which is more sensitive to the contradictions within state policies and within women's lives, and an understanding of women as political agents. Eisenstein distinguishes in her analysis between a *patriarchal family* and a *social patriarchy*, that is, 'between the hierarchical sexual organization for the reproduction of sex–gender as it exists in the family and the organization of sex–gender as it exists throughout the society understood as a totality'. This distinction has contributed to the development of a more complex framework of analysis for studying the transformation of the sexual power hierarchy, and sexual power relations in the advanced welfare state.

The concept of patriarchy has been much debated among feminists. Radical feminists have embraced it, while many Marxist feminists have argued that the term 'patriarchy' should be reserved for 'the rule of the father' in pre-capitalist societies, and that it cannot be extended to designate 'the power of men over women' in modern capitalism (Barrett, 1980; Beechey, 1979). Zillah Eisenstein and Heidi Hartmann have been among the best-known Marxist-feminist scholars arguing that it is important to maintain the concept of patriarchy defined as a system that reproduces the power of men over women and re-define and specify it in relation to different modes of production.[4] It is, however, still an open question, whether it is possible to develop a unified theory that can explain the sexual power relations and the sexual hierarchy in contemporary society using patriarchy as the key concept.

As a political scientist and an American, Eisenstein is very sensitive to the meaning and importance of liberal ideology as an important part of the dominant political culture. Her analysis of the importance of liberalism for the development of women's sexual class consciousness as working mothers is a good illustration of that. She argues that although there are still important class differences among women, the economic class reality of the majority of women today tends to unite women across classes because the family forms have become more dynamic. The term 'sexual class position' refers to women's position as providers of the basic necessary activities of society: reproduction, child rearing, nursing, consuming, domestic labour, and wage earning. The term 'class' refers to the fact that women's activities of reproducing and sustaining society are fundamental and necessary to the present social order. Women's sexual class identity, then, is constructed primarily in the realms of human reproduction and sexuality. State activities are at present trying to mediate between the needs of the capitalist market and the patriarchal need for the institution of motherhood. She argues that when middle-class women come into the market-place as workers they start to press for reforms of equality for the equal rights and opportunities promised in the liberal ideology. It is the highlighting of women's differentiation from men in the market sphere that begins to create a consciousness one can name feminist. Today, therefore, it is the working women who have the potential for change. While liberalism is currently in a crisis, feminism is generally accepted by a large majority of men and women. The 'gender gap' in politics – whereby women tend towards a specific voting profile that is different from men's on important issues, such as the peace question and the question of government spending on public welfare programmes – is explained in this perspective as 'a reflection of and a reaction to women's sexual class position, particularly in terms of the way one's economic status is defined in terms of it' (Eisenstein, 1981).

I find Eisenstein's contribution important in several ways. Contrary to many feminist scholars, her main emphasis has been on the changes in male domination and in the relations between the patriarchal family and social patriarchy; she has focused on political motherhood and on the patriarchal need to maintain women as mothers, mediated by the activities and policies of the state. This emphasis on the political dimension of women's oppression, on the sexual power relations in the family and society, and on the collective interests of men from different classes in maintaining the sexual power hierarchy, has been an important contribution to both a feminist and a Marxist theory.

There are, however, many open questions in connection with her concept of the patriarchal state, with her functionalist approach to the family and the state, and with her concept of sexual class. First of all, historical analyses make it doubtful whether the family and motherhood as social institutions have been mainly functional for capitalist patriarchy. Apparently families have served important positive functions for women (and men) as well (Humphries, 1977). Secondly, Eisenstein has described the state (and the family) as a predominantly oppressive institution and has underplayed the possibility that state actions and policies have also served as instruments of liberation for women from patriarchal dependence in the family. The state is portrayed as 'the' great oppressor, as an instrument of either capitalism or patriarchy or both. The structural approach to power underplays women's political activities and tends to regard women mainly as powerless victims of patriarchy. Furthermore, the concept of sexual class understates the socio-economic differences and the power differences among women. Finally, the analysis of the meaning and importance of the liberal culture for women has a rather strong American bias which makes it difficult to use her framework in a Scandinavian perspective. In the political cultures of the Scandinavian countries liberalism has competed with other values of equality and solidarity, and today a strong welfare ideology has become an important part of the dominant political culture (Siim, 1987).

Other Marxist-feminist approaches have used the concept of patriarchy in ways that have been more sensitive to historical changes in the relationship between state and family to the role of

women's organizations in transforming or reproducing the patriarchal power system. Eli Zaretsky has stressed the role of women's
organizations, especially feminist reformers of the progressive era in
the USA, in the development of the welfare state in its present
form. He argues that the modern family cannot be explained exclusively as an expression of either capitalism or patriarchy. The state
has not emptied the family of functions but the state and the modern
family have expanded together: the form in which the welfare state
expanded was public, the context private (Zaretsky, 1982). The
central role of the state in transforming patriarchy from the power
of men in the families to the power of men through the state has also
been explored by other Marxist-feminist scholars (Brown, 1979;
Boris and Bardaglio, 1983). Boris and Bardaglio argue that the state
moved historically to replace the family as the main force that
structured patriarchy in the broader society. They define social
patriarchy as 'the organization of hierarchical gender-roles and
relations throughout society', and they describe the welfare state as
a form of state patriarchy.

In the different historical approaches there seems to be a more
complex and dialectical understanding of the state–family relationship and of the relations between women and the state. The
conclusion from the historical studies seems to be that there is a
double and contradictory relationship between the state, women,
and the family: the state has historically helped to undermine the
authority of the family in society, but at the same time it has also
helped to foster familial autonomy. The state has helped to weaken
the familial authority of the father, but at the same time it has also
helped to institutionalize the power of men over women in the wider
society. I find it important to develop a more dialectical framework
along these lines, one that has the ability to transcend the dualist
and functionalist approaches that focus either exclusively on the
state as the oppressor or on the family as the ideal 'haven in a
heartless world'.[5]

From Private to Public Dependence for Women

Helga Marie Hernes's comprehensive empirical analyses of
women's position in the Scandinavian welfare states have also made
an important contribution to our theoretical understanding of the
modern welfare state (Hernes, 1982; 1984). While Marxist feminists
have concentrated on women's economic oppression either by the
state or in the family, and liberal feminists have focused primarily
on the relationship between the public and the private sphere,
Hernes has focused primarily on women's position within the

institutional structure of the state and in the formal political system. She is specifically concerned with sexual power relations, that is, women's lack of power within the corporate state structure, and with women's absence in the political process.

Hernes has emphasized that the development of the Scandinavian welfare states with the increasing 'socialization' of the family after the Second World War has been part of a political process which has taken place mainly under male leadership. The institutional structure of the welfare state has become increasingly corporatist, and the corporate leadership of interest groups, politicians, experts, and professionals is the most hierarchical and the least participatory of all political decision-making centres. On this basis she has argued that we find in Scandinavia a sexual power hierarchy, where men have been the participants and women the receivers in the political process: 'From this perspective one can describe the Scandinavian stateform as a tutelary state for women since they have had a minimal role in the actual decision-making process concerning the distribution of power' (Hernes, 1983: 7). Women have gradually improved their representation in the parliamentary system from 10 per cent in 1960 to 25 per cent in 1985, which is the highest percentage in the world, but she argues that this increase in women's representation has not necessarily given women more power in relation to men, because the centres of power during the same time have shifted from Parliament to the corporatist organization, where women's representation is only 10 per cent. She finds a historical explanation of the unequal power relationship between men and women in the political process related to the fact that women were politicized – that is, made the objects of politics – before they were mobilized, while for men it was the other way around.

Hernes argues that the corporate channel of influence has a patriarchial character for the following reasons:

1 There is an alliance between working-class men and the men of the bourgeoisie.
2 Men were integrated directly into the political process and women only indirectly.
3 Men and women have a different participational profile on the formal labour market.

The Scandinavian welfare states have been characterized by a process she describes as 'reproduction going public', and this development has had different consequences for men and women. It has changed fundamentally women's position in society, and women have moved from a private dependency on their individual husbands to a public dependency on the state. The new dependency on the state is connected to women's three different but interrelated relations to the welfare state as clients, as employees, and as citizens. First, women have become dependent on the state as public employees within the public service sector. Second, women have come to rely on public institutions and public agencies. And third, women have become dependent on the state as citizens, because they do not have strong and powerful organizations to defend their interests. This is the basis for Hernes's argument that women have today become more dependent on the state than men, and for her main thesis that there has been a shift from private to public dependency for women. Although the development of the Scandinavian welfare states has given women important social and economical advantages, there is still a strong sexual power hierarchy in the formal political system. Women have become incorporated into the public sphere as clients, workers, and citizens, but they have become subordinated to a qualitatively new sexual power hierarchy within state institutions. In the corporatist state it is an individual's professional status that determines his/her status as citizen and client, and therefore it becomes crucial to improve women's professional status in order to improve women's collective position as citizens.

Hernes's analysis of the sexual power hierarchy within the formal political system and of women's object status and lack of participation in the political process is very stimulating and has challenged many beliefs about the Scandinavian systems held by feminists and the Left: first and foremost, the belief that the influence of the Labour Party on the institutional structure and the policies of the welfare state has necessarily made it a more participatory democracy and that Scandinavian welfare states are in all respects the most advanced in relation to women (Ruggie, 1984). She has challenged feminism by shifting the emphasis away from the sexual power hierarchy in the family to the sexual power hierarchy in the formal political system, and by focusing for the first time on the theoretical and practical meaning of the Scandinavian experience for women. Whether we find that women's growing dependency on the state is a good or a bad thing, there is a growing need for both a theoretical analysis of the sexual power relations and sexual power hierarchies in the current welfare state and for empirical studies of how the institutional structure, political culture and concrete policies of different kinds of welfare states affect women.[6]

On the empirical level Hernes's approach has no doubt emphasized important characteristics of the modern welfare state. It seems to me, however, that women's dependency on the state and the sexual hierarchy in the corporatist state are two different things, with different origins and different consequences, and that they should therefore also be separated analytically: the corporatist character of the state has exacerbated a hierarchical decision-making process. Women's dependency on the state is, however, not necessarily a thing to be avoided and should be studied in connection with the concrete character of the state and with the meaning of a social citizenship (Hernes, 1984, 1986; Siim, 1986).

There is a need for further empirical analyses of the contradictory aspects of the institutional structure of the welfare state and of the different nature of women's dependency. First of all, women's dependency on the state as workers and citizens is in important ways different from their dependency as clients. There are still important socio-economic cultural and power differences among women. Some women have improved their position as workers within the different parts of the public power hierarchy, especially within the social, educational, and health sectors. As workers they have become organized and today they have at least the potential power to influence the decision-making process through collective struggle. These capabilities can influence their position as citizens.

There is also an important difference between being dependent on the state as consumers of public services and being dependent on social welfare benefits as clients. The social stigma, political control, and economic dependency are primarily connected with the position as clients, whereas consumers of the public services, as for example day-care services, often have power to influence the decisions of the service workers directly at the local level, and they may try collectively to improve the services by influencing the political decisions at the local level as citizens. Secondly, I find that the corporatist structure is only one part of the institutional structure of the welfare state and her analysis understates the importance of the administrative structure and concrete policies of the social state.[7] Finally, there are important differences between the different Scandinavian welfare states. I have argued elsewhere that Norway in some respects resembles Britain more than it resembles Denmark and Sweden in the organization of human reproduction. The family still plays a much larger role in Norway and England in relation to child care than in Denmark (Borchorst and Siim, 1987).

It is important to emphasize that in the modern welfare state there is no alternative to women's dependency on the state. Historically the wife was economically dependent on her husband, but today the alternative to dependency on the state is women's dependency on market forces as wage-earners and not, as liberal ideology suggests, individual autonomy. It is therefore wrong to associate a strong welfare sector like the Danish, with a strong dependency on the state. For women, I would argue, it is actually the other way around: a strong public service sector seems to be one precondition to avoid becoming solely dependent on the welfare system of the state as clients. In Denmark and Sweden women have to a greater extent come to rely on the state as consumers of public services, and only to a smaller degree as social welfare clients. The opposite is true in Britain and the USA, where women have come to rely on the state primarily as clients, because it has proved impossible for them to rely solely on market forces or the family for support for themselves and their children (Sapiro, 1986; Erie, Rein, and Widget, 1983; Ungerson, 1985).

On the theoretical level there is a need to analyse further what determines the actions and policies of the state and what are the fundamental values of the political culture. What exactly makes the political culture, institutional structure, and concrete polices of the welfare state patriarchal? What have been women's interests in relation to politics and in what ways have women's interests and activities influenced the decision-making process in the formal political system?

Hernes's approach has concentrated on women's participation in the formal political system and on women's lack of power. It is equally important to explore women's activities and participation in the informal political system and the empowering of women in social movements, trade unions, and local associations, where women seem to be as active as men at least on the basic level. Hernes's approach to women and politics has focused primarily on politics and power from above, but analyses of women's relation to politics and to power from below, focusing either on women's activities in social movements or on women's political interests and values, would no doubt give a more positive picture of women's relation to politics. This approach would also disclose power differentials among women of different classes and cultures (Peterson, 1985a).

Patriarchal Power Relations in the Advanced Welfare State

There has been a strong disagreement among feminist scholars about the nature of the state, approaches to empirical analyses of, and concrete strategies towards, the present welfare state (for an overview see Sarvasy, 1985; Eisenstein, 1984). One important question has been whether the expansion of the welfare state has been primarily an expression of patriarchal male interests dominating the decision-making process, or whether public policies have been the passive response to more general socio-economic changes, such as growing demand from the economy for married women's labour power and the parallel breakdown of the one-earner family.

Feminist scholars, who have emphasized the capitalist character of the state, have studied women's economic position and the tendency toward a feminization of poverty in the modern welfare state. Other feminists, who have emphasized the patriarchal character of the state, have focused primarily on sexual power relations and on sexual politics. These differences have often resulted in conflicts about strategies: a pro-state position has emphasized women's growing economic dependency on the state and the growing need for an expansion of state services and welfare benefits to women and their children in the economic crises (Ehrenreich and Fox-Piven, 1984), while an anti-state position has emphasized the negative aspects of the state policies governed by male interests and their power to control women's lives (Elshtain, 1983; Ferguson, 1983). The discussion about the Scandinavian welfare state has to some extent accentuated these differences between pro- and anti-state strategies, because pro-state advocates have used the Scandinavian experience as a 'model' for the advancement of women's social and economic welfare (Ehrenreich and Fox-Piven, 1984; Ruggie, 1984).

On the basis of my own comparative study of women's position in Denmark, Britain, and the United States I have argued that the state has today become a crucial factor influencing women's lives, because women have become integrated into the public sphere and increasingly have come to rely on incomes from the three different welfare systems: the state, the labour market, and the family. The comparison between Denmark and other welfare states, like Britain and the USA, has made it clear that there has been no simple economic determination at play. On the one hand, socio-economic forces have in all welfare states resulted in an integration of married women into the workforce and a parallel breakdown of the one-earner family as the dominant family form. On the other hand, the differences in social policies in the three welfare states, especially in relation to motherhood and care work, make it clear that there has been ample room for the different political forces to act as mediators between these socio-economic forces and the social needs and interests of different social groups (Siim, 1985; 1986).

In spite of important differences in the institutional structure, concrete policies, and political cultures in Denmark, Britain, and Sweden, there is a sexual power hierarchy and a sexual division of labour in all three welfare states. This does not necessarily mean that the state policies have been primarily concerned to ensure male domination. There is an important analytical difference between the immediate objectives of state policies, the assumptions and interests that have shaped them and their consequences for women that must be acknowledged in empirical analyses. The immediate objectives have all reflected to a certain extent what has been called separate state interests in economic growth, ensuring an international position or securing internal stability, but they have always been mediated by specific interests and concrete characteristics and priorities of the particular political system. I would argue that state policies can be said to reflect male dominance to the extent they have incorporated the dominant male assumptions and have been governed mainly by male interests and, therefore, have not permitted any real threat to male supremacy (for a discussion, see Randall, 1982; Siim, 1986; Jaquette and Staudt, chapter 10). Whether or not that is true of concrete policies must be analysed separately.

There have no doubt been important changes in male domination with the advance of the modern welfare state, which has shifted the locus of oppression from the private to the public sphere. Today sex is no longer a legitimate source of power, but there is still a strong male domination in all the central spheres of economic and political life. Women have been neither victims of state policies, nor have they been passive supporters of the modern welfare state, but they have in different ways and often with different political profiles been engaged in struggles to improve women's position in society and to create greater equality between men and women as workers and citizens. Therefore it becomes important to look at sexual relations and at women's political activities as citizens, and discuss women's role in the contemporary restructuring and future development of the welfare state.

I find that the Scandinavian experiences cannot be used as a model for women's social and economic welfare. On the contrary, I argue that the complexity of the Scandinavian experience points to the necessity to transcend the analytical categories of individualism and class used by liberalism and Marxism. It is important on the one hand to combine an analysis of women's socio-economic position with an analysis of the sexual power relations, and on the other hand to combine an analysis of women as objects of patriarchal oppression with an analysis of women as social and political agents of change. In the following, I illustrate this point very briefly with examples from my own research.

Social Patriarchy or a New Form of Social Citizenship?
In the modern welfare state I find it is crucial to look at the question of sexual power relations and their effect on the integration of

women as citizens and the content of citizenship. In my comparative analysis I have found that there are important institutional and cultural differences in the organization of social reproduction of individuals and households in relation to care for children, the sick, the old, and the disabled. These institutional and cultural factors can explain important variations in women's position as mothers, workers, and citizens in Denmark, Britain, and the USA. I have argued that the development of the modern welfare state in Denmark has brought a new form for partnership between the state and the family – and to some extent between women and the state. In contrast, the British welfare state is still predominantly familiast in the sense that the family still plays the main role in human reproduction, and there is legislation built on the assumption of women as mothers and carers (see also McIntosh, 1979a; Ruggie, 1984).

In Denmark an important part of a new partnership has been a growing state responsibility in relation to care for children, the old, and the sick and disabled during the 1960s and 1970s. Under the leadership of the Social Democratic Party the state has formulated a conscious policy of socializing important parts of the reproductive work by building a network of public institutions, and it can be argued that motherhood and care work in this way have become a part of social citizenship. The general meaning of social citizenship was to secure the universal rights of the individual vis-à-vis the state. The term has been defined as 'the right to a modicum of economic welfare security regardless of the position on the labour market and the right to share to the full of the social heritage and to live the life of a civilized being according to the living standards prevailing in society' (Marshall, 1983). This right of the individual, originally formulated by Marshall, became a working-class ideal about equality that was nowhere automatically extended to include women. It is therefore remarkable that the Social Democratic Party in Denmark developed an understanding of citizenship that accepted motherhood and care work as a part of the social responsibilities of the state and subsequently built a net of institutions to support these ideas (Siim, 1986).

The Scandinavian development of the social state, which has been most advanced in Denmark and Sweden, has been interpreted in completely different ways. One interpretation has, like Ruggie, stressed the socio-economic improvements in women's situation as an illustration of the importance of the social state and of the strength of the Scandinavian 'model' in relation to women. Another interpretation has, like Hernes, focused on the unequal power relations and on women's object status and lack of power in the corporate state structure and in the central political and economic institutions of the state, and has argued that Scandinavian welfare states are still dominated by patriarchal power structures. Both interpretations cover important aspects of the contradictory nature of the Scandinavian experience for women, and must therefore be included in a theoretical framework of analysis.

An expansion of our understanding of the concept of power makes it possible to analyse the social state in terms of power relations. In this perspective it can be argued that the partnership between the family and the state has been one of the preconditions for the empowering of women as workers by integrating women into the public sphere of work as a permanent part of the workforce and for the empowering of women as mothers by decreasing women's economic dependence on their individual husbands. This interpretation of social citizenship transcends the liberal understanding by changing the concept of citizenship from the right of the individual to the collective rights of women, and thereby stressing the empowering of women as a group and not as individuals. It transcends the Marxist understanding by changing the concept of citizenship from a working-class right to the collective rights of women, and thereby stressing the empowering of women as a separate group and not as part of the working class.

The Scandinavian experiences reveal that looking at women's socio-economic position as mothers and workers does not give an adequate picture of women's situation, if it is not combined with studies of sexual power relations and of women's relation to the political power structure. The development of the Scandinavian welfare states has apparently been a very contradictory experience for women: women have to some extent become empowered as mothers, workers, and citizens, but at the same time women have become subsumed under a new kind of sexual power hierarchy within the administrative and political system of the welfare state. The old sexual power hierarchy and the old power relations have been transformed and replaced by a new, more complex and subtle sexual power structure. The welfare state can be said to be patriarchal and paternalistic to the extent that women are absent from the decision-making process and to the extent that public policies are governed by male assumptions about women as mothers and carers. But women have also become empowered as workers, mothers, and citizens to the extent that motherhood and care work have become part of social citizenship in the modern Scandinavian welfare states. The Scandinavian experiences have illuminated the two contradictory aspects of the welfare state in relation to women: the oppressive side and the supportive side. During the 1970s there has been on the one hand a growing political mobilization, especially of younger, well-educated women, and on the other hand a growing economic marginalization and a tendency toward a feminization of poverty among older, unskilled women workers. These contradictory tendencies in the welfare state and the ensuing class and power differentials among women have been exacerbated during the economic crisis and mass unemployment (Hernes, 1986; Fraser, 1985; Sapiro, 1986).

New Research Strategies

The contradictory character of the Danish and Swedish welfare states and women's contradictory experiences as workers, mothers, and citizens must be kept in mind, for it points towards the need for more comparative research about the specific character of the Scandinavian welfare states from women's perspective, and about women's experiences in the different welfare states (Adams and Teich Winston,1980; Siim, 1985; 1987). Future research must to a greater extent combine and confront analyses of women as objects of oppressive patriarchal power structures and male-dominated politics with analyses of women as collective political agents, and also study the political mobilization and empowering of women.

On the emphirical level we need to develop approaches that to a greater extent explore differences in women's political activities, interests, and values, and that to a greater extent focus on power differentials among women of different classes and cultures and between women in different welfare states. In this perspective we need to develop approaches that are able to combine the study of the economic power relations with the study of sexual power relations in the labour market, in the family, and in the formal and informal political system. We also need more comprehensive analyses of the different institutional structure and political content of both the corporatist and the social state that can help us determine more precisely the new character of male domination within the institutional structure, the concrete policies, and the political culture of the modern welfare state. How has the development of the modern welfare state influenced the position and experiences of women? And how and in what way have women's increasing representation and participation in the administrative and political system and growing political activities influenced the social political institutions of the modern welfare state?

On the theoretical level, feminist scholars such as Carole Pateman, Helga Hernes, and Zillah Eisenstein have focused on the relationship between the family and the state, between the private and the public sphere, and have begun to rethink and reconceptual-ize central concepts in political theory such as power, interests, and citizenship. They have even started to question the concept of politics, re-defining it to include both struggles and co-operation about power and values with the perspective of maintaining or changing social institutions and male domination. Given the enormous task it is not surprising that there is not yet any agreement on what the feminist project looks like nor how it can be accomplished.

Today there is a growing interest in transcending the old liberal and Marxist paradigms and in developing new concepts and approaches sensitive to the problems that women face in the modern welfare state. One of the crucial questions for many feminists has become the need to mobilize and empower women in relation to political and economic life. There is a growing body of research attempting to re-conceptualize power in a way that trans-forms the concept away from the emphasis on the negative aspects of power – as power to control other people – towards an emphasis on the positive aspects of power – to determine one's own destiny and to change one's life through collective actions.[8]

The changes in the nature of male domination with the advance of the modern welfare state appear to have shifted the locus of oppression from the private to the public sphere, and have today made it more important than ever that women strive collectively to be present as women within public institutions and organizations as one precondition for a transformation of the values, public policies, and institutional structure of the welfare state in ways that make it more responsive to women's needs and interests (Jónasdóttir 1985a). Women's integration into the administrative and political institutions has today become one precondition for the empowering of women as mothers, workers, and citizens in the sense that it enables women to determine their own destiny and define their own interests.

In the modern welfare state there seem to be strong socio-economic, cultural, and political factors that both divide and unite women (Luker, 1984; Eisenstein, 1984; Stacey, 1983). Radical feminists have emphasized experiences that tend to unite women in connection with motherhood and care work, whereas Marxist feminists have emphasized structural class and power differentials among women. Zillah Eisenstein's concept of sexual class, which emphasizes women's common interests in the modern welfare state as working mothers is an interesting contribution to this debate. Further research needs to explore to what extent, how, and in what ways women can overcome their cultural, class, colour, and generational differences and unite around common interests as workers, mothers, and citizens.

Notes

1. The state plays an important role regulating all dimensions of women's social existence, but here I focus especially on sexual power relations in relation to women's situation as mothers, workers, and citizens. This emphasis underplays questions related to women's sexuality and relations of desire. See Jónasdóttir, 1985b.

2. See Jean B. Elshtain, 1981; 1983. While Elshtain understands her critique of the public–private split as a socialist critique, feminists like Judith Stacey have criticized Elshtain as a new conservative. See Judith Stacey, 1983.

3. Friedrich Engels' classic work *The Origins of the Family, Private Property and the State* was rediscovered by Marxists and feminists at the beginning of the 1970s. Feminists gradually challenged the prevailing conception of reproduction that focused primarily on the reproduction of the working class, and instead emphasized the social and human aspects of reproduction. See Jan Gough (1977); Elisabeth Wilson (1977); Mary McIntosh (1979a, 1979b).

4. The 'classical' Marxist-feminist texts arguing that patriarchy as a social system still exists next to the capitalist system are Heidi Hartman (1979, 1981) and Eisenstein (1978, 1981, 1983). For an alternative understanding of patriarchy that attempts to combine the Marxist-feminist and radical-feminist insights see Anna Jónasdóttir, 1985b.

5. J. Donzelot (1977) and Christopher Lasch (1977) have both argued that the state has primarily controlled the family and invaded family life. Feminists have usually been rather critical of this argument; see, for example, Barrett and McIntosh (1982) and Mary McIntosh (1984). See also, for a critique of the family as a revolutionary potential, Peterson (1985b) and Jones (forthcoming).

6. I have in my own work been much inspired by Helga Hernes's analysis. Although the emphasis in my own work on the development of the social state has been somewhat different from Hernes's (which should be clear from the following pages), I find that it is today crucial to analyse the relationship between the corporate and the social state. In later articles Hernes has developed a more positive understanding of the Scandinavian welfare state, and especially of the social state. In a recent article (Hernes, 1986) she argues that it is necessary to develop a concept about a philogenic (women-friendly) state. See also chapter 9.

7. The term 'social' state is usually defined in relation to social policies in a broad Anglo-Saxon sense meaning 'education, health care, social security, housing and social services'. Hernes (1986) has analysed the ambiguities of the social state in terms of social policies. Nancy Fraser (1985) uses the term 'the judicial–administrative–therapeutic state complex' (JAT) for the social domain of state activities and has also stressed the complexities and ambiguities of the social state.

8. The works of Richard Sennet (1982) and Michel Foucault (1980) have been an important inspiration for feminists. We need, however, to be aware of the dangers of a new kind of dualism, where the negative aspects of power tend to become identified with 'male' power and the positive aspects of power tend to become identified as 'female' power. This tendency is perhaps most visible in the work of Marilyn French (1985).

References

Adams, Carolyn Teich, and Kathryn Teich Winston (1980) *Mothers at Work, Public Policies in the U.S., Sweden and Britain*. Princeton, NJ: Princeton University Press.

Barrett, Michele (1980) *Women's Oppression*. London: Verso.

Barrett, Michele and Mary McIntosh (1982) *The Anti-Social Family*. London: Verso.

Beechey, Veronica (1979) 'On Patriarchy', *Feminist Review* 3: 66–82.

Borchorst, Anette and Birte Siim (1984) *Kvinder og velfærdsstaten – mellem moderskab og lønarbejde i 100 år*. (Women and the Welfare State – between Motherhood and Wagework in 100 years.) Aalborg: Aalborg University Press.

Borchorst, Anette and Birte Siim (1987) 'Women and the Advanced Welfare State – a New Kind of Patriarchal Power?', in Anne Showstack Sassoon (ed.), *Women and the State. The shifting boundaries of public and private*. London: Hutchinson.

Boris, Eilien and Peter Bardaglio (1983) 'The Transformation of Patriarchy: The Historic Role of the State', in Irene Diamond (ed.), *Families, Politics and Public Policy*. New York: Longman.

Brown, Carole (1979) 'Mothers, Fathers and Children. From Private to Public Patriarchy', in Lydia Sargent (ed.), *Women and Revolution*. New York: Pluto Press.

Donzelot, Jacques (1977) *The Policing of Families*.

Ehrenreich, Barbara and Frances Fox-Piven (1984) 'The Feminization of Poverty' *Dissent* 31(2).

Eisenstein, Zillah (1978) *Capitalist Patriarchy and the Case for Socialist Feminism*. New York: Monthly Review Press.

Eisenstein, Zillah (1981) *The Radical Future of Liberal Feminism*. New York: Longman.

Eisenstein, Zillah (1983) 'The State, the Patriarchal Family and Working Mothers', in Irene Diamond (ed.,) *Families, Politics and Public Policy*. New York: Longman.

Eisenstein, Zillah (1984), *Feminism and Sexual Equality, Crisis in Liberal Feminism*. New York: Monthly Review Press.

Elshtain, Jean (1981) *Public Man – Private Woman. Women in Social and Political Thought*. Princeton, NJ: Princeton University Press.

Elshtain, Jean (1982) *The Family in Political Thought*. Brighton: Harvester Press.

Elshtain, Jean (1983) 'Antigone's Daughters: Reflection on Female Identity and the State', in Irene Diamond (ed.), *Families, Politics and Public Policy*. New York: Longman.

Engels, Friedrich (1948) *The Origin of the Family, Private Property and the State*. Moscow: Foreign Languages Publishing House.

Erie, Steven, Martin Rein, and Barbera Widget (1983) 'Women and the Reagan Revolution: Thermidor for the Social Welfare Economy', in Irene Diamond (ed.), *Families, Politics and Public Policy*. New York: Hutchinson.

Evans, Judith *et al.* (1986) *Feminism and Political Theory*. London; Beverly Hills: Sage.

Ferguson, Kathy (1983) 'Bureaucracy and Public Life. The Feminization of the Polity', *Administration and Society* 15(3).

Ferguson, Kathy (1984) *The Feminist Case Against Bureaucracy*. Philadelphia: Temple University Press.

Foucault, Michel (1980), *On Knowledge and Power*. New York: Basic Books.

Fox-Piven, Frances (1984) 'Women and the State. Ideology, Power and Welfare', *Socialist Review* 74 (March-April).

Fraser, Nancy (1985) *Feminism and the Social State*. Working paper, forthcoming in *Salmagundi*.

French, Marilyn (1985) *Beyond Power*. New York: Summit.

Gough, Ian (1977) *The Political Economy of the Welfare State*. London: Macmillan.

Haavio-Mannila, Elina *et al.* (1985) *The Unfinished Democracy, Women in Nordic Politics*. Oxford: Pergamon Press.

Hartmann, Heidi (1979) 'Capitalism, Patriarchy and Job Segregation by Sex', in Zillah Eisenstein (ed.), *Capitalist Patriarchy and the Case for Socialist Feminism*. New York: Monthly Review Press.

Hartmann, Heidi (1981) 'The Unhappy Marriage of Marxism and Feminism', in Lydia Sargent (ed.), *Women and Revolution*. London: Pluto Press.

Hernes, Helga (1982) *Staten – kvinder ingen adgang* (The State – No Admittance for Women). Oslo: Universitetsforlaget.

Hernes, Helga (1984) 'Women and the Welfare State – the Transition from Private to Public Dependence', in Harriet Holter (ed.), *Patriarchy in a Welfare State*. Oslo: Universitetsforlaget.

Hernes, Helga (1986) 'Den todelte Socialpolitikken: En polemik' ('The Two Faces of Social Policy: A Polemics'), in Stein Kuhnle (ed.), *Statsvitenskap i Norge 1950–85 (Political Science in Norway 1950–85)*. Oslo: Universitetsforlaget.

Humphries, Jane (1977) 'Class struggle and the Persistence of the Working Class Family', *Cambridge Journal of Economics*, 1(3): 241–58.

Jónasdóttir, Anna (1985a) 'Kvinnors interessen och andre værdien' ('Women's Interests and other Values'), *Kvinnovetenskaplig Tidsskrift nr. 2. (Journal for Feminist Science)*.

Jónasdóttir, Anna (1985b) 'Beyond "Oppression". On the Exploitation of a Sex/Gender System'. Paper prepared for ECPR conference, Barcelona.

Jones, Kathleen (forthcoming) 'Socialist-Feminist Theories of the Family', *Praxis International*.

Lasch, Christopher (1977) *Haven in a Heartless World*. New York: Basic Books.

Luker, Kristin (1984) *Abortion and the Politics of Motherhood*. Berkeley: University of California Press.

McIntosh, Mary (1979a) 'The State and the Oppression of Women', in Kuhn and Wolpe (eds), *Feminism and Materialism*. London: Routledge.

McIntosh, Mary (1979b) 'The Welfare State and the Need of the Dependent Family', in Sandra Burman (ed.), *Fit Women for Work*. London: Croom Helm.

McIntosh, Mary (1984), 'The Family, Regulation and the Public Sphere', in G. McLennan, D. Held, and S. Hall (eds), *State and Society in Contemporary Britain. A Critical Introduction*. Cambridge: Polity Press in association with Basil Blackwell, Oxford.

Marshall, T.H. (1983) 'Citizenship and Social Class', in D. Held (ed.), *States and Societies*. Oxford: Oxford University Press.

Pateman, Carole (1983) 'Feminism and Democracy', in Duncan Graham (ed.), *Democratic Theory and Practice*. Cambridge: Cambridge University Press.

Pateman, Carole (1985a) *The Problem of Political Obligation. A Critique of Liberal Theory*. Oxford: Polity Press.

Pateman, Carole (1985b) 'Women and Democratic Citizenship'. The Jefferson Memorial Lectures, Berkeley, CA.

Peterson, Abby (1985a) 'The New Women's Movement – Where Have All the

Women Gone? Women and the Peace Movement in Sweden', *Women's International Forum* 8(6).

Peterson, Abby (1985b) 'The Revolutionary Potential of the "Private": A Critique of the Family as a Revolutionary Force Position'. Working paper, University of Umeå, Sweden.

Randall, Vicky (1982) *Women and Politics*. London: Macmillan.

Ruggie, Mary (1984) *The State and Working Women. A Comparative Study of Britain and Sweden*. Princeton, NJ: Princeton University Press.

Sapiro, Virginia (1986) 'The Gender Basis of American Social Policy', in *American Political Sciences Quarterly* 10(2).

Sarvasy, Wendy (1985) 'Rethinking in the Welfare State, An Overview with Some Policy Implications'. Working Paper, San José State University.

Sennet, Richard (1982) *On Authority*. New York: Vintage Books.

Siim, Birte (1985) 'Women and the Welfare State – between Private and Public Dependence'. Working paper, Center for Research on Women, Stanford University, California.

Siim, Birte (1986) 'Women and the Welfare State. A Comparative Perspective on Care Work in Denmark and Britain', forthcoming in Clare Ungerson (ed.), *Women and Community Care, Gender and Caring in the Modern Welfare State*. London: Wheatsheaf.

Siim, Birte (1987) 'The Scandinavian Welfare States – towards sexual equality or a new kind of male dominance', *Acta Sociologica*, no. 3–4.

Stacey, Judith (1983) 'The New Conservative Feminism', *Feminist Studies* (Fall): 555–84.

Ungerson, Clare (1985) *Women and Social Policy, A Reader*. London: Macmillan.

Widerberg, Karin (1985) 'Ett kvinnosperspektiv på vældfærdsstaten marknaden och det civile samhälle' ('A Women's Perspective on the Welfare State, the Market and the Civil Society'), in *Veldfærdsstatens krise 2*, Gløder nr. 9 (Aalborg University).

Wilson, Elisabeth (1977) *Women and the Welfare State*. London: Tavistock.

Zaretsky, Eli (1982) 'The Place of the Family in the Origins of the Welfare State', in Barrie Thorne and Marilyn Yalom (eds), *Rethinking of the Family*. New York: Longman.

9

The Welfare State Citizenship of Scandinavian Women[1]

Helga Maria Hernes

The concept of citizenship has traditionally expressed the rights and duties attached to membership in the state. It refers to the bonds between state and individual citizen as well as to the bonds among individual citizens. These bonds are circumscribed by law, which spells out the rights and duties attached to membership; by custom, which expresses shared societal values and political culture; and by the material resources available to individual citizens, resources accrued in the labour market, through government transfers or by private provision. The dimensions of citizenship are determined by these bonds of membership and by the institutions which are designed to incorporate, defend, and administer them. They are, in addition, circumscribed by the political situation prevailing at any point in time. All the dimensions are gendered in a variety of ways, and states differ along all three dimensions: the nature of legal, social, and material bonds among citizens; the nature of the institutions which define and defend these bonds; and their capability of handling political crises. This chapter is concerned with the interdependence of the core dimensions of citizenship in Scandinavia: the bonds of membership; the institutional balance within which these are formed; and how these in turn affect women.

The assertion that welfare states empower women is not uncontroversial. There is general agreement that the material welfare of women (and children) is increasingly dependent on public policies rather than exclusively on private provision. However, there is no consensus as to the implications this might have for the political power of women, whether social welfare and political empowerment are related to each other, and if they are, how. The thesis that material welfare is the basis, or at least the precondition of welfare state citizenship, which is basic to the social democratic paradigm, is challenged by the thesis that the material basis of welfare state citizenship leads to dependence and clientilization, which is basic to the liberal and conservative paradigm.

This chapter indirectly addresses both these issues, and analyses Scandinavian policy and institutional development in regard to the content of citizenship, especially the citizenship of women. It thus enters a dialogue with both feminist and mainstream welfare state analysts who often regard the state as 'villain', with Marxist analysts who regard the market as 'villain', and those feminists who regard the patriarchal system, that is, the alliance between state, market, and male providers as 'villain'. If I may place myself in this partly ideological, partly scientific landscape I might describe myself as a state-friendly feminist in search of the women-friendly state and as part of the rather optimistic, pragmatic, social-democratic tradition of Scandinavian welfare state analysis.

I shall concentrate on the institutional basis of participatory rights since it is within this context that women's empowerment is occurring. The interplay between material and participatory rights is presented by way of an introduction. Let me state my conclusion at the outset: it is the institutional base of citizenship which is the decisive factor in women's gradual empowerment. This development has had three characteristic features (1965–1985):

1 The mobilization of women through the state and the public sector.
2 The process of administrative decentralization and devolution which has moved the welfare state to the local level, and involved women in a variety of ways.
3 The absence of the public/private split or rather the fact of institutional symbiosis in Scandinavian systems. This is a consequence of protracted social-democratic rule which has made it possible to carry out long-term policies, to establish a corporate system of governance, and to make an ideologically lasting impact on the political culture. For women the policy of integrating social and labour market issues, and of issuing gender equality acts, has been of decisive importance; corporate structures are two-edged swords; while the ideology of equality and universalism has been positive in terms of material welfare.

Material and Participatory Rights of Citizenship

Theories about the democratic state should ideally deal with the state's smallest unit, the individual citizen, and with the institutions which support central public values. Yet there exists a serious gap between theories of the welfare state (a state form which portends to be democratic) and democratic theory, both on a theoretical level and on the level of empirical operationalization. This poses problems for the study of citizenship, especially in the advanced, highly differentiated welfare states of Scandinavia. Recent democratization policies have added an aspect of citizenship – in other words, participatory rights guarantees of personal autonomy and material entitlements – to almost all relationships between the state and the individual within a great variety of institutional settings. The welfare state literature, to the extent that it deals with individual citizens, treats those aspects of citizenship which are related to social policy entitlements. Democratic theories and empirical studies of democratic politics emphasize the participatory aspects of citizenship. Any adequate account of contemporary citizenship in Scandinavia must include all these dimensions in order to grasp the interplay between material rights, multi-level participation, and political identities. As states have changed so have the content and meaning of citizenship changed for the individuals living within their borders. Yet most theories do not attempt to combine the answers to the central questions of modern citizenship: (a) Who participates in the institutional life of society and the state and what are the rights and duties attached to this participation? (b) Which values and resources are institutionalized, defended, and distributed by public authorities?

Congruence across institutions and between the three levels of society – individual, organizational, and institutional – can therefore be assessed only with great difficulty. Yet from the point of view of democratic citizenship such congruence should be a normative as well as a practical prerequisite in order that citizens may make use of their rights, and live up to their duties as citizen, and in order to enable citizens to identify with the political system on all three levels. Such congruence exists to much greater degree for men than for women. Women's formal rights and status as persons and as citizens have not led to fundamental changes in social institutions which are designed to defend central societal values, changes which would enable them to make use of their rights and fulfil their duties as persons, members of society (*bourgeois*) and citizens (*citoyen*). The ambiguously transmitted expectations and role conflicts which women experience even today are the products of a process of socialization which reflect the double messages women receive from the social and the political system. Contemporary women have formal rights of access, but experience difficulties in using these. This is true to a lesser degree in Scandinavia when it comes to their political rights, but is still the case in regard to economic life.

Ideals of citizenship have differed from each other throughout history on a variety of dimensions, most of which can be explained in institutional terms. Greek, liberal, Marxist, and social-democratic ideals of citizenship differ from each other. The *full-time citizenship* ideal of Aristotelian Athens fused public and private identities; patriotism and solidarity were one and the same, and there were no competing loyalties to those of life in the *polis*. Machiavelli's ideal citizen was the Roman legionnaire, the *citizen soldier* whose private life and values were irrelevant and of no concern to the Prince. The *part-time citizenship* ideal of liberal society places self-realization and the good life outside the public realm; private pursuits of salvation and capital accumulation are more important than life in the political community. The liberal state is expected to guarantee rights of personal integrity of body and mind, and certain forms of personal autonomy. It should enable the citizen to have 'a quiet life and not much trouble', an ideal fostered by Benjamin Constant in the last century, as well as by the British Liberal Party in ours (Holmes, 1979; 1985). The fact that liberal values and institutions deny women equal citizenship has been forcefully put by Carole Pateman (Pateman, 1985).

Marxist ideals of citizenship often seem limited to one goal, namely to increase the amount of free time at one's disposal. Liberation, according to one recent interpretation, lies in a maximum of free time available (Przeworski, 1985). The abolition of the state is naturally accompanied by the *abolition of citizenship*, an absence of public commitment and communal ideals which seems far removed from social-democratic ideals of citizenship.

The *activist, participatory, egalitarian ideal of social-democratic citizenship* differs from these former ideals. The historical basis of citizen involvement is to be found in the waves of social movements which have formed Scandinavian history since the middle of the nineteenth century, movements which were based on direct participation, but which were absorbed into the representative structure only to be followed by new waves of movements (Heckscher, 1951). Social democratic hegemony has concentrated its attention almost totally on the citizen as worker. Trade union members were until recently the prototypical social-democratic citizen. The social-democratic citizen is the *citizen worker,* a male family provider, a working-class hero. *His* rights, identities, and participation patterns were determined by *his* ties to the labour market, and by the web of associations and corporate structures which had grown up around these ties. This is changing, only to a small extent, because unions are empowering women. The participatory ideal grapples with a segmented reality both on the individual and on the institutional–systemic level (Olsen, 1978: 122; Hernes, 1982: 78–83).

The social-democratic state has until now placed great emphasis on guaranteeing citizens certain standards of material well-being. There is a new interest in civil rights and the protection of personal autonomy. The democratization policies of the past decade in combination with the high standard of material well-being might well have led up to this new interest in individual rights. Yet the main image in contemporary Scandinavia is one of *segmented and fragmented citizenship patterns*, whose combined effect on the individual level is unclear. These are a direct consequence of corporate institutional structures and of decentralization policies designed to increase the channels of access to decision making. Representation and participation occur in innumerable settings, in part expressing what Tocqueville termed 'the independent eye of civil society' through activities in voluntary organizations and social movements; in part taking the form of traditional electoral and party politics; and in part the exercise of work-place democracy. The positive consequences of the decentralization which local particpation rights have involved are increased autonomy, both on the personal and the organizational level. But decentralization has also inescapably led to decreased central control over national policy aims, including equality legislation on the systemic and organizational level, and fragmented participation patterns on the individual level. Citizenship is among other things still gendered.

Social democracy fosters a time-consuming and sometimes burdensome ideal which in itself can lead to new inequalities. Institutional participation patterns may on the other hand be the clearest expression of citizens' perceived feelings of obligation vis-à-vis their various memberships, expressing loyalties, support, feelings of duty and obligation as much as self-interest or the joy of self-expression. Those few studies which compare the motivations for membership and participation in various organizations seem to indicate that the motivational base differs from one institutional setting to the next. These do show gender differences: women participate more often in order to work for a cause or work for others than men do. This reflects also their greater investment in time-consuming memberships in humanitarian organizations and in movement politics such as the peace or the environmental movement (Hernes, 1987, ch. 3).

In the wake of Scandinavian development very little attention has been paid to membership duties, although these of course do exist. There is the duty to pay taxes, to do military service, and the duty to accept a job even if this means moving home and family. In the past all of these have concerned men more than women, but today the duties of membership are most visible to social clients, many of whom are women, and to young men doing military service. In general, the state makes few claims on its citizens, but membership rights on the other hand have grown at an almost exponential rate, and become more universal in nature. The actual status and content of many newly won rights is, however, debatable and the constitutional status of many welfare rights such as 'the right to work' which is guaranteed by the new Swedish constitution is rather unclear. Material claims on the state, the distribution of material rights, and the content of ideological bonds which form public identities, personal autonomy, and the level of information about the workings of society, as well as patterns in societal participation differ clearly according to group, and at this point in history especially according to gender. After twenty years of equality policies on various levels, women's and men's life patterns have changed but they still differ, and women still have considerably less societal power. Most social clients are women. Most full-time workers – the powerful 'indirect citizens' of corporate structures – are men. Most voters are women, most representatives are men. Women are the direct participants in an increasing number of citizen roles, men are either represented indirectly or are those who fill representative posts at least in the majority of cases.

There have so far been no empirical studies which would trace to what extent these differences are the result of conscious choice and preference, and to what extent they reflect the absence of choice and consciousness. Women's strategies will, regardless of their underlying motivations, bring about societal transformations, including shifts in the balance of institutional power. Women's activities are revitalizing electoral politics and thus the institutions of representative democracy. They are also increasing the level of activity in movement politics, and expanding the base of corporate decision making. The fluidity of the political situation is at least in part due to the activities of women. It is too early to say whether women's concentration on electoral politics, on the democratic power base of representative institutions, rather than the indirect power base of the corporate system will contribute to the renewal of the parliamentary power base. Parliaments and thus established political parties have become of decisive importance for women, since their political aims involve fundamental redistributions. Their political mobilization, which is a fact in all Nordic countries, may thus have the revitalization of parliaments as one of their most important institutional consequences, and citizenship patterns may once more be directed primarily at one institution at the national level. Even though I stated at the outset that there is at this point no single institution whose 'conquest' would lead to a permanent shift in the power balance between women and men, a conscious and strategic use of parliamentary power could bring about fundamental redistributions. The political identity of women is tied closely to the state, in both its democratic and in its administrative aspects.

Yet citizenship encompasses not only the bonds between state and individual, but also bonds and relations among individual members. This development has legal aspects, but in addition it shapes group formation and affects group consciousness. This group consciousness has in most European countries taken the form of patriotism or nationalism, while Scandinavia's long social-democratic history has resulted in widespread feelings of solidarity, in other words, communal bonds towards one's fellow-citizens rather than towards the state or the nation. These bonds are usually seen as the result of great societal, historically based homogeneity, yet attitudes towards social equality which are among the most important ingredients of Scandinavian homogeneity are as much a result of conscious policy over several decades. Scandinavian citizenship has not only the state but many societal memberships as its point of reference. Citizenship expresses not only, or even mainly, legal and national bonds, but social and political bonds in many institutional contexts. Swedish and Norwegian society score rather high on measures of solidarity, that is, bonds between citizens when measured in terms of support for equality. There are many indications that Scandinavian citizens form a 'material community' in terms of claims, rights, and entitlements, and most importantly standards of just distribution. The comparatively universalist nature of the material base for this community has been of decisive importance when it comes to the economic aspects of citizenship. There are also many indications that Scandinavian citizens form a 'political–legal community', a civic culture in the sense that Almond and Verba (1963) used the term (Allardt, 1975).

Political reforms have added social and economic rights to the traditional legal rights, to use the language of T.H. Marshall's classic (Marshall, 1964). These reforms have increased citizens' material ties to the state and provided them with 'property rights' to collective goods. They form, so to speak, the material base of welfare state citizenship. Membership now guarantees certain measures of social and economic equality in addition to political equality. Mutual dependence between state and citizen is considered a social good, and preferable to older private forms of dependence, such as those between a male head of family and his wife, or between capitalist and worker. The fact that the goods distributed on the basis of these rights are often scarce and access to them is limited has led to discussions of distributional justice of a rather complex nature, especially among those inside and outside the labour force. For that reason most distributional issues are gender issues at the present time.

Normative questions of distributive justice lie at the heart of Scandinavian welfare state development, and are thus also closely related to political ideologies. As elsewhere in Europe there is the underlying assumption, almost never expressed openly, that universal welfare state services and transfers must not exceed those earned in the labour market. In addition, there is the fact that many material rights are contingent at least in size on labour market participation. There is also the fact that those who are better off often also receive a disproportionate share of services such as day care. In the language of Michael Walzer, there occurs perhaps an unjust conversion of resources (Walzer, 1983). Yet there have occurred lasting redistributions among classes and social groups. Although membership rights are not equal – that is, identical, but dependent on one's contribution – there is a political struggle between women and men to count also certain types of unpaid work as a legitimate basis for welfare rights (Hernes, 1987; chapter 5).

Reforms have, however, not only taken the form of increased material benefits. There have been a number of reforms aimed at giving citizens access to decision structures in many different institutional settings, especially the work-place (Lafferty, 1986). Yet this development has gone much beyond the confines of workplace democracy, and includes all public roles and relations. The social-democratic policy aim described as the 'democratization of all areas of social life' should first of all be interpreted as an effort to reduce the potential for paternalism endemic to all welfare systems. It has given many forms of activity an aspect of citizenship. Participatory rights have been added on to various public roles as client, consumer, and worker. Advocacy has been built into the system. Political reforms have had a participatory profile. 'Citizens', or rather members of different public or semi-public institutions and all places of work above a certain size, and in certain instances those directly affected by particular activities, can participate in the relevant decision field. This has widened the recruitment base of the corporate system as well and given new groups access to many new decision structures from which they were formerly excluded. There are in the present situation two different reasons for women's limited representation in the corporate and institutional decision-making fields: women will on the whole lose out to men in those cases where competitive struggles for positions occur; and women have also, given the prevalence of part-time work among them, less access to nominations, and full-time working women will often, given their combined greater work load, be reluctant to accept nominations.

Participation rights in many different institutional contexts have thus developed parallel to and sometimes even in connection with increases in material rights. The special interplay between participatory and material rights is one of the hallmarks of Scandinavian political development. One of its central aims has been to reduce the dangers of clientilization which more paternalistic systems have been subject to. Whether this aim has been achieved is a question open to empirical validation. The question is whether this participatory ideal realized through a series of reforms is in agreement with popular preferences, to what extent citizens can live up to such high participatory ideals, and whether the present system's legitimacy rests on high participation rates. Another question is whether individual autonomy is sufficiently protected in a system which sets such a high premium on participation. The dangers of participatory democracy rewarding those with 'the most evenings to spare' has been discussed by Michael Walzer in his essay on 'A Day in the Life of a Socialist Citizen' (Walzer, 1970). Yet participatory rights have added components of procedural, formal justice to the material, substantive justice of social and economic rights (Bertilsson, 1987). Potentially they counteract clientilization, that is, welfare state paternalism, and give those who have the most pronounced 'client profile' citizen competence, that is, a feeling of self-worth and belonging.

Another important question to be raised is whether the participatory channels which have been created at the grass-roots level – the local corporatism of the decentralization strategy – find their counterpart in the representative systems of national corporate bodies, or whether the vertical segmentation described by Johan P. Olsen and his associates (Olsen, 1978), is also accompanied by a horizontal segmentation between national and local decision-making arenas. The fourth question which will not be addressed here is whether the bureaucratic structures which have been democratized lose as much legitimacy as they gain, whether bureaucratic and democratic legitimacy can be mixed.

Participatory Corporatism and Segmented Citizenship

Despite the fact that one's status as citizen of the state is the most inclusive and comprehensive, it is rarely the most dominant in citizens' consciousness. More autonomous activities within groups outside the boundaries of the 'state' in the strict sense of the word create stronger bonds of belonging and solidarity. Data from the

European Value Study show for example that Norwegian citizens identify more readily and strongly with their municipality than the country as a whole. Material claims on the state on the basis of rights, ideological bonds which form our public identity, information about the workings of society, and participation patterns which circumscribe our perception of personal influence and power, all give content to various aspects of citizenship, and all are transmitted and occur within different institutional contexts.

Most institutional contexts have for a variety of reasons become either gender specific or a gender dimension has been added to them. Women now occupy one-third of all representative elected positions. In Norway they occupy one-third of all positions in the corporate system of decision making, in Sweden about one-fifth. One-third of all civil servants in the large municipal administrative system are women, and in Norway this is true also for the lower ranks of the central civil service (Hernes, 1987). The public sector's welfare bureaucracies are dominated by women, especially in the lower ranks of course, but the feminization of relevant professions is now progressing at such a rate that women will soon occupy central decision-making posts. Women's advance in traditional professions such as medicine and the law is causing some dismay among men who fear for the declining status and subsequent declining income potential. Gender segregation has thus clear institutional aspects. Women have gained, if not parity, at least enough power in welfare state administration and in the electoral part of the political system, to affect priorities in these two spheres; they are still powerless in the private market, and are losing legal ground in the family. Women's limited market power is reflected in their limited union power, but they are now gaining power in professional and public sector unions. Women are quite clearly an important factor in party politics as well as in movement politics, as authors, as journalists, and as prominent athletes. Their influence on economic policy is, however, limited and their corporate power not comparable to their electoral power. We are dealing again with gender-specific institutional contexts.

Welfare reforms may have limited the economic power of capitalists over workers and of individual men over their wives, but these reforms are often implemented by bureaucratic organizations which become power bases in themselves. The institutional contexts within which we act have become ever more important in determining the content and the quality of our lives. To counteract bureaucratically induced apathy one has democratized many different types of large-scale organizations. The fact that women's client, employee, and taxpayer roles also come into conflict with each other complicates both individual lives and the political process. These cross-cutting loyalties may also create layers of solidarity with various groups and commitment to a variety of values, and Scandinavian political culture and institutions offer a greater variety of public citizen roles – if not private roles – to both women and men than most other cultures do. Social homogeneity is offset by political heterogeneity. Yet the organizational fit between the variety of individual citizen roles and motivations and the corporate actors whose purpose it is to mediate between citizens and large-scale institutions is at issue today.

Welfare bureaucracies have been subject to the most extensive criticism. This has led to public sector reforms which are aimed at increasing the efficiency and the accessibility of public services. Such criticisms reflect the problematic aspects of the status of client and of consumer rights. The exercise of social and economic rights has increased the number of state-related conflicts, and the level of these sometimes reaches the intensity of private-market-related conflicts of earlier decades. Although concerted action is still easier in one's role as employee or voter than in one's role as client or consumer of public services, there have been some instances of concerted action between clients, consumers, and employees – especially in Denmark, but also in Norway and Sweden. The client and consumer-related power of citizens is thus circumscribed by the institutional setting within which these rights are received and exercised. It seems thus quite clear that women's identities especially are shaped by their multiple roles in regard to the political–administrative system, roles which include bureaucratic and democratic elements. Women's claimant role is thus often combined with an employee or political role, and women's power is increasingly associated with bureaucratic power.

This is not to say that citizens' client and consumer power is not also related to the resources they possess in each instance, and by the degree of professional autonomy and discretion various institutions have been able to build up. Wresting control over parts of the social and health sectors from the male-dominated medical profession has been an important strategy of the semi-professions dominated by women. In the wake of such struggles women do of course compete with each other as well. Clients and welfare bureaucrats do not always see eye to eye on perceived needs and the legitimacy of claims or the desire for personal autonomy in Scandinavia any more than in most welfare states. For example, single providers, 90 per cent of whom are women, have notoriously fewer rights, less influence on the content of their client role, less sense of their own personal worth in the public realm than other women. They are also the group least likely to be organized for collective action. Still, their life strategy – being a social client, rather than an exploited worker – is often the result of conscious choice and preferences.

The external pressures created by democratization policies have also slowly affected large corporate actors such as unions. Despite the fact that the transition from social movement to powerful corporate actor has led to passivity among members, there is no doubt that the symbolic value of the 'club' ('facket' in Sweden, 'klubben' in Norway) is still very high. But new social movements, such as the environmental protection movement, the peace movement, and others have more emotive meaning among the younger generation and among women, and many different types besides economic interest organizations (which originally grew out of the 'second wave' movements) are now gaining access to corporate decision-making structures.[2] The corporate system which until relatively recently was a purely national decision-making system is reproducing itself on the local level (Hernes and Selvik, 1981). It is also for a variety of reasons changing from an arena of economic planning and income negotiation into a multipurpose system of decision making. The complex implications of this cannot be discussed here. In this context it must however be pointed out that it was the corporate system of economic interest articulation and negotiation which created, and even in part implemented, the material rights attached to welfare state citizenship. Whether it now can be turned into the system of implementing and orchestrating the participatory rights which have been the next wave is the question at hand. Does corporatism lend itself to direct and broadly based participation? Will such participation be meaningful in terms of impact and citizen influence? Can and should corporatism be participatory?

Citizenship in contemporary Scandinavian society is tied to a variety of organizational and institutional settings within state institutions, districts or municipalities, places of work, trade unions, numerous voluntary organizations, social movements, spontaneous issue-oriented activities, and neighbourhood associations. The citizen roles tied into these settings do not have equal status either legally or in terms of personal identity, but they all impinge upon the content of contemporary citizenship. Individual participation is (in other words) highly institutionalized, entrenched in a system which could be described as 'participatory corporatism', one phase beyond what Swedish historian Rolf Torstendahl terms 'corporative capitalism' which, according to him, characterizes the present phase in the history of European capitalism, and two phases beyond what he termed as 'participatory capitalism' (Torstendahl, 1984). Each phase of Torstendahl's four-stage model consists of four related factors; technological change and its impact on labour processes; the division of labour, especially the division into blue- and white-collar labour; the economic structure of society; and the organization of labour and the class struggle. His work is highly suggestive in terms of the interrelationship between technological, economic, and political changes. Yet his analysis stops short of incorporating two recent developments which have had lasting and irreversible impact and which affect each of his four factors: the expansion of the public sector, and the influx of women into the labour market. Most public sector work is carried out by women. It cannot be automatized or rationalized in the way new industrial work can, since it is 'people work'. The 'technology' of the public sector should definitely be an integral part of any analysis of the present phase of economic development. Secondly, labour markets are segregated along gender lines as well as sector lines, and solidarities among workers occur now as often along sector lines and thus gender lines, as they do along wage lines. Thirdly, the economic structure of society is largely determined by this division into private and public sectors, and it is often a moot point which sector receives greater state support. In terms of 'crisis management' in its mild Scandinavian form, there are clearly stated aims both of limiting the growth of the public sector and of letting non-profitable industries fall prey to market forces. In reality, however, there are few public sector cutbacks, and those that do occur are in the communications and transport sector rather than the social sector. Private sector unemployment is staved off by active labour market policies and continued support to non-profitable industries (especially in Norway). Various forms of co-determination increase worker participation in the public and the private sectors. This is one aspect of what in this chapter is termed 'participatory corporatism', one stage beyond Torstendahl's 'corporative capitalism'. Fourthly, labour struggles have intensified, there has been a significant increase in strike activity. Yet these struggles now often take the form of gender struggles, both in terms of wage policies and when it comes to state support of the economy. Class struggles and gender struggles intertwine in complex ways. Public and private sector competition is in reality often a competition between groups dominated by male and female labour and job categories. In addition, a number of reforms open up for participation in a variety of institutional settings, giving individuals access to decision-making structures, to information about administrative procedures and the opportunity to lodge complaints. The participatory profile of reforms and their decentralizing consequences have affected the organization of labour as well.

Defining the rules for such institutional or corporate citizenship can in itself pose problems of justice and autonomy. What are the rights of students vis-à-vis university authorities, the rights of patients vis-à-vis health professionals, the rights of workers in nationally owned plants threatened by bankruptcy? According to democratic theory, membership implies equality of access to decision-making structures (Dahl, 1986; Walzer, 1983). It is quite clear that these newly won participatory rights do not guarantee such equality and that there exist hierarchies of influence which are considered legitimate by many. This is, for example, the case in regard to the rights of ownership within the confines of work-place democracy. Until recently the rights of full-time and part-time labour were not equal, but that has been challenged successfully in some instances. Participation rights in many institutional contexts have thus developed parallel to and sometimes in connection with the increase in material rights, designed to give citizens the right to co-determine the content and oversee the implementation of their various rights.

Participatory corporatism extends beyond work-place democracy, and affects many areas of public life. One must, however, raise the question to what extent this decentralization policy has added real power either to new groups which now are represented, or has resulted in a real shift of power from the centre to the periphery. One possible thesis is that political power becomes limited partly because of collusion among powerful organizations, partly because organizational, bureaucratic, and political power become fused through laws which delegate a great deal of discretionary power to administrative organs. What we might be observing in this process of devolution is a loss of power on all parts, and certainly on the part of (electorally based) political institutions. After a protracted period of increasing state power, which was especially marked in Scandinavia, we are witnessing the dissolution of power. Women's increase in political power, especially in parliaments, has of course often been seen in connection with the perceived loss of institutionalized political power. Men who are interested in power no longer compete for political posts, it is feared.

But decentralization has also inescapably led to fragmentation and decreased central control over national policy aims, including gender equality implementation. Corporate decision structures, especially those on the regional levels, are designed for piecemeal reforms, implementation, and local adaptations, not for innovation or major redistributions. Also issue-oriented politics often concentrate on the grass-roots level. There is, in other words, a definite possibility that a relatively high level of activity on the local level will detract energies from the realization of women's major policy aims. There are, however, certain indications that active women have a wider political repertory than men have. That is to say, women have a more political citizen profile, while men have a more professionally based, corporate citizen profile.

To this negative interpretation one might pose the following counterthesis: participatory corporatism and decentralized popular and organizational participation as they are practised in Scandinavia today, especially on the local level, are appropriate for the creation and innovation of political culture and thus for the formation of new solidarities. While it is a political arrangement which quite clearly is not very appropriate for large-scale reforms or redistributions, it might well be an appropriate institutional solution for building up trust and dialogue among a wide variety of actors such as bureaucracies, organizations, movements, local action groups, and political parties. The sources of legitimacy are thus maintained and renewed. We are witnessing a new wave of incorporation of citizens and issues, similar to the one experienced at the end of the past century (Rokkan, 1967; 1970). Establishing new procedures and building institutions around these procedures is itself an important aspect of political life. Phases of policy innovation and reform are different from those phases that build up new procedures for creating mutual trust and thus legitimacy. The long period of political reforms of the sixties and seventies has added new actors, especially women, and new policy areas, especially in the area of reproduction, which must be absorbed and incorporated. Both are intimately connected with the organization of daily life, and thus lend themselves more naturally to decentralization to the local level than most other policy areas. In addition, decentralization and participation, while not very efficient or result-oriented in the short run, may give political newcomers, mainly women, both the time and the opportunity to become political innovators in the long run. Precisely the lack of localized political power to which Torstendahl (1984) refers, the 'non-transparency' of the political situation of which Habermas (1985) complains and the loss of steering power of which Claus Offe writes (1984c), in short the fluidity of the political situation, combined with a comparatively high level of participation from an international perspective, may all be well suited to create new sources of legitimacy based on communal ties and to increase the political power of women. These could expand the base of solidarity which trade-union-defined, working-class solidarity had narrowed down.

'State feminism', feminism from above in the form of gender

equality and social policies as well as the feminization of welfare-state-relevant professions, have their counterpart and challenge in the 'feminization from below' among women activists in political and cultural activities. Women are making their presence felt both in terms of numbers and of clout. Women are, so to speak, exchanging economic powerlessness for political power, or at least the opportunity to gain political experience, and to steer the implementation of their newly won rights. Women's and men's different individual priorities, preferences, attitudes, and values are becoming visible. The cognitive, behavioural, and emotive aspects of citizenship differ among women and men from one context to the other. Women are very marginal in the private sector of the economy where men still are the dominant gender – this applies not only to positions of power but also to their consumer roles. In the family, women's legal power is being reduced through legislative measures in the name of gender equality, even though the actual division of labour is still quite uneven. Women and men compete for the custody of their children who have, one might say, become one of the major scarcities, in emotional terms.

The Institutional Balance between State and Society

Institutional interdependence and a 'public/private mix' rather than a 'public/private split' (which characterizes more liberal Western systems) and thus the absence of clearly defined institutional boundaries are among the hallmarks of Scandinavian historical development (G. Hernes, 1978; H.M. Hernes, 1982; Hedborg and Meidner, 1983; Olsen, 1983; Sejersted, 1984; Torstendahl, 1984; 1986; Nybom, 1986). They present the core of the Scandinavian model with its three cornerstones: the corporate system, the public sector, and the amalgam of social movements and political parties of democratic (partly electorally based) institutions. The interface between the political–administrative system and the market is institutionalized in the national corporate system. The interface between the political–administrative system and the family has found its expression partly in the public sector administered by a local form of corporatism. This sector of course also provides infrastructures for the private sector, that is the 'market', in the strict sense of that term. The interface between political and social movements, which have been the main source of political innovation throughout the past century, is not as clearly localized or circumscribed. They have acted as a link between a variety of arenas: trade unions have mediated between market and state, earlier in their history between market and family as well;

traditional humanitarian organizations have directed social policy demands at the political–administrative system as well as political parties and parliaments. They have been instrumental in the integrative process between state and society, and political–administrative institutions. The state, the market, the public sphere of opinion formation, and the family are thus the four major institutional settings.

The state has been the dominant institution designed to administer this mix since the turn of the century, increasingly mitigating state power as the only decisive base for political power. In respect to this dominance of the state the Scandinavian model parallels the nineteenth-century Prussian model of industrial development (Torstendahl, 1986). Increasing the power of working-class men was part of the Swedish pre-war settlement (the Norwegian settlement had to wait until after the war). The fact that the Swedish settlement took place before the Second World War is probably a more important cause of the stability of the system than is usually acknowledged (Nybom, 1986). With the rapid expansion of the public sector in the 1960s, the family (and thus, women) became an integral if weak partner in the institutional network. In no other part of the world has the 'state' been used so consistently by all groups, including women and their organizations, to solve collectively felt problems.

Until the 1960s women had mainly been confined to the family. Now they move increasingly among all four spheres. Individual patterns of movement and involvement over the life course are gender specific. Women's evolving profile of citizenship reflects the institutional interface between state and family, their employment in the public sector, and their political mobilization. Women have become mobilized through their varied ties to the state, much as men a hundred years before were politically mobilized through their ties to the market. These two modes of mobilization as well as their socialization effects differ from each other, and account in part for the gender divisions of contemporary Scandinavian societies and for differences in the modes of citizenship of women and men.

Scandinavian institutional and political development differs from that of other countries in two important respects: the 'welfare state' is not a sector, a state within a state, but rests solidly on the institutional balance between the corporate system, the public sector, and the family; and secondly, the mobilization and political incorporation of working-class men which provided the political base for the first phase of welfare state development is now followed by the mobilization and political incorporation of women who provide an important political base for the second phase of welfare state development. The following discussion will refer to these differences in a variety of contexts.

Many observers, including some feminist analysts, refer to the dominance of the state in Scandinavian political development as the most prominent example of the 'pathology' of welfare states, which has led to the 'atrophy' of societal forces, both social and economic. This negative interpretation of welfare state development rests in part on a political–cultural critique and in part on assumptions of liberal economic theory which states that only the 'market', that is, the private sector, can be responsible for the creation of public and private goods. Its concomitant social-democratic policy assumption is that only full employment and growth can save the welfare state. In economically based theories the welfare state is almost solely defined in terms of a social policy sector dependent on the health of the private market economy. The social policy model of welfare state development, though often combined with reference to the historic incorporation of the working class, sees citizens as 'claimants–consumers–clients' whose demands have led to fiscal overload and bureaucratization. The 'citizen' is thus implicitly and even explicitly viewed as a profit maximizer rather than as political participant with multiple visions and goals. The richness of previous frameworks (Rokkan, 1970; 1974) on which much of this modernization research is based is lost. The political and cultural base of mobilization into citizenship is marginalized and economic concerns of personal security which dominate the social policy drive are overemphasized.

Furthermore, feminist welfare state analysts stress the 'clientilization' of women through welfare state development and view social policy, and thus the welfare state, as an instrument for the control of women (Ergas, 1982; Riedmüller, 1982; Frazer, 1986; Pateman, 1987). Few agree that women's client status and their dependence on – or rather integration into – the public distribution system bears in it the seed for new citizen status. Nor do they agree with the assumption that there exists a natural alliance between women and the welfare state (Hernes, 1984; 1986; Piven, 1985; Piven and Cloward, 1985: 179). Most feminist theorists claim that the private sphere of kinship and family rather than state and market is the locus of women's oppression, and they rarely look to state or market as problem solvers. These are described as public and private patriarchies, impersonal and exploitative, seldom regarded as amenable to reform. Instead feminists tend to opt for separatist, public, non-state organizations in order to guarantee control by women. Scandinavian political culture expresses a more benign view of the state as an instrument of popular will, which is used to control the private forces of market and family. It is these that are regarded as the sources of social and economic inequality. Scandinavian feminists act in accordance with their own political culture in turning to the state, even in those instances where they wish to build alternative institutions. The logic of feminist argumentation is usually that women have as much right of access to public goods as men do. Political organization and collective action by women are considered the effective antidote to 'clientilization'. Most general models of welfare state development do not consider the participation and incorporation of women to be an indicator of structural and thus institutional change. Women are usually subsumed under the gender-neutral category of 'new groups' or 'welfare state claimants'; they are considered to be agents of crisis, threats to working-class solidarity, burdens on the public purse, and so on.

In contrast to the more narrowly conceived social-policy-oriented models there is one comprehensive theory which combines several levels of analysis, the work of Jürgen Habermas (Habermas, 1981; 1985). His theory gives one the opportunity to discuss the interdependence of various institutions and individual roles and statuses within them, and provides a good framework for an analysis of the political and social incorporation of a plurality of citizen roles; yet he shares the widespread distrust of the state as an institution. His distrust of the state and his fear of citizens' clientilization are an analytical challenge from the point of view of Scandinavian citizenship. Habermas analyses the interplay between four respectively public and private spheres: the 'system' which consists of the public administrative system and the private market, and the 'life world' which consists of the public sphere of opinion formation and the private sphere of intimacy and the family. This fourfold set of public/private and system/life world institutional settings are the parameters within which he describes welfare state development.

His welfare state citizenship theory is one of clientilization, yet ideally democratic citizenship consists for him of the capacity to form independent opinions and the opportunity for intellectual autonomy. These are formed not in the state, but in the 'life world' through primary socialization in the family and in the educational system, later through participation in the public sphere of opinion formation. In the 'system' we are mainly clients, legal subjects, and wage-earners, dependent on the power and discretion of an impersonal state apparatus and market. The uncontrolled expansion of state and market power have, according to Habermas, increased the 'system's' control over our lives and limited our ability to control our lives and our capacity for self-reflection. Our 'inflated' client role and acquisitive worker and consumer roles are much more pronounced and dominant than our 'citizen role' in the public sphere. He denies (or ignores) thus the citizen aspect of client, consumer, and worker roles, that is to say, the participatory rights, guarantees of personal autonomy, and material rights which combine into citizenship. Only within the public sphere as it is defined by him can we act as 'citizens'. The 'colonization of the life world' by the system lies at the core of his cultural critique of the welfare state, a colonization which excoriates our citizen role. Conservative critics of welfare state development parallel Habermas's colonization thesis, in which the state undermines the creativity of society, with an 'invasion' thesis of the market in which the state destroys the creativity of the market. This invasion deprives the market of its innovative and creative adaptability. All these analytical traditions – liberal, feminist, critical, and conservative – thus share a fear of the state. They share this attitude with those 'left functionalists' who, according to Piven and Cloward, claim that 'welfare state programs incapacitate people for political action' (1985: 176). Scandinavian optimism departs on this point from most of the literature.

Habermas's thesis about the political and economic system's dependence on the life world for its own legitimation rests on the assumption that state and society form distinct and even dichotomous categories of social discourse and relations. The assumption is that meaning is produced only within the latter, and that the economic foundation for the welfare state is produced only within the former. Habermas denies the possibility of the norm-, symbol- and meaning-producing capacity of institutional settings within the 'system'. He also ignores the production of welfare services (public goods) by women in the family and by voluntary institutions in the life world. For Offe it seems as though meaningful political activity is carried on mainly within political movements rather than other political institutions, and that the public sector 'feeds' on the private sector for its survival (Offe, 1985; 1987). Both these theorists assume that the 'life world' (or society) is the sphere where meaning is created and where attitudes towards the system of power and money are formed. Habermas has in his latest important essay on the crisis of the welfare state as a legal–bureaucratic machinery relied almost exclusively on Offe's analyses of political development (Offe, 1984a, b, c; Habermas, 1985). Offe, on the other hand, has carried his own analysis of the decline of the post-war settlement further in terms of the structural disintegration of the labour market, of 'work' as we have known it during the industrial age, and thus of the bases for solidarity. The strength of Offe's most recent work lies in his analysis of the tension between 'welfare state' and 'political democracy'. Its limitation lies in the fact that, despite his attention to social movements (1985), he continues to view the labour market as the only real basis for solidarity, and for the formation of group consciousness and identity (Offe, 1987).

The notion of the 'state' carries for both of them almost exclusively repressive or at least deeply alienating symbols. In the light of Scandinavian historical developments one must at least consider the possibility of political identity formation within the legal–administrative system. This is especially relevant in the case of women who have so many different points of contact with the state. Legal and political reforms have in some ways developed in such a way that they have mobilized rather than distanced individuals from the system. Clients of the system, most of whom are women, have become more active in negotiating both the content and the forms of delivery of their entitlements, which are considered an integral part of welfare state citizenship. There is in addition the mediating role of political movements. One might at least hypothesize that this trust is in part a result of the democratization of core institutions and of policies which aim at increasing the participatory element of corporate structures, a development towards 'participatory corporatism'. Although the institutional balance between state and society has in Scandinavian social democracies quite clearly gone in favour of the state, there is thus an awareness of the dangers of alienation which has resulted in important participatory reforms at all levels, involving individuals in their functionally limited corporate roles.

Do segmented citizenship patterns then necessarily imply fragmentation and alienation on the individual level? Or do they develop intra-personal pluralism and foster the growth of citizen competence in a variety of legal, organizational, and institutional contexts (the 'segments' of corporate states)? This is the normative question of contemporary Scandinavian citizenship. Scandinavian policy has intended to democratize all four socio-political processes and the institutions attached to them: market, bureaucracy, political institutions, and the corporate bargaining system (Dahl and Lindblom, 1953). There is no agreement as to which of these regulatory and co-ordinating principles is the most decisive one today. One might claim that the intended democratization and increase of polyarchal elements has not succeeded; that we witness rather a strengthening of the corporate bargaining structure where leaders control each other. The 'crisis' is accordingly a deadlock among leaders and of the institutional balance, not one of declining solidarities. It is a leadership crisis which may at some point become a serious crisis of democratic legitimacy.

Solidarity crises are of a different nature. They refer to waning bonds among citizens, rather than waning trust between citizen and governing institutions. Solidarity and legitimacy are ultimately related, because strong bonds of solidarity among and within citizen groups affect institutions and determine the institutional balance within society. Yet it is a moot point where there exists a crisis of changing solidarities among citizens, of deep-going changes in the social structure and of processes of mobilization which have characterized Scandinavian societies (Svallfors, 1986; Martinussen, 1988).

Marx's theory of the socializing effect of the market has been echoed in a variety of theories of modernization and mobilization. There is little doubt that the market and the industrial epoch have determined much of the content of citizenship of the past hundred years, and that European images of citizenship are formed by this interplay between democratic participant and claimant roles. Practically all theories of political development assume that mobilization for citizenship is mediated through the market, and cannot occur directly in confrontation between the state and its citizens. If this becomes the primary mode, it is assumed that client status and negative dependence will result. Most models are based on the historic incorporation of working-class men, even though they claim universal and even future validity. As a consequence of the second phase of welfare state development referred to above, women have become mobilized through the state. These two modes of mobilization as well as their socialization effects differ from each other, and account in part for differences in modes of citizenship, not only among women and men, but among several 'new groups' and the proto-typical 'citizen worker'. The traditional incorporation occurred through unions and parties and was directed at parliaments. Today more and more citizens have direct ties to the state as employees of the public sector, as client and consumer of public services and transfers, as taxpayer, as lodger of complaints, and as political participant. These roles intersect. Citizens 'meet themselves at the door' in innumerable settings and direct their support, demands, and complaints at a growing number of organizations and agencies. As the mediating role of unions wanes new organizational buffers between citizen and state and citizen and market develop. Yet is it is difficult to foresee the final outcome of these organizational realignments, and even more difficult to foresee which of the co-ordinating principles – the bargaining–

negotiating one of corporatism, the competitive one of the market, or the political one of polyarchy – will prevail.

One might hypothesize that the stability of the Scandinavian system until now has not been based on any of these or even a mixture of them, but has rather been conditioned by a *fifth principle of co-ordination*, i.e. namely that of '*community*', of a deeply felt 'felleskap' (*Gemeinschaft*) and 'habits of the heart' to cite the title of a recent book (Bellah *et al.*, 1985). We have stated above (p. 193) that there are many indicators that Scandinavians form a 'material community' in terms of claims, rights, and entitlements, and of standards of just distribution. This has been of decisive importance for women. We have also stated that they form a 'political legal community', a civic culture which has recently opened up to women. A case can also be made that they form an 'ethical community' of shared meanings, identities, and symbols which waning solidarities have not yet undermined. The idea of the 'folkehemmet' (the people's home, *Heimat*) is one of those common symbols, common because Swedish social democrats already in the 1930s were able to capture it as a national political symbol. (Hentilä, 1978). It is a term which, like the general Scandinavian term 'felleskap', cuts across the state/society distinction. In Swedish and Norwegian public discourse the words 'society' and 'state' are used interchangeably, and not as dichotomies as in other languages (Hernes, 1985). The altruistic impulse of Erik Allardt's *Having, Loving, Being* (1975) might be as strong as the competitive, acquisitive, combative, and bargaining impulses of other aspects of citizenship.

The Future of Citizenship

A good case can be made that more fundamental aspects of Scandinavian institutional arrangements and political culture account for the increasing political power of women. The fluidity of institutional arrangements; the lack of 'separateness' and the corresponding mutual permeability of state, market, family, and public sphere; the intermingling of different principles of rationality within one and the same institutional context – all of these are basic characteristics of the Scandinavian model. The separation of private and public, personal, and communal aspects of life in most Western societies is usually regarded as one of the major stumbling-blocks for the emancipation of women. Scandinavia is a deviant case in this regard, and its deviance is consciously institutionalized. In the international literature on Scandinavia attention is usually paid to the economic settlement between capital and labour, the core of the corporate arrangement. In fact such negotiations occur between a variety of groups and on an increasing number of subjects far beyond narrowly defined economic planning. Women in their various institutional capacities have in the wake of welfare state developments become important bargaining partners. State feminism is nothing more nor less than the result of negotiations and 'contracts' between the state and women; it represents the results of an alliance between women and the state. As with all political outcomes, it is based on compromises which are re-negotiated at regular intervals. The public sector as 'the family writ large' is the major subject of negotiations and thus the major battle scene. Citizen power for women at this point of economic and political development is largely synonymous with influence over the future of the public sector. As Therborn has pointed out: 'Welfare states have very important effects on the conditions of human reproduction, and above all on the position of women . . . the growth of the welfare state should increase the independence of women' (Therborn, 1986: 160). Women are partners as well as challengers and claimants vis-à-vis the state, and alliances among different groups of women constitute the force of 'feminization from below', which expresses itself in co-operation and coalitions among different groups of women. Scandinavian polities are today characterized as much by divisions of gender as by divisions of class. This is at least in part due to the success of social-democratic parties in both Sweden and Norway in reducing class differences. As class differences have been reduced, women have begun to compete with men and inequalities between them have become obvious and even exacerbated. The real challenge for Scandinavian political tradition is not, however, to eradicate this new inequality. Scandinavian political traditions and institutions are rather well equipped to reduce inequalities. The challenge for these homogeneous societies is rather to design a gender equality policy which allows for pluralism and gender difference while guaranteeing equality. And this task is a political one which can be solved only through political discourse. What Scandinavian women are fighting for today is thus political power – the power to define, to circumscribe, to give content to policies – not material welfare. It is for these reasons that the political reforms which have added citizen aspects to all our public roles are so important for women. The expansion of representation rights to include many societal institutions have incorporated women and simultaneously increased gender conflict. Women's entry into public space has been facilitated by the absence of clear and decisive institutional boundaries. Institutional integration rather than segregation has made it possible for women to move from one sphere to the other, and to combine more roles than the institutional arrangements of other countries have allowed for.

Notes

1. This article is reprinted in slightly revised form from my book *Welfare State and Women Power: Essays in State Feminism*. Oslo: Norwegian University Press, 1987.
2. This loss of monopoly on the part of the unions may be related to the demographic crisis and its demands on citizen's potential 'care-taker pool' which is organized and expressed in settings other than unions.

References

Allardt, E. (1975) *Att ha, att älska, att vara (Having, Loving, Being)*. Lund: Argos.
Almond, G. and S. Verba (1963) *The Civic Culture*. Princeton, NJ: Princeton University Press.
Bellah, R.N., R. Madsen, W.N. Sullivan, A. Swidler, and S.M. Tipton (1985) *Habits of the Heart*. New York: Harper and Row.
Bertilsson, M. (1987) *Social Justice and Social Theory*. Uppsala: Swedish Centre for Advanced Study in Social Sciences.
Dahl, R. (1986) 'Procedural Democracy' in R. Dahl (ed.), *Democracy, Liberty and Equality*. Oslo: Universitetsforlaget.
Dahl, R. and C. Lindblom (1953) *Politics, Economics and Welfare*. New York: Harper and Row.
Ergas, Y. (1982) '1968–1979 – Feminism and the Italian Party System: Women's Politics in a Decade of Turmoil', *Comparative Politics* 14, 253–79.
Frazer, N. (1986) 'What's Critical About Critical Theory? The Case of Habermas and Gender', *New German Critique* 35: 97–131.
Goul Andersen, J. (1984) *Kvinder og Politik (Women and Politics)*. Aarhus: Politica.
Goul Andersen, J. (1986) 'Electoral Trends in Denmark in the 1980s', *Scandinavian Political Studies* 9(2): 157–74.
Habermas, J. (1981) *Theorie des Kommunikativen Handelns (Theory of Communicative Action)*. Frankfurt: Suhrkamp.
Habermas, J. (1985) 'Die Krise des Wohlfahrtsstaates und die Erschöpfung Utopischer Ideen', in *Die Neue Unübersichtlichkeit (The New Intransparency)*. Frankfurt: Suhrkamp.
Heckscher, G. (1951) *Staten och organisationerna (States and organizations)*. Stockholm: Liber.
Hedborg, A. and R. Meidner (1983) *Folkhemsmodellen (The People's-Home-Model)*. Stockholm: Raben and Sjögren.
Hentilä, S. (1978) 'The Origins of the Folkhem Ideology in Swedish Social Democracy', *Scandinavian Journal of History* 3: 323–45.
Hernes, G. (ed.) (1978) *Forhandlingsøkonomi og blandingsadministrasjon (Bargaining Economy and Mixed Administration)*. Oslo: Universitetsforlaget.
Hernes, G. and A. Selvik (1981) 'Local Corporatism', in Berger (ed.), *Organizing Interests in Western Europe*. Cambridge: Cambridge University Press.
Hernes, H.M. (1982) *Staten – Kvinner ingen adgang? (The State – Women No Access?)* Oslo: Universitetsforlaget.

212   *The political interests of gender*

Hernes, H.M. (1984) 'Women and the Welfare State: The Transition from Private to Public Dependence', in H. Holter (ed.), *Patriarchy and the Welfare Society*. Oslo: Universitetsforlaget.

Hernes, H.M. (1985) 'Norden – idealer og realiteter' ('Norden: Ideal and Reality'). Oslo: Forbruker- og administrasjonsdepartementet.

Hernes, H.M. (1986) 'Die Geteilte Sozialpolitik' ('Dual Social Policy'), in Haujsen and Nowotny (eds), *Wie Männlich ist die Wissenschaft? (How Male is Science?)* Frankfurt: Suhrkamp.

Hernes, H.M. (1987) *Welfare State and Woman Power*. Oslo: Norwegian University Press.

Holmes, S.A. (1979) 'Aristippus in and out of Athens', *The American Political Science Review* 73: 113–29.

Holmes, S. (1985) 'Differenzierung und Arbeitsteilung im Denken des Liberalismus' ('Differentiation and the Division of Labour in Liberal Thought'), in Luhman (ed.), *Soziale Differenzierung (Social Differentiation)*. Opladen: Westdeutscher Verlag.

Lafferty, W. (1986) 'Varieties of Democratic Experience'. Oslo: Department of Political Science. Mimeo draft.

Listhaug, O., A. Miller, and H. Valen (1985) 'The Gender Gap in Norwegian Voting Behavior', *Scandinavian Political Studies* 8: 187–206.

Marshall, T.H. (1964) *Class, Citizenship and Social Development*. New York: Doubleday.

Martinussen, W. (1988) *Solidaritetens grenser* (The Limits of Solidarity). Oslo: Universitetsforlaget.

Nybom, T. (1986) 'The Making and Defense of the Social Democratic State', University of Uppsala: Department of History.

Offe, C. (1984a) *Arbeitsgesellschaft: Strukturprobleme und Zukunftsperspektiven (Working Society: Structural Problems and Perspectives of the Future)*. Frankfurt: Campus.

Offe, C. (1984b) *Contradictions of the Welfare State*. London: Hutchinson.

Offe, C. (1984c) 'Korporatismus als System Nichtstaatlicher Makrosteuerung', ('Corporatism as a System of Non-State Governance'), *Geschichte und Gesellschaft* 10: 234–56.

Offe, C. (1985) *Disorganized Capitalism*. Cambridge: Polity Press.

Offe, C. (1987) 'Democracy Against the Welfare State?', *Political Theory* 15(4): 501–37.

Olsen, J.P. (1978) *Politisk organisering (Political Organization)*. Bergen: Universitetsforlaget.

Olsen, J.P. (1983) *Organized Democracy*. Bergen: Universitetsforlaget.

Oskarson, M. (1987) 'Gender, Social Structure and Party Choice in Sweden 1985'. Gothenburg: Department of Political Science.

Pateman, C. (1985) 'Women and Democratic Citizenship'. The Jefferson Memorial Lectures, University of California, Berkeley.

Pateman, C. (1987) 'The Patriarchal Welfare State', in A. Gutman (ed.), *Democracy and the Welfare State*. Princeton, NJ: Princeton University Press.

Piven, Frances Fox (1985) 'Women and the State: Ideology, Power and the Welfare State', in Rossi (ed.), *Gender and the Life Course*. New York: Aldine.

Piven, F.F. and R.A. Cloward (1985) *The New Class War: Reagan's Attack on the Welfare State and its Consequences* (rev edn). New York: Pantheon Books.

Przeworski, A. (1985) *Capitalism and Social Democracy*. Cambridge: Cambridge University Press.

Riedmüller, B. (1982) 'Frauen haben keine Rechte' ('Women have no rights'), in Kickbusch and Riedmüller, *Die Armen Frauen (Poor Women)*. Frankfurt: Suhrkamp.

Rokkan, S. (1967) Introduction, in Lipset and Rokkan, *Party Systems and Voter Alignments*. New York: Free Press.

Rokkan, S. (1970) *Citizens, Elections, Parties*. Oslo: Universitetsforlaget.

Rokkan, S. (1974) 'Dimensions of State Formation and Nation Building', in Tilly (ed.), *The Formation of National States in Western Europe*. Princeton, NJ: Princeton University Press.

Sejersted, F. (1984) *Demokrati og Rettsstat (Democracy and Rule of Law)*. Oslo: Universitetsforlaget.

Svallfors, S. (1986) *Offentlig sektor (Public Sector)*. Stockholm: Institute for Social Research.

Therborn, G. (1986) 'Karl Marx Returning', *International Political Science Review* 7(2).

Torstendahl, R. (1984) 'Technology in the Development of Society. Four Phases of Industrial Capitalism in Western Europe', *History and Technology* 1: 157–74.

Torstendahl, R. (1986) 'Staten, samhället och den organiserade kapitalismen' ('State, Society and Organized Capitalism'), *Historisk Tidskrift* 4: 502–11.

Walzer, M. (1970) 'The Problem of Citizenship', in Walzer (ed.), *Obligation*. Cambridge, Mass.: Harvard University Press.

Walzer, M. (1983) *Spheres of Justice*. New York: Basic Books.

10
Politics, Population, and Gender:
A Feminist Analysis of
US Population Policy in the Third World

Jane S. Jaquette
and Kathleen A. Staudt

In the 1960s and 1970s, the goals of two very different movements – the women's movement and the worldwide campaign to limit population growth – seemed compatible. It was thought that increased availability of contraceptives would serve the feminist ends of increasing freedom of choice for women, and reducing male control over women's bodies. Fewer children, it was argued, would improve women's health, extend female life expectancy, and give women more time and energy to invest in their families or to seek income-generating opportunities. Because reproductive rights and increased access to 'male' jobs were top priorities for feminists in the United States, family planning programmes for Third World women seemed a logical extension of women's liberation to traditional societies where, as the stereotype had it, women were 'even more oppressed'.

Beginning in the mid-1970s and into this decade, the women's movement has nevertheless become quite critical of US population policy. Feminists have found it too narrow in its focus on women's reproductive decisions, coercive in its pressure to increase contraceptive use or promote sterilization, and damaging to women's health in its disregard for the negative consequences of promoting women's use of technologies that endanger their health. More recently, a feminist case has been made for women's maternal rights and for the recognition of the fact that women have children for themselves and not just in response to 'patriarchal' demands.

This chapter reviews the evolution of population policy in the United States from the early 1960s to the present, and examines the arguments surrounding its adoption and implementation. It has two aims: the first is to highlight the sexist assumptions that were present from the beginning in US population policy and to analyse why feminists ignored these biases; second, and more important, we argue that analysing the process by which the policy was developed provides a good case-study of the intersection of gender and politics. From the beginning, the primary emphasis was on women as the 'target population' whose behaviour should be changed. The ways in which the issue was defined, policies were advanced, and programmes were established and implemented, suggest critical points in the (American) political process where we can observe the interaction of gender and politics. A closer reading of this interaction will show how difficult it is to avoid the issue of how to define women's interests and make it possible to move more purposefully towards the goal of a politics that is sensitive to gender.

Looking back on the development of US population policy reveals how much progress has been made in developing an awareness of political patterns likely to be harmful to women's interests. Although it was argued then, and the case can still be made, that women's ability to control their own fertility is an essential prerequisite to women's empowerment in modernizing societies, it is clear to us that population policy evolved in ways that we would now recognize as actually dangerous and disempowering for women.

The development of population as an *issue* took place in a climate of near-hysteria generated by books like Paul Ehrlich's *The Population Bomb* (1968), which mobilized individuals who, with the intensity of true believers, sought policy changes that would affect the lives of others who were outside the US political system, and thus outside of a political feedback loop that might have softened the policy's excesses. In this case, one of the virtues of a *pluralist political process* – that those affected by policies are actively involved in setting those policies and monitoring their implementation – was absent.

Furthermore, there were a number of danger signals at the *implementation* stage. The US Agency for International Development (AID) worked to convince Third World recipients of US aid to accept population limitation as a part of their development plans. This inevitably increased the state's involvement in reproductive decision making and, depending on whether the response was positive or negative, heightened its pro- or anti-natalist efforts. The availability of a technological 'fix' in the form of new contraceptive technology guaranteed that population policy would be administered in ways that distanced the implementing agencies from the women they were trying to reach. In addition to the hierarchical relationship between bureaucracy and client (Ferguson, 1984), the fact that contraceptive technology was a medical expertise put doctors in charge. This meant that the legitimacy of the conventional doctor/patient relationship – that of authority and dependence – was not questioned at any level (Delamont and Duffin, 1978; Ehrenreich and English, 1973).

When it became clear, as the policy evolved, that contraceptive supply did not generate sufficient demand, social scientists were called in to study the factors affecting contraceptive use, and to advise the bureaucracy on how to create more effective programmes. Social scientists did expand the focus and look at women in a much broader social, political, and economic context. The result, however, was not to enhance women's power but rather to increase the effectiveness with which the state could manipulate women's reproductive behaviour. This chapter explains how we can learn from the failure of good intentions. Feminist goals, 'visible' women, committed staff, and engaged social science do not necessarily add up to good outcomes for women.

Making Population an Issue

Although both movements can claim important gains in the early 1960s,[1] public awareness of the feminist movement and the population issue both increased dramatically in the late 1960s. There were some obvious affinities between the two movements. Both were part of the wave of popular movements of the 1960s and both were in part reactions against the rapid economic growth of the postwar period. Both identified imbalances between technology and nature, and both shared a goal of human empowerment. Population activists argued that human beings could anticipate disaster and act rationally to avert it, and feminists saw women rising up to break the chains of 'two thousand years of oppression'.

Many argued that there was a positive connection between the two movements, pointing out that feminism owed much of its promise to recent advances in contraceptive technology. Because the Pill had liberated women from obligatory childbirth and thus from the inevitability of dependence on men, women's liberation and sexual liberation were seen as positive and mutually reinforcing goals.

On the one hand, the population issue captured the imagination of many women, few of them declared feminists, but many drawn to the movement as particularly relevant to their experiences and in need of their skills. On the other hand, the voluntarist and individualistic implications of the population campaign appealed strongly to liberal feminists, then as now the core of the movement. To them it seemed obvious that the obligation to have children was in direct conflict with the goal of having women succeed in careers hitherto dominated by men.

Some feminist theory expressed a real ambivalence about women's bodies and their reproductive capability. From radical feminists who traced women's oppression to biology (Firestone, 1970) to anthropologists for whom reproduction and ensuing domestic responsibilities explained women's 'universal subordination' (Rosaldo, 1974), contraception was seen as a means to freedom and a necessary prerequisite to full equality. The family was criticized as an oppressive institution, a way of keeping women down. Others, like Gloria Steinem, could argue that women's reproductive capacity should be used as a sort of a bargaining chip in the battle between the sexes. For Steinem, women's ability to have children, or to refuse to have them, is women's 'turf'. The ability to give or deny that turf could become the basis for a conscious strategy of female empowerment.[2] This could be a particularly important source of power for Third World women because, where traditional values prevail, women lack the legal and political means to improve their status.

Ehrlich's intent in *The Population Bomb* was to awaken the American public to the depth and imminence of the disaster that would occur should population growth rates, especially in the Third World, continue unabated. Re-reading Ehrlich today clearly reveals the racist and sexist biases of *The Population Bomb* and the political rhetoric it popularized. By creating a crisis mentality, one that later proved to be vastly overdone, Ehrlich encouraged policies in which the goals were given: the necessity of limiting population growth was an article of faith, not subject to review. As a result, strategies of implementation could offer little space for participation by those whose behaviour was to be changed – that is, by Third World women themselves. Such policies were necessarily highly manipulative, with debate focused solely on the issue of how to be more effective at behavioural manipulation, and not on whether to engage in the effort.

The Population Bomb began on a doomsday note: 'The battle to feed all of humanity is over. In the 1970s and 1980s hundreds of millions of people will starve to death in spite of any crash programs embarked upon now' (p. xi). Ehrlich used 'scenarios' that assumed drastically changed conditions and supplied dialogues to justify the changes in policies and attitudes that would be required to avoid a global disaster. In one such scenario, 'Professor Gilsinger' is explaining to his wife, 'Jane', how population pressures will produce famine in the United States as well as in the Third World: 'Even with rationing, a lot of Americans are going to starve to death, unless this climate change reverses. We've seen the trends clearly since the early 1970s, but nobody believed it would happen here, even after the 1976 Latin American famine and the Indian

"Dissolution." Almost a billion human beings starved to death in the last decade, and we managed to keep the lid on by a combination of good luck and brute force' (p. 53).

Behind the campaign to lower birth rates lay not only the altruistic desire to rescue 'Spaceship Earth' but also the fear of what would happen to the standard of living in the United States should the benefits of development be literally eaten up by rapid population growth and international politics become a zero-sum battle for resources. The population explosion would make conflict between the rich and the poor inevitable, undermine the legitimacy of capitalism as a growth strategy, and leave the United States in a position where it could rely on little more than 'good luck and brute force'.

Fear of Third World instability has remained a strong rationale for US efforts to limit population growth. Fear that the expansion of non-white populations might tip the balance against the existing racial power structure has been a domestic as well as an international issue in the United States and in the European 'North'. Ehrlich's thinly disguised racism was neither new nor surprising.

But there was also a deep and obvious strain of sexism in *The Population Bomb* which women ignored and feminists overlooked. 'Professor' Gilsinger is portrayed as the wise male who has come to recognize the gravity of the crisis, and for his wisdom is paid as a government consultant. 'Jane' is the housewife who cannot engage in a rational discussion of international politics because she is so preoccupied with how she will feed her family 'with beef at $12 a pound'. Despite her interest in the topic, Jane could not understand 'what the failure of the corn crop had to do with beef prices' (pp. 52–3). In Ehrlich's scenarios, men think while women emote only men are scientists and only men are capable of political action. For Ehrlich as for Aristotle, domestic responsibilities turn women into 'idiots' – that is, individuals who cannot understand the world, much less act in it (Elshtain, 1981: 47).

But women do give birth and do make decisions about their fertility, so women must be dealt with. Ehrlich had to struggle to find an explanatory model for uncontrolled population growth that ignored cultural and religious values, side-stepped the often-cited theory of 'demographic transition' (the view that as societies become wealthier and more urbanized, the birth rate falls), and avoided any mention of the status of women. His choice was an evolutionary model that neatly avoided political, economic, and cultural questions; he even put the blame on women as the biological 'first cause' of the population problem.

According to Ehrlich, human evolution had taken the path of

increased brain size. But, because women's bodies did not evolve to accommodate full brain development during pregnancy, babies are born helpless and require years of care. However, this too creates problems:

> How could the mother defend and care for *her* infant during its unusually long period of helplessness? She couldn't, unless Papa hung around. The girls are still working on this problem, but an essential step was to get rid of the short, well defined breeding season characteristic of most mammals. The year-round sexuality of the human female, the long period of infant dependence on the female, the evolution of the family group, all are at the roots of the present problem. . . . Our urge to reproduce is hopelessly entwined with most of our other urges. (p. 14, emphasis added)

Women have 'power', but it is a negative power that uses 'year-round sexuality' to manipulate men into joining 'family groups'. This assumes that families exist only to manipulate men into taking on the 'female' responsibility of raising the new generation – after all, Momma bears and praying mantises let males off the hook.

In the end, Ehrlich's messages come through loud and clear: social scientists are the kind of humans who have the skills to foresee disaster correctly and act to prevent it. They are men. Women's biological and domestic roles make them unfit to be scientists or activists. If Jane Gilsinger is the norm, they are part of the problem, not architects of the solution. Innocent but dangerous after millennia of evolutionary moulding, they cannot be engaged as conscious actors; they must be manipulated into changing their behaviour.

The Inundation Policy and Critical Response

As the public perception of a population crisis developed, newly mobilized lobby groups put pressure on Congress to make the dissemination of birth control knowledge and technology in the Third World a high priority of US foreign policy. Congress agreed and passed legislation to be implemented by AID, the US bilateral foreign assistance agency, and supplemented by support for the United Nations Fund for Population Activities (UNFPA) and the International Planned Parenthood Federation (IPPF), an international federation of private organizations modelled on Planned Parenthood in the United States.

Because it feared Roman Catholic opposition in Congress, AID's predecessor agency had placed contraceptive devices on the list of items ineligible for contraceptive assistance in 1948. By 1963 the mood had changed sufficiently to allow a person who advocated birth control to become the head of AID's health programme in an administration headed by a Roman Catholic president. By 1965, interest on the part of both President Kennedy and President Johnson had resulted in small family planning programme ($2.5 million); by 1969 this programme had grown to $50 million. In response to strong popular support and increased Congressional interest, AID's population budget increased throughout the 1970s, levelling off at about $200 million by the end of the decade. A special Bureau of Population and Humanitarian Assistance was created in 1972 (Jaquette and Staudt, 1985: 14).

AID's mandate, as outlined in Title X of the Foreign Assistance Act of 1967, was to establish 'voluntary family planning programs' to provide individual couples with education and contraceptive techniques to 'plan their family size in accordance with their own moral convictions' (p. 9). Half the funding was administered directly through AID and half went to multilateral organizations like UNFPA and IPPF, as well as to similar organizations seeking innovative techniques to increase the effectiveness of population programmes.

The strength of the population effort can be measured not only by the size of the budget but also by the ways in which population criteria were institutionalized across AID's organizational structure. Regional bureaux hired population specialists, and projects and programmes were to take account of population impacts. The head of the Bureau, later the Office of Population, Dr Ray Ravenholt, was a tireless advocate of family planning. During his period of service, from 1966 to 1980, Ravenholt backed a policy of contraceptive *inundation* – that is, of putting AID's resources behind a maximum effort to increase the supply of contraceptives available in the Third World. He felt strongly that, although the supply was increasing rapidly, there would always be more demand for contraceptives than the supply could match. Efforts to probe the social or economic causes of fertility patterns or programmes that drew on research about the inverse relationship between the status of women and fertility, were seen as diversionary and inefficient. Others might push for a more contextual approach to the issue, but Ravenholt stuck to his guns, backed in Congress by key sectors of the population lobby.

Despite its racist and sexist overtones, the population campaign received very little attention from feminists, even as women's health care became the object of strong and effective criticism within the United States (Rogow, 1986). As population budgets continued to grow during the 1970s, the most formidable opposition came from the Third World. At the first UN Conference on Population, held in

Bucharest in 1974, many nations joined in a chorus of radical criticism, arguing that the population campaign was directed only at coloured people, and that the focus on population was merely a Northern ploy to divert attention from the South's demands for a New International Economic Order. In Bucharest, the Chinese took a leading role in arguing that birth rates fall only after a substantial degree of economic development is achieved. They characterized US efforts to make family planning programmes a precondition for development assistance as not just misguided but self-serving, and argued that the United States should commit its resources to development, not population control (Finkle and Crane, 1975).

Congressional hearings in 1978 sparked feminist concern that the United States was responsible for 'dumping' unsafe contraceptives in the Third World. This culminated in a major feminist critique, an article by Barbara Ehrenreich, Mark Dowie, and Stephen Minkin in *Mother Jones* (1979) that accused the US government of 'gynocide'. The article attacked AID for continued distribution of the Dalkon shield intra-uterine device after it had been taken off the domestic market by the FDA in the face of mounting evidence that the shield caused perforation of the uterus, pelvic inflammation, and babies born with birth defects. Ehrenreich also attacked AID for supporting family planning programmes that provided Depo-Provera, an injectable contraceptive with negative side-effects sufficient to prevent its being marketed in the United States.

These revelations sent shock-waves through the American feminist community. An AID exhibit on women and development at the National Women's Studies Association was verbally 'trashed' by irate feminists, despite the fact that the Women in Development Office in AID took the lead in criticizing the inundation approach and the single-minded focus on 'women as reproducers' within the Agency. Within the feminist movement in general, there was increased awareness of the coercive aspects of US policy and a new understanding that the resistance of Third World women to population programmes should not simply be dismissed as a form of 'false consciousness' that would be overcome once feminism became an international movement.

The Bureaucratization of the Population Campaign

In addition to its ideological aspects which, as we have shown, are both racist and sexist and legitimize the disempowerment of women, the process of implementing population policy through the creation of bureaucratic mechanisms deserves closer analysis. Kathy

Ferguson's 'case against bureaucracy' has alerted feminists to the ways in which bureaucracies disempower citizens by creating hierarchical relations both within the bureaucracy and between the bureaucracy and its 'clients'. She, along with Barbara Nelson (1984), Wendy Sarvasy (1986), and Adele Mueller (1985) have done much to popularize Michel Foucault's thoroughgoing critique of bureaucracies in the 'welfare' state.

Bureaucracies convert knowledge into power and empower knowledge élites – the so-called 'experts'. Experts do battle with each other, not merely to establish the 'truth' – which in Foucault's view cannot be discovered, in any case – but over whose definition of the problem will prevail. A particular definition of a problem tends to privilege a set of solutions, and the choice of solutions in turn determines who will set social norms, and who will control the flow of resources that society commits to solving the problem. Since the battle for truth is in fact a battle for power, the victory of one expertise over another rarely alters the hierarchical relationship between the bureaucracy and its clients, though it will determine which set of experts gains or loses.

Just such a conflict between approaches occurred within AID. The dominant expertise, represented by the Population Office under Ravenholt's leadership, called for an inundation strategy. Doctors were the professional corps on whom the approach relied. The narrow focus on medical technique allowed the Office to steer clear of the conflicts that might have arisen had issues of economic development and equality, or moral or religious values been raised. Ravenholt's inundation approach also represented a powerful strategy within the bureaucracy. The more single-minded the task, the easier it is to prove that a particular strategy is 'cost-effective'. The Office had a clearly defined mission with measurable goals, which turned out to be very useful in maintaining Congressional support or budget increases against the claims of competing approaches and against other offices within AID that tried to encroach on its territory. The experts whose power was reinforced by the inundation strategy were the doctors and health professionals who both set policy and implemented it via networks of maternal and child health programmes. The relevance of the feminist critique of the medical profession needs little elaboration here. We simply note that the hierarchical aspects of Western medicine are heightened in the Third World, where indigenous medical practices (often controlled by women) are being replaced by 'scientific' medicine (dominated by men). The asymmetrical power relationship between the male doctor and the female patient in the Third World is usually exacerbated by class, racial, and urban/rural distinctions.

Women need and seek medical advice, either for themselves or to help their children, and they are vulnerable to manipulation because of that need. AID programmes often reached women just after they had given birth and, despite language emphasizing women's rights and choice, AID's own accounts of their post-partum programmes reveal the distance between the 'experts' and their patients. Women were seen in depersonalized terms as 'acceptors' or 'targets', or as 'at-risk reproducers'. Goals for contraceptive use were quantified in terms of 'number of monthly cycles' used; IUDs and sterilization were seen as more desirable because they cannot be reversed and their effectiveness is not limited by human ambivalence or lack of knowledge about proper use.

The focus on medical techniques had a significant advantage over other approaches in appealing for the co-operation of Third World leaders. Improvements in health are a positive result from development that few question, in contrast to the scepticism with which urbanization, assembly line production, or consumerism are greeted. Within the countries that participated in population programmes, improvements in health care and the introduction of medical technology were eagerly welcomed. Many governments that were constrained by religious and cultural values from giving direct state support to population programmes none the less tolerated contraceptive education and distribution through private organizations.

Third World criticisms of US population policy primarily stemmed from the political opposition of the 'South' to the 'North's' monopoly of power and resources in the international arena, and specifically to the failure of US and European policy makers to respond to Third World demands for a larger share of the international economic pie; the racist implications of the policy were a secondary theme, with no attention whatsoever paid to the manipulative, disempowering, or sexist elements of population policy vis-à-vis women.

Despite its appeal, however, the inundation strategy did not go uncontested. Within AID and its support staffs of consultants, demographers stood ready to challenge the hegemony of the doctors. As early as 1967, Kingsley Davis (1967) attacked US policy as too technological and drew attention to the problems of leaving population programmes in the hands of 'respected medical personnel':

> In viewing negative attitudes toward birth control as due to ignorance, apathy and outworn tradition, and [in seeing] 'mass communication' as the solution to the motivation problem, family planners tend to ignore the complexity of social life. If it were admitted that the creation and

> care of new human beings is socially motivated, like other forms of
> behavior, by being a part of the system of rewards and punishments that
> is built into human relationships, and personal interests, it would be
> apparent that the social structure and economy must be changed before
> a deliberate reduction in the birth rate can be achieved. (p. 103)

The changes that would be necessary, Davis concluded, would be
changes in the 'structure of the family, in the position of women,
and in sexual mores' (p. 103).

The gauntlet was down, but it was not until 1976 that the
Population Office yielded any turf. In that year Congress passed
Section 104d of the International Development and Food Assistance Act; it called on AID to address the issue of demand for
contraceptives and to design projects that would modify the social
and economic conditions which kept birth rates high. Internally,
new procedures were implemented that required all projects to be
reviewed for 'fertility impacts', with oversight in the hands of the
Policy Planning Bureau rather than the Population Office. Substantial funds were made available to study the social and economic
determinants of fertility.

The attempt to put population policy in a broader developmental-
ist context was welcomed by many, including those who felt that the
inundation strategy had been pursued too zealously, to the
detriment of women's health. Others saw this as an opportunity to
redirect economic resources to women who had remained largely
untouched by AID's programmes of investment and training.

The emphasis on socio-economic criteria changed the terms of the
debate and empowered a new group of demographers and social
scientists who sought the 'determinants' of women's fertility
behaviour. But the search for a few key variables was frustrating.
Attempts to correlate 'status of women' variables, particularly
women's work, with reduced fertility did not prove conclusive and
thus did not provide an ironclad case for increasing women's
employment opportunities (Birdsall, 1976). Part of the problem was
methodological; there are simply not enough solid data on women's
employment to ensure that the statistics are reliable.

But a feminist critique of the role of social science as a
handmaiden to government policy must probe further. As a social
'science', demography employs a methodology that abstracts
researchers from the objects of their research, in this case, Third
World women. It derives key hypotheses from the experiences of
the Western researcher, not the web of interconnections, economic
constraints, or moral sensibilities of the women whose behaviour it
studies – and ultimately seeks to change. Demography provides the
policy maker with new 'tools', that is with social and economic
variables that are thought to be more amenable to control than are

women's fertility decisions themselves. It is reasonable to assume that those who make use of demographic techniques find social engineering a more efficient and less politically risky task than education or social mobilization. We sit up and take notice only when demography produces results that lead to policy prescriptions that run so counter to our values that we find them shocking – as when it is suggested that we should cut back on health care or basic human needs for women because women who are sick and starving produce fewer babies.

It has been suggested that, because most development programmes and social policies are manipulative, the way to improve population policy is to ensure that women are in key administrative positions where it is expected that they will be more sensitive to women's concerns (Tangri, 1976). We would counter that affirmative action may help the professional careers of women bureaucrats and social scientists, but it does not change the power of the bureaucracy vis-à-vis the client. The fact that women manage population programmes does not eliminate class, race, or cultural differences that distinguish the interests, experiences, and vulnerability of the professional women from those of the women whose fertility they are 'managing'. Unless the top-down orientation itself is changed, and programmes are designed to empower women in this and other arenas, the effect can only be to divide women and to perpetuate the model (see Jones and Jónasdóttir, chapter 1).

Giving a more prominent role to social scientists broadened the context in which population policies were considered, but it reinforced rather than challenged the hierarchical bureaucratic relationships that were institutionalized under the medical approach in the early years of the programme. It is not surprising that Kingsley Davis's very trenchant criticism of the medical technological approach was offered not to empower women by improving their status but to move policy away from the relatively benign but ineffective 'family planning' effort toward full-scale population control. Davis's suggestions for implementing such a policy included strong sanctions against unwed mothers, active government intervention to provide economic rewards and punishments, and rewriting school-books to recast social values. It is hard to imagine a clearer example of modernizing patriarchy or a more rigid prescription for strong state intervention regardless of women's interests or needs.

The Reagan Administration

In 1984, for reasons that had to do with domestic politics, US population policy shifted dramatically. At the second UN Conference on Population, held in Mexico City in August 1984, the US delegation, headed by New York Senator James Buckley, reversed twenty years of unequivocal US support for population programmes.

The new approach, as outlined by Buckley and his hastily assembled delegation, took the view that the United States no longer considers the relationship between population growth and economic development to be necessarily a negative one.[3] If the Third World nations are running out of food and unable to supply their populations with a steady increase in material goods, the problem is not due to ecology (resource scarcity relative to population) or dependency (the unfair international distribution of wealth) but to the historical pattern of too much state intervention in Third World economies. With this one stroke the Reagan administration was able to pay a debt to the moral majority, which was sensitive to the abortion component of some international family planning programmes, underline its rejection of Third World demands for a New International Economic Order, reject the 'negativism' of the Carter administration's emphasis on the limits to growth, and reinforce its message that capitalism is the only economic model that works. Ironically, the United States and China reversed the polar positions they had held in Bucharest ten years before, with China taking the view that population control is a *sine qua non* for development and the United States taking the position that economic development – to be achieved under capitalism, of course – would solve current and future population pressures (Finkle and Crane, 1985). The switch in US population policy had practical as well as rhetorical consequences as the United States moved to withdraw its funding from UNFPA and other international agencies and to question the anti-maternal and technology-dependent biases of its own policies.

The movement away from a narrow and arguably racist and sexist focus on the population issue in our relations with the Third World would appear on the surface to be a positive shift that feminists would applaud. With the pressure reduced, it is less likely that women will be coerced or manipulated into accepting contraceptives that are harmful to them or that they do not want, or that US support for development programmes will be conditioned on a country's willingness to participate in population limitation programmes. The bureaucratic excesses that have characterized the implementation of population policies will presumably be curtailed, though many of the same committed people are still working on those programmes and their values presumably have not changed overnight. It is possible that, without a consensus on the single-minded goal, policies and delivery systems will truly become more open to contextual factors, not the least of which should be the felt needs of the women themselves.

By the same token, however, those feminists who have been fighting for a change have got some of what they want, but not the way they wanted it. The interests of the Far Right and of women do not coincide. Feminists may fear coercive and manipulative programmes that disempower women and subject them to unnecessary and often unexplained health risks, but they do favour the idea of reproductive choice. To abandon the attempt to reach women with contraceptive information, maternal and child health programmes, and a range of other services that can be provided by these delivery systems, such as legal aid and income-generating opportunities, is to abandon women to the vagaries of the market system (in which women are often disadvantaged) and to the pressures of cultural habits (by which women are also coerced). Feminists should take the Reagan administration's attack on population programmes as an opportunity and a breathing space, but hardly as a solution to the problem. In the end, despite feminist scepticism, responsive bureaucracy is likely to be much better than no bureaucracy at all.

Conclusions: Some Thoughts on Gender and Politics

Analysing how US population policy evolved reveals some useful insights for feminist political practice. At each stage in the political process – from the definition of the issue, to its reflection in the pluralist politics and, finally, in the bureaucratic implementation of that policy – there are important lessons to be learned.

In the first stage, when an issue is being defined, a policy designed to met a crisis is predictably simplistic. Key actors are stereotyped, especially if the 'target groups' are poor, of another race, female, or foreign. Stereotyping and simplistic solutions – in this case the dissemination of contraceptive technology – are unlikely to take into account the effective participation of those whom the policy is intended to reach, and by narrowing the range of alternatives considered, reduce the flexibility of policy design and implementation. The fact that the subject of population policy is women's reproductive behaviour, and that the 'objects' of policy were Third World women, exacerbated but did not cause the underlying problems. Of course, without a public perception of crisis it is difficult to command legislative attention, create political consensus, or ensure the commitment of new resources. The question for feminists is how to reduce the damage that can happen when policies are made under the pressure of crisis, and to be especially vigilant about global solutions that focus on changing the behaviour of 'others'. The emphasis must be placed on participation, on resisting group stereotyping, and on re-defining the problem in ways that reflect the needs of those who are most affected by implementation efforts.

In terms of the political *process* itself, we see that the actors were individuals who could be mobilized because the goals and means of the campaign seemed to be congruent with liberal, humanitarian, and even feminist values. In general, it can be said that pluralist politics does not work as it is theoretically supposed to for gender issues. The long-term institutionalization of male issues poses special barriers to a female voice and to putting women's issues on the political agenda. When women's issues are included, it is often for the 'wrong' reasons: men legislating 'for' women in the name of a social cause. In this case, because Third World women are geographically excluded, not merely politically marginalized, their response did not form part of the 'feedback loop' characteristic of pluralism; groups that were organized to lobby effectively often amplified the crisis orientation of the population issue and thus contributed to the top-down flow of power.

Finally, and this is crucial, those who were responsible for *implementing* policies did not have unambiguously positive incentives to reflect the reactions of the women whose behaviour they were trying to change. On the contrary, it was easier and entirely credible for them to attribute failures in policy implementation to the persistence of 'traditional' values among Third World women rather than to take responsibility themselves or, more radically, to question the goal itself or the measures of its success or failure. US feminists, who certainly acquiesced in the expansion of US-funded population programmes abroad, can be faulted for equating their interests and their perceptions with those of Third World women. This is not due solely to racism in the feminist movement – though there was surely some of that present, consciously or unconsciously – nor is it solely due to a blind drive to 'export' feminism, although that motive too must be recognized and confronted. The simple truth is that pluralism reflects well only the interests of those who can organize themselves and maintain the pressure to influence policy and monitor implementation. Third World women were not directly involved, and US feminists did not organize to represent them.

We have emphasized and contrasted two sets of policy and implementation strategies, those based on medical technology and those relying more on social science analysis. We concluded that, although it might seem that social scientists would be likely to offer more sensitive and contextual approaches to understanding women's fertility decisions, the assumption of both the social scientists and the policy makers was that social science could and should be used for social engineering.

Changing the model (which, in any event, put only a minor dent in the operations of the Office of Population) did not change the hierarchical relationship between bureaucracy and client. On the contrary, it may have helped to legitimize the notion in the minds of some Third World élites that the state can and should manipulate its citizens' private behaviour. The stereotype of women as non-participants, as 'irrational' or as a threat to 'modern' values – shared by population experts and congenial to many Third World bureaucracies – may have helped overcome the cultural constraints against letting the state meddle in this very intimate arena.

If we posit that a feminist politics would emphasize caring, connectedness, and context (Gilligan, 1982; Tronto, forthcoming), it is clear that such a feminist conception is not well served by liberal politics-as-usual. At each point, from the way an issue is defined, to the processing of that issue through interest group interaction and Congressional legislation to the bureaucratic implementation of that policy, the process favours narrowing and simplification, often stereotyping the causes of the problem. This in turn makes it easier to seek one-dimensional, easy-to-administer solutions that can be applied, 'cost-effectively', to a range of cases, and minimizes the mechanisms for effective feedback.

It is possible to imagine a concept of bureaucracy that builds in feedback, that uses its 'delivery mechanisms' to empower rather than disempower its client groups, and that accepts as likely the result that definitions of the problem and of the solutions will and should change over time. Social scientists can play a role in challenging the social engineering biases of the 'welfare' bureaucracy.[4] But given the reality of narrowly defined goals, hierarchically ordered bureaucratic institutions, and a political system that is unresponsive, it is easy to understand why women are often driven to anti-statist strategies and to self-help. Despite our criticisms of US population policy, we would argue against withdrawal and the resulting depoliticization. The state can be a vehicle for change, and policy implementation can be a process of empowerment. It is only through the state that feminists can legitimize new norms and more open political processes for all of society.

It has become very fashionable to dismiss any bureaucratically implemented policy as hierarchical and exploitative, and to argue that the solution is decentralization and seek alternatives that emphasize decentralization and 'community'. We would argue that decentralization does not necessarily solve the problems of hierarchy (Freeman, 1974) and that it may in fact reinforce the norms of control rather than the norms of empowerment. When self-help is self-imposed isolation, it ceases to be an argument for systemic change. In our view, it is inconsistent – and self-defeating – to hold a revolutionary vision that we implement just for ourselves, even if that were possible.

It can be argued, perhaps, that the questions raised here about the politics of population are peculiar to this issue, and cannot be used to draw conclusions about the interaction of gender and politics. Germaine Greer (1984) and others have pointed out that the focus on women's sexuality, a focus shared by feminists as well as population policy makers, is itself disempowering. Fertility decisions are, as Irene Diamond puts it, inappropriately 'excised from a moral context'. Controlling the consequences of fertility through 'technologized' service delivery systems 'diverts attention and resources from gender education about social and political equalities' (1983). Population programmes are a means by which the state can modernize patriarchy, substituting modern norms and practices for the traditional controls enforced by kinship groups, using the appeal of scientific medicine and the popular support for economic growth to disguise the extension of its power.

We would agree that an overemphasis on controlling fertility misreads women's interests, but that the issue of population policy is not atypical; on the contrary, it merely highlights tendencies that are commonly present in gender politics. Defining women as reproducers makes them, like the poor, the targets rather than the authors of policy, which is why population programmes easily become manipulative and even coercive. Modern states are defined in part by their ability to set norms and practices in the traditionally 'private' sphere, that is, in areas once under the control of families. Making public policy in this arena is quite different from setting economic regulations or directing foreign policy. In the process, women are made the target rather than the authors of legislative 'solutions' to social 'problems'.

Yet the original feminist goal of increasing women's power by giving women control over their own fertility was not a misguided one. This case of an empowering motive gone awry should serve to focus our attention on the hard task of reconstructing our political process and on making the bureaucracy function in ways that broaden options, that seek to engage women in defining their own problems and in deciding their own interests. Bureaucracies have the potential to create connectedness and engender community in ways that the market-place, which is the only realistic alternative to bureaucracy, does not. Changing norms and redistributing resources, not giving up on politics and abandoning bureaucracy, are appropriate tools for feminist revolution.

Notes

1. The Kennedy administration established a Commission on the Status of Women (which did not, however, support the ERA), and Betty Friedan's *The Feminine Mystique* was published in 1963. Population assistance became an official part of US foreign policy when President Kennedy endorsed it in April 1963; the programme was expanded by President Johnson in 1965. See Jaquette and Staudt (1985).

2. Of course, the fact that child-bearing is the major source of power for women in traditional societies makes it unrealistic to expect that they will withdraw this resource, Lysistrata-style, from men, as Steinem suggests. Germaine Greer's mother-centred arguments in *Sex and Destiny* (1984), which was written from her experience in India and which angered many women working in the population field, parallels some of the arguments now being made by Irene Diamond (1983) and others, drawing on the work of Michel Foucault. 'Maternal feminism', which elevates women's unique qualities and perspectives as mothers, has now become a recognized position in feminist theory. See, for example, Elshtain (1983) and Friedan (1981).

3. Finkle and Crane (1985) quote Richard Benedick using the 'old' language in the spring of 1984:

> The United States Government's concern about demographic developments is based on our traditional respect for human dignity and on our interest in worldwide economic development and political stability. The changes and imbalances being brought into play by unprecedented population growth in many countries are contributing to an increased potential for political instability, social unrest, extremism, mass migration, and possible conflicts over scarce land or resources.

4. This analysis owes much to feminist critiques of science, especially the work of Sandra Harding (Harding, 1986; Harding and Hintikka, 1983; Keller, 1984).

Editors' note

Both authors worked in the Women and Development Office at AID; Staudt during 1979 and Jaquette from 1979 to 1980, under the Intergovernmental Personnel Exchange Act.

References

Birdsall, Nancy (1976) 'Review Essay: Women and Population Studies.' *Signs* 1: 699–712.

Davis, Kingsley (1967) 'Population Policy: Will Current Programs Succeed?', *Science* 158(3802) (Nov.).

Delamont, Sara and Laura Duffin (1978) *The Nineteenth Century Woman: Her Cultural and Physical World*. London: Barnes and Noble.

Diamond, Irene (1983) 'American Feminism and the Language of Rights and Bodies'. Paper presented at the Annual Meeting of the American Political Science Association.

Ehrenreich, Barbara and Dierdre English (1973) *Witches, Midwives and Nurses.* New York: Feminist Press.

Ehrenreich, Barbara, Mark Dowie, and Stephen Menken (1979) 'Gynocide, The Accused: The U.S. Government', *Mother Jones* (Nov.).

Ehrlich, Paul (1968) *The Population Bomb.* Published under the auspices of the Sierra Club by Ballantine Books, New York.

Elshtain, Jean (1981) *Public Man, Private Woman; Women in Social and Political Thought.* Princeton, NJ: Princeton University Press.

Elshtain, Jean (1983) 'Antigone's Daughters: Reflections on Female Identity and the State', in I. Diamond, *Families, Politics and Public Policy.* New York: Longman.

Ferguson, Kathy (1984) *The Feminist Case Against Bureaucracy.* Philadelphia: Temple University Press.

Finkle, Jason and Barbara Crane (1975) 'The Politics of Bucharest: Population, Development and the New International Economic Order', *Population and Development Review* 1: 1 (Sept.).

Finkle, Jason and Barbara Crane (1985) 'Ideology and Politics at Mexico City: The United States at the 1984 International Conference on Population', *Population and Development Review* 11(1) (March).

Firestone, Shulamith (1970) *The Dialectic of Sex.* New York: Bantam Books.

Freeman, Jo (1974) 'The Tryanny of Structurelessness', in Jane S. Jaquette (ed.), *Women in Politics.* New York: John Wiley.

Friedan, Betty (1963) *The Feminine Mystique.* New York: W.W. Norton.

Friedan, Betty (1981) *The Second Stage.* New York: Summit Books.

Gilligan, Carol (1982) *In a Different Voice.* Cambridge, Mass.: Harvard University Press.

Greer, Germaine (1984) *Sex and Destiny: The Politics of Human Fertility.* London: Secker and Warburg.

Harding, Sandra (1986) *The Science Question in Feminism.* Ithaca, NY: Cornell University Press.

Harding, Sandra and Merrill Hintikka (1983) *Discovering Reality.* Boston: Reidel.

Jaquette, Jane and Kathleen Staudt (1985) 'Women as At-Risk Reproducers', in Virginia Sapiro (ed.), *Women, Biology and Public Policy.* Beverly Hills: Sage.

Keller, Evelyn Fox (1984) *Reflections on Gender and Science.* New Haven, Conn.: Yale University Press.

Mueller, Adele (1985) 'The Bureaucratization of Feminist Knowledge: The Case of Women and Development', *Resources for Feminist Research* (Canada), 15(1) (March).

Nelson, Barbara (1984) 'Women's Poverty and Women's Citizenship: Some Political Consequences of Women's Economic Marginality', *Signs* 10(2).

Rogow, Deborah (1986) 'Quality Care in International Family Planning: A Feminist Contribution'. New York: The Population Council.

Rosaldo, Michelle (1974) 'Woman, Culture and Society: A Theoretical Overview', in Michelle Rosaldo and Louise Lamphere, *Women, Culture and Society.* Stanford, CA: Stanford University Press.

Sarvasy, Wendy (1986) 'Gender, Race, Class and the Contradictory Legacy of the Feminist Welfare State Founders'. Paper presented at the Western Political Science Association Meeting.

Steinem, Gloria (1975) Quoted from a film on the UN Conference on Women, Mexico City, 1975: 'What do Women Want?' Produced and edited by Pat McMurray and Jane Jaquette.

Tangri, Sandra S. (1976) 'A Feminist Perspective on Some Ethical Issues in Population Programs', *Signs* 1(4).

Tronto, Joan (forthcoming) 'Women's Morality: Beyond Gender Differences to a Theory of Care', *Signs*.

Index

Index compiled by Peva Keane